Uitlander English:
Identities, Memories, Belonging to
]

Patricia Johnson-Castle

Langaa Research & Publishing CIG
Mankon, Bamenda

Publisher:
Langaa RPCIG
Langaa Research & Publishing Common Initiative Group
P.O. Box 902 Mankon
Bamenda
North West Region
Cameroon
Langaagrp@gmail.com
www.langaa-rpcig.net

Distributed in and outside N. America by African Books Collective
orders@africanbookscollective.com
www.africanbookscollective.com

ISBN-10: 9956-554-91-x

ISBN-13: 978-9956-554-91-1

© Patricia Johnson-Castle 2025

Front cover image, InZync Poetry Performance at Amazink in Kayamandi, 2017; back cover image, Statue of Jan Marais on the Rooiplein at Stellenbosch University, 2017.

All rights reserved.
No part of this book may be reproduced or transmitted in any form or by any means, mechanical or electronic, including photocopying and recording, or be stored in any information storage or retrieval system, without written permission from the publisher

Dedication

This book is dedicated to everyone who has cried from injustice; has been pushed down, and stood back up; has been told there was no point in trying, but tried anyway; who felt love in their hearts, and wanted to use it to take away the suffering of others. A better world is possible. It is never too late to try.

> In time, we shall be in a position to bestow on South Africa the greatest possible gift: a more human face.
> Steven Bantu Biko

> We have been taught to fear the very things that have the potential to set us free.
> Alok Menon

> I imagine one of the reasons people cling to their hates so stubbornly is because they sense, once hate is gone, they will be forced to deal with pain.
> James Baldwin

Acknowledgements

There are so many people to thank. This thesis was only made possible by the support of:

My parents for their emotional and financial support;

My supervisor, Francis Nyamnjoh, for his insights and intellect; there was never a dull moment with you, Francis;

Chris Machelm-Peters, for helping me keep track of all my lost items (there were many);

The Anthropology Department of the University of Cape Town, but particularly Helen Macdonald and Fiona Ross, for their support during my darker days;

My Anthropology cohort (in no particular order): Anita, Chloe (Shain & Cormack), Robyn, Mystecia, Sabelo, Lesago, Philani, Qiniso, James, Julia, Terena, Shannon, Minga, Laura, Yusra, Raisa and Jodi;

My participants (including those who did not get quoted in this thesis) namely, Amy, Ané, Anneke, Cathelynne, Catherine, Chantelle, Christoff, Du Toit, Freddie, Hugo, Jason, Justin, Kara, Lauren, Lia, Liza, Luigia, Marc, Megan, Melissa, Philna, Randy, Shane, Siphe, Wanijuk, and Wiaan; your conversations and interviews provoked my thoughts and provided me clarity;

My support system in Cape Town: Alex, Barry, Kira (who also gets credit as my banker), Yash, Hannah, Jordan, Emma (Gates-Pottinger, Buckland & Tiffin), Belle, Limpho, Abigail, Lidija, Michael, Marli, Tonio, Sindi, Brynde, David, Nathan, James, Landile, Rob, and Nick;

My support system in Stellenbosch: Anneke, Lucy, Farai, Julian, Rabia, Faith, Maxine, Skhu, Claire, Stephané, Willem, Kara, and the USDV;

Particular thanks to Raisa and Maythe for their proofreading;

And my ancestors, for all the sacrifices they made for me to be and be brought to this point in my journey.

Table of Contents

Acknowledgements v
List of Table and Figures ix
Abbreviations xi

Chapter 1: Introduction 1
    Welkom by/ Welcome to/Wamkelekile eStellenbosch 1
    Methodology 9
    Ethical Considerations 31

Chapter 2: Settling On Settler-Colonialism 37
    Introduction 37
    African, Colonialism, & Settler-Colonialism 40
    Settlers & Language 55
    Settlers & Land 73
    Shades of White: Class Politics 82
    Conclusion 83

Chapter 3: Afrikaans, English & Africa:
A Story of Love And Hate 85
    Introduction 85
    Struggles in Stellenbosch 92
    Historical Afrikaans & English
    Relations in Broader South Africa 104
    South African Language Beyond
    English and Afrikaans 114
    African Language Debates: Empire,
    Achebe, Ngugi and Beyond 116
    Conclusion 128

Chapter 4: Routes to Stellenbosch 133
    Introduction 133
    Setting the Scene at Stellenbosch University 135
    Conclusion 158

Chapter 5: Silent Walls: Black and White,
and the Grey Areas of the Making and
Re-Making and Maintaining of
Interracial Friendships 159
    Introduction 159
    Whiteness & South African Whiteness 160

'Place' in Theory 164
Characteristics of Friendship 167
Challenges of Making Friends 169
Whiteness Isn't Only Skin Deep…
Sometimes, It Has Little to Do with the Skin....................178
Social Spaces in Stellenbosch 189
Conclusion..194

Chapter 6 : "You Can't Just Leave Us Here"– Caught Between Bloemfontein and Perth... 197

Introduction 197
Mediums of Instruction..203
Being White/African/Afrikaner:
History and Obligation..207
'Should I Stay, or Should I go?':
Emigration and Remaining 211
Discussion and Hierarchy among
White-Afrikaans People..213
Language and Identity at Stellenbosch................................215
Don't Rock the Boat..225
Learning & Flexibility 230
Conclusion..234

Chapter 7: Ndiyazama Noko.. 239

Conclusion..239

Reference: 247

List of Tables and Figures

Figure 1: Location of University of Stellenbosch (L) and Location of University of Stellenbosch (Zoomed) (R)	26
Figure 2: The Synonymy of the University and the Town on the Internet	27
Figure 3: Demographic Distribution of Stellenbosch	27
Figure 4: Europe	28
Figure 5: Replanting of Flowers in Stellenbosch	135
Figure 6: Jan Marais on His Plinth	136
Figure 7: The Sunken Entrance to the Library	138
Figure 8: The Wolfpack Tank	140
Figure 9: Local Performance on the Train from Cape Town to Stellenbosch	147
Figure 10: Idasvallei	152
Figure 11: Lush Green Trees, Smooth Pavement, Being Protected by Police	153
Figure 12: Language Protest on the Rooiplein	154
Graph 1: 1980 Home Language among White South Africans (L), Parliamentary Seat Count of the National Party (R)	23
Table 1: Demographic Change at Stellenbosch University from 2015-2023	**240**
Table 2: Demographic Change At Stellenbosch University 2000-2012	241

Abbreviations

BA Building: Faculty of Arts and Social Sciences Building, Stellenbosch University.
DWA: Department of Water Affairs
GBB: Gereformeerde Blues Band
NG Kerk: Dutch Reformed Church
NPR: National Public Radio
PSO: Private Student's Organisation
RDP: Reconstruction and Development Programme
SAHO: South Africa History Online
TRC: Truth and Reconciliation Commission
UCT: University of Cape Town
UNISA: University of South Africa
USDV: University of Stellenbosch Debating Union
VOC: Dutch East India Trading Company
VSBC: Vluytjeskraal Share Block Company

Chapter 1

Introduction

Welkom by/Welcome to/Wamkelekile eStellenbosch

> The masquerade [...] not only moves spectacularly; but those who want to enjoy its motion fully must follow its progress up and down the arena. This seemingly minor observation was elevated into an Igbo proverb of general application: *Ada-akwu ofu ebe enene mmuo*. That is, "You do not stand in one place to watch a masquerade" – *Chinua Achebe* (1988: 65)

During my fieldwork, I attempted to watch a dancing masquerade at Stellenbosch University: *the unfolding of the politics of race and language*. I entered Stellenbosch University from the perspective of an outsider with activist tendencies. As my education— formal and informal— continued, I realized that I would need to be more engaged with my environment to keep up with the multifaceted debates about language. Fortunately, I found informants who shared their experiences with me and helped me understand some perspectives on language at the University. Language is deeply tied to race and ethnicity in South Africa, as it is in many places around the world. I hope this text is read beyond the borders of South Africa as I have learned so deeply from the ability to think broadly between my upbringing in St. John's, Newfoundland, and my experiences here in Cape Town.

There are challenging questions facing the born-free generation of South Africans – those born in or after 1994, the year Apartheid officially (politically and legally) came to an end. Most broadly this work probes for how and where students at Stellenbosch imagine a future for themselves. After the legal barriers against racial mixing have been removed, it brought me to the question: what does it mean for South Africans to be able to live together? I examine how Stellenbosch, as a place, impacts the choreography of friendship and to what extent it prevents people from finding dance partners (figuratively and literally) from racial groups other than their own. Though this book is based on my time in Stellenbosch from 2015-2017, it remains relevant to the struggle over the future of Stellenbosch University. The university itself stands in for a microcosm of the struggle of transformation from a non-democratic White supremacist Apartheid state to a state founded on democratic values explicitly of non-racialism and non-sexism; as well as human dignity, the achievement of equality, and the advancement of human rights and freedoms (SA Constitution 1996, 3). Chatting with a young White South African of English descent at a dog park in Cape Town, I told her about studying Stellenbosch and she replied, "Oh yes, Orania-lite". Orania is an infamous Afrikaner nationalist town with an all-White population in the Northern Cape Province. This town is examined in more depth in my second chapter but it is significant that this woman in her early-twenties identifies Stellenbosch as "Orania-lite" as it indicates the continued connotation of the town and university as a "Whites-Only" space. For the first time in 2023, White people are no longer the majority at the University by 0.2% (Stellenbosch University 2023). This demographic change has clearly not altered the discursive understanding of Stellenbosch.

In January 2024, a scandal made the whole country catch its breath: the initiation practices of the Wilgenhof residence—home to "many elite Afrikaner leaders in its 120 years" (Ruiters 2024) – were revealed. The residence was described by News24 as a "house of horrors" which contain two "strafkamer" or punishment rooms. The rooms were used in initiation rituals to "break-in" first-year students to create loyalty to the Wilgenhof residence. The rooms contained Ku Klux Klan-like hoods, and sexually explicit drawings. A former resident turned whistleblower described having to "drink a toxic mixture of linseed oil and aloe crystals, and having a liquid with a "urine-like odour" poured over his body" in 2022 (Ruiters 2024). In its most basic formation, power is the asymmetrical ability for an individual or group to create consequences for another, when the Other could not possibly create similar consequences. First-year students are younger, likely living away from home for the first time, and do not have a strong network of friends or support system, which means their ability to pull off any similar horrors to their upper-class men is extremely low.

Student Paul Joubert tried to sound the alarm on the practice when he was a Master's student in the Philosophy Department describing how members of the residence formed an extra-judicial 'disciplinary committee' and would dress up in black Ku Klux Klan uniforms to punish "any resident who they felt transgressed the official or unofficial code of the residence" (Ruiters 2024). Joubert described to journalist Tracy-Lynn Ruiters: "This punishment reportedly always took place past 1am, in the form of dragging residents out of their beds, beatings with broken glass bottles, being forced to give humiliating speeches admitting 'guilt' while naked, and performing extremely punishing physical activities for hours on end" (2024). This is not the first time these practices have been revealed at Wilgenhof. An expose was also written in the student newspaper nearly 40 years ago. Constitutional law expert Pierre De Vos described similar practices when he lived in the residence in 1984 and 1985 (Ruiters 2024). In his own column, De Vos noted that initiation practices were done in the name of "*koshuis gees* (residence spirit) as part of a larger project to ensure broad acceptance of the Afrikaner Nationalist culture, a culture steeped in violence, obedience to authority, and fear and hatred of the Other" (2024).

Stellenbosch University was under fire for lack of inclusion of Black students when I arrived in South Africa in 2015. These issues have also continued into the present. In 2022, Theuns du Toit peed on fellow student Babalo Ndwayana's study material. The incident was caught on film which led to du Toit's expulsion (De Kock 2024). When asked about his action replied: "It's a white boy thing" (Mkentane 2022). As I write in Cape Town during 2024, a trial will soon begin in the Western Cape High Court to determine whether Stellenbosch University Central Disciplinary Committee had grounds to expel du Toit from the University (De Kock 2024). Shortly before du Toit urinated on the belongings of Ndwayana, an Indian student attending the Faculty of Law's dance requested an Indian song be played by the DJ which was met with racist remarks. The Indian student was then laughed at by a White student who she had turned to for help (Chetty 2022). These incidents culminated in the creation of the Commission of Inquiry into Allegations of Racism at Stellenbosch University, headed by retired Constitutional Court Justice Sisi Khampepe. The purpose of the Commission was to examine:

> The current state of diversity, equity and inclusion within the university campus culture, with specific reference to racism. [...] whether the current structures of the university and its material university policies, rules and processes are sufficient and most effective to address the lived experience of students and staff with regard to racism in all its guises. [And r]elated issues and concerns that may arise in the course of the inquiry, including the need for further investigation or consideration of related issues (Charles 2022).

The same year, after the establishment of the Commission, another White student urinated on the belongings of two Black students in the Eendrag residence at Stellenbosch (Baloyi 2022). There was a third incident related to urination in 2022 that did not seem to be racially motivated based on my research, rather it seems that an incredibly drunk student urinated on himself while sitting in his roommate's chair (Mthethwa 2022). All the articles about instances of urination mention the excessive drinking of alcohol. The excessive use of alcohol was not particularly surprising. Though it does not come across in the research presented here, binge drinking was a very normalised part of weekend life in Stellenbosch. It is difficult to speak to exactly why these incidents of urination began making news in 2022. Was the student in October inspired by du Toit? This does not come across in any media coverage. Have students in the past had their belongings urinated on but did not feel safe enough to speak up about it? Plenty of alumni of colour from the university shared incidents of racism they endured with journalists, but there does not seem to be a urine theme in the past.

In May of 2022, Leslie van Rooi, the senior director of Social Impact and Transformation at Stellenbosch University, connected the racism at the University to history: "Historically, the town has a very specific depiction of being the bedrock of Afrikaner nationalism, of which the university of course played a very central role. And linked with that the understanding that it's a very exclusive town, a town limited to an understanding of nationalist Afrikaner ideals." As reported on by Morné Esben, some of what van Rooi sees as preventing transformation in Stellenbosch "are "dinner table conversations", coupled with disillusionment with the government and an overriding sense of fear that the new South Africa won't allow white people space to play a role in the future of the country". This book explores some of the issues explored in these dinner table conversations as well as the perspectives of Black, Coloured, and Indian students to consider what it means to and for these students living in a South Africa which is still largely segregated but rhetoric aims for integration. Van Rooi observed that "These conversations with family and friends and in schools often feed the insecurities. These conversations are based on fear, pain, uncertainty and perhaps also an over-emotive understanding of place and identity in South Africa," and identity forms a significant exploration of this work.

The observations of van Rooi are echoed in the findings of Justice Khampepe's final report for the Commission Of Inquiry Into Allegations Of Racism At Stellenbosch University which emphasized the historical attachment of the white Afrikaner community:

> The history of the University and the symbolic meaning that it has acquired for certain members of the White, Afrikaans community poses challenges to transformation at the University. This is because there are people, both within and outside of the University, who believe that the University is culturally significant to Afrikaners and that the status quo should accordingly be preserved. These sentiments manifest in external pressures being exerted on the University by alumni and various political and interest groups, and in resistance from White, Afrikaans students who attend the University hoping to have the same experience of university life that was on offer at the University many years ago (2022, 11).

During the research for this work, I found myself in a rabbit hole related to the continuities between the present and the past at the University and in the village due to exactly what Justice Khampepe outlines above. I could not understand the dynamics I was witnessing without understanding the past of the place where I found myself. I was truly astounded by the social power that continued to be wielded by the White minority that was magnified in this winelands village. As a person who is and whose ancestors were Indigenous to the Canadian Arctic, I feel an immense responsibility to my ethnic community due to the struggles of my ancestors to get me to where I am now. My indebtedness to my ancestors made me curious about how particularly White South Africans thought of their relationship to their ancestors. Working through this thesis research process I was grappling with understanding how my South African peers were understanding and navigating to what responsibilities do historical crimes of their ancestors (for White South Africans) impose upon them today?[1] And how were Black, Coloured, and Indian students coping and creating community in a place that many found viscerally violent. Justice Khampepe connected her findings to the struggle to achieve transformation in the university:

> The crux of these findings was that the University has made impressive theoretical strides towards transformation, but that these simply are not translating adequately into the lived experiences of students and staff. In other words, although the University appears to have in its arsenal a formidable transformation apparatus, Black students and staff members still feel unwelcome and excluded at the University (2022, 10).

These feelings of exclusion and a lack of welcome to Black, Coloured, and Indian students and staff was at the fore when I arrived during the RhodesMustFall movement in 2015. When Open Stellenbosch– a sibling- or cousin-movement so to speak to RhodesMustFall– formed, the Afrikaans-language offerings and their implementation were raised as a primary barrier to the advancement of transformation.

Afrikaans has been touted by some as a barrier to entry for Black students into Stellenbosch University; and by

---

[1] The phrasing of this question is inspired by the work of Peter Seixas and Jill Colyer's curriculum project called "The Historical Thinking Project" (2014).

others as the only way rural, impoverished Coloured students can enter the University and make the best of their higher education. Undeniably, there is a tension created by increasing English offerings in the historically Afrikaans-speaking universities, as pointed out by one of my participants, Christoff:

> On the one hand, it's just a matter of people hav*e* to understand what happens in class; that's just non-negotiable. On the other hand, you get people who want to Anglicize so that they can leave… it's not easy to be White in South Africa now, that's not saying it's easy to be Black… but if you're White you have to carry historical baggage… that's something that's going to happen to you and it's not something you should shy away from, it's something that you should embrace. The way forward for White people as a collective […] is not just throw away everything, you know forget that history ever happened. […]
> If you institute a policy in this country that everyone has to do from grade 2 or grade 3, you have to do a third language, an indigenous language, that would mean that White people have to learn a Black language, I think the uproar you would get would be tremendous, people would be enormously upset. Because why? Because what am I going to do with that in the international community? You don't live in international community, you live here. You are the international community and you decided to come here. Please just do something for the people here. That's so frustrating. So, English becomes easy compromise because they [White people] want to be international and go to Perth and they [people who are Black, Indian, or Coloured and do not speak Afrikaans] want to understand what's going on in class, so now they have a common way forward. But they come from completely different: One is patently disloyal and the other is marginalized, end up benefitting from the marginalized's needs. It's quite sickening for me. [2]

Christoff speaks to how a focus on international connections exists at the cost of improving local connections.

My interviews went in waves starting in October 2016, December 2016, then in February 2017, and finally in August

---

[2] Interviewed 2 November 2016

2017. However, due to my involvement with Open Stellenbosch and the fact that I began a romantic relationship with someone in Stellenbosch, I consistently spent time at the University and in the village starting from June of 2015. As they appear in the text I'll continue to introduce my informants but offer an overview here of the people whose collaboration in large part created this book. My initial interview with Christoff was instrumental in how this book took shape. The interview opened my eyes to the broad possibilities of the spectrum of beliefs and nuances possible in the subject at hand. When we met, Christoff had just finished his first year of Masters in Biochemistry but was a history enthusiast, particularly of his people: the Afrikaners. He grew up in Bloemfontein and had been the Prim[3] at a men's residence at the University. I was connected to him through my friends who had joined a student group called *Volksverraaier*, a loaded term in the Afrikaner community meaning "betrayer of the people".

Megan was another informant associated with *Volksverraaier*. She was enthusiastic about changing how white-Afrikaans-speaking students were engaging on campus. Around the same time, I met Wanijuk. She was a Black-Kenyan who supported the goals of Open Stellenbosch but did not take part in any protest action out of fear of losing her study-visa. Anneke was also a huge help to me, because of her insights but also letting me sleep at her house and helping me meet participants. She was a White-Afrikaans, fluently bilingual in English. We met through the USDV[4]. I also interviewed Catherine and Kara from the USDV whom I also interacted with socially. After hearing about Du Toit from Catherine, I was introduced to him by a friend in the InZync Poetry Collective.

The second wave of interviews were mostly from connections I made while attending an event at one of the men's residences in early February 2017. I met Jason, Freddie, Philna and Justin at that event. Ané was interviewed around this time because we had tried to meet before the holiday-break, but our timing did not work until the following school year began. Megan introduced me to Ané. Siphe and Shane

---

[3] The head of the residence committee.
[4] The University of Stellenbosch Debating Union.

were acquaintances I had met while facilitating a workshop with their residence's house committee. The last wave of interviews in August 2017 were follow-up interviews with Du Toit and Catherine. Hugo, a student I met while playing PokemonGo on the Rooiplein one night, was the last interview I conducted. The rest of this chapter outlines the methodology and ethical approach I used.

Methodology: *Layers upon Layers*

This is an ethnographic study of the relationship between identity and belonging at Stellenbosch University. I begin this section by describing my methodological approach with regards to my day to day during fieldwork, how I found my participants, and the method I used to try keeping my own biases in check. Every researcher, in every field (no matter how "scientific") is steeped in the biases of their society and positionality.[5]

Participant observation is a methodological cornerstone of ethnography. I used participant observation to investigate the students of Stellenbosch through experiencing what they experience. Participant observation is a special kind of attentiveness to everyday life. It is a subjective tool, as it draws from one's own experience, and is also objective, as anthropologists develop methodological tools to verify subjective experience, personal observations and interpretations (Ross 2010:10). As such, participant observation helps reduce the problem of people changing their behaviour when they know that they are being studied (Bernard 2011: 265). I have drawn on my own personal experiences of inhabiting Stellenbosch as a key source of data by combining an understanding of de Certeau's "Walking the City" (1988) and the hermeneutic circle of Hans-Georg Gadamer to be able to critically understand how I experienced Stellenbosch. Keeping track of my experiences through fieldnotes was a way of creating my own story. I am opening "a legitimate theatre for practical actions" (de

---

[5] For example, in the 2010s engineers who developed the motion sensing tapes – who were mostly White– failed in their testing phase to test their tapes on a diverse enough sample of people so the taps didn't work for people with darker skin tones (Plenke 2015).

Certeau 1988: 125, original emphasis). Stories can cut across barriers, and narratives create bridges in their place.

I found participants for my research through my established social network in Stellenbosch. I also attended some events where I made an effort to speak with people. Most of my interviews were semi-structured, focused around general themes with broad, open-ended questions so that participants were able to answer in ways that allowed them to express what they believed to be most significant (Bernard 2010: 156). My early interviews had a set structure, beginning by asking people about growing up and school, then moving into questions about the University. I gave myself the liberty of deviating from the questions that I had formed when my informants opened up about particular issues or brought up subjects other than those I had prepared. Hence, this required an attention to detail in the words my participants used. Additionally, I carried a small notebook in which I jotted things down as well as the notes application on my phone when I observed moments that seemed significant to me.

The hermeneutic circle I used to understand my story in Stellenbosch was based on the work of Hans-Georg Gadamer (1960). Gadamer argued humans always have particular prejudices (information that shapes our ability to make judgements). He understands prejudice as a prejudgment that occurs while we are interpreting information. Prejudgments, however, are always themselves open to revision as long as we foreground that they are there. Insofar as human understanding involves prejudices, to understand it, we must involve ourselves in a dialogue that encompasses our understanding of ourselves as well as of the matter at hand. At the end of the day, I did my best to write up a journal entry of significant events and then reflect on how I understood those events using a Gadamerian hermeneutic circle.

Theoretical Framework for Identity

Stuart Hall defines 'identities' as points of temporary attachment to the subject positions which discursive practices construct for us. To understand expressions of individual or collective identity, he argues, we must look for their roots not in any particular 'history' or 'culture' but rather in present-day discursive structures, as notions of the 'self' and 'society' are becoming increasingly supple (1996: 6). This understanding of identity was built from his earlier work in which 'cultural identity' is conceived of in two distinct ways. The first is understanding it as a shared culture that acts as a collective 'true' self, hiding beneath layers of superficial or artificially imposed 'selves', which people with a shared history and ancestry hold in common (Hall, 1996: 223). The second way is understanding that while there are many points of similarity, there are also "critical points of deep and significant difference which constitute 'what we really are'- or rather, since history has intervened, 'what we have become'" (Hall, 1996: 235). In this second sense, cultural identity is a matter of 'becoming' as well as of 'being'.

Both forms of understanding concern the different ways in which people are positioned by or position themselves within narratives of the past (Hall, 1996: 235). To position myself using Hall's concept, since my grandmother was victimized by the structural violence of the Canadian state's project of assimilation of Labrador Inuit, she did not share her language or much of her culture with my father; while I am Inuk[6] through my blood memory and the reclaimed cultural practices shared with me by my father but also because I am in the process of becoming Inuk through my own pursuits such as learning our language— Inuttitut— and building ties with Inuit community.

Elsewhere, Hall encourages us to think about the tension between 'roots' and 'routes': how that culture embeds one in place or in a context of recognition; and culture as the different staging posts that people go through in their lives, collectively and individually (Hall, 1997). He pushes us to think about the related idea of identification as "the moment when we invest in how we are hailed from the outside". Each identification is an act of symbolic power that excludes the 'other' (Hall, 1997). I intend to use Hall's understandings of language and culture — as a way of situating oneself in particular moments, as a process of 'becoming', and as a way of 'being' — to see how people position themselves in particular instances. This study is about how young Afrikaners are adapting to an increasingly anglicized

---

[6] *Inuit*: people in Inuttitut, *Inuk*: Person in Inuttitut

Stellenbosch and how students who would have been historically excluded from the University (namely Black, Coloured and Indian students) position themselves in an Afrikaner-created space.

Identities are often understood as narratives: the stories people tell themselves and others about who they are (and who they are not). Generally, collective narratives of identity underpin more individual narrative. Each generation reproduces narratives in a selective way. Identity narratives can shift, be contested, and occur in multiple ways. "They can relate to the past, to a myth of origin; they can be aimed at explaining the present and, probably above all, they function as a projection of a future trajectory" (Yuval-Davis, 2006: 202). This mobile understanding of identity is meant to work against me "carry[ing] on about the people (others) we [anthropologists] study, assumed to be 'immobilised' by frozen tradition and customs and confined to particular geographies and spaces" (Nyamnjoh, 2016b: 30).

Ideas of 'belonging' are political, and the politics of belonging "comprises specific political projects aimed at constructing belonging in particular ways to particular collectivities that are, at the same time, themselves being constructed by these projects in very particular ways" (Yuval-Davis 2006: 197). Simplistically, "belonging can be an act of self-identification or identification by others, in a stable, contested or transient way" (Yuval-Davis 2006:199). Many scholars, including Bell, Fortier and Butler, argue that belonging is constructed to include a performative dimension. That is, performance through "specific repetitive practices, relating to specific social and cultural spaces, which link individual and collective behaviour, are crucial for the construction and reproduction of identity narratives and constructions of attachment" (Yuval-Davis 2006:199) It is in this way that free floating emotions 'stick' to particular social objects (Yuval-Davis, 2006: 203). Understanding belonging as performance therefore, should be combined with the idea of identity as transition, always producing itself through the combined processes of being and becoming, belonging and longing to belong. This duality often appears in narratives of identity (Probyn, 1996: 19). Additionally, Simon Harrison (2003) points out that identity can be constructed as much against difference as through similarity and resemblance. In Stellenbosch, I have investigated how the performance of identity differs for people who occupy different identity positionalities.

Race and Anthropology

This study uncovers aspects of and attitudes toward English at Stellenbosch University, where White people are the overwhelming majority of students and staff. In this section, I consider the relationship between anthropology and concepts of race as well as grappling with Apartheid categories

There are more professors named Johan than professors who are Black (Open Stellenbosch Collective 2015), even as some Blacks are named Johan. Considering the national demographics of South Africa, I want to acknowledge the demographic anomaly that is the University space as it is strikingly White. As I am entering this space, I believe the benefits of anthropological studies that include White people should be considered. Historically, anthropology focused on the racialized other (see Deloria 1969; Nyamnjoh 2012a&b, 2013). Dyer explains that the consequence of concentrating on the racialization of those on the margins of society has fixed attention on "others" as the problem needing explanation; that is, they are the ones who must come in line with those thought to be the centre. This dynamic allows the centre to construct itself as the norm, an unproblematic standard point of reference (Dyer 1988: 44).

Etienne Balibar provides insight on the cause and consequence of anthropology's relationship with the concept of race and the racialized other. He described the relationship between the "wrong use of the scientific category of race or from mythical construction of a pseudo-biological notion (a superstition) that had no empirical content but transposed cultural and linguistic differences" which was then "extended into ethnology and anthropology, against the background of European colonial expansion and its project of civilising barbarians" (2008, 1632). Studying the powerful is important to disrupting the use of anthropology to construct 'otherness', to move the discipline further away from projects of "civilising barbarians". After the existence of biological races was decisively disproven, there was an ideological shift within anthropology to explain that instead of being from different races that:

> [...] humankind is not a racially diverse species but a species capable of racism, perhaps inevitably pushed into the construction of racist [...] attitudes, either by some sort of transcendental illusion or as a consequence of their historical development in communities, separated cultures, and societies caught in objective relations of domination (Balibar 2008, 1635).

Moving away from a racialist analysis –which accepts the existence of races– meant turning the discipline instead closer towards one which examines power, how it is leveraged in ways expected and not. Positively, Balibar constructs anthropology as:

> a program of self-cognition or self-recognition by humankind, an identification of the humanity of the human. It is a project of answering questions of identity and relations in the human (historic, geographic, cultural) world: who we are and where we are with respect to one another (2008, 1635).

If we continue to study within the same sets of power dynamics with regards to social class, race, gender, religion, etc, then we are not furthering our understanding of who we are and where we are with respect to one another. Studies of non-traditional subjects –whiter, wealthier, more powerful humans– highlight new questions of identity and relations in the human world.

The category of racism "is taken for granted, all the more because the study of racism has become an essential sociological and political object, and what are mainly discussed are different definitions and theories and the conditions of their application" (Balibar 2008, 1630). Balibar argues we must consider and question the "obvious" related to racism. From the perspective of South Africans of many different backgrounds, there are countless "obvious" things with regards to "race" and racism. All the more reason to be undertaking anthropology to make these "obvious" knowledges visible.

The demographics of Stellenbosch mean it is haunted by questions of race and racialized language hierarchies as well as interethnic relations ordered around the same logic of racialized hierarchies. What makes a language sit higher in the hierarchy is not the level of sophistication but rather the closeness to the language spoken by White people. Specific laws from apartheid entrenched these hierarchies of language and race like the *Group Areas Act* (1950) which was used to reserve the town centre of Stellenbosch (including the University), for those classified by the apartheid regime as White. A way of understanding how people think about race is as Mary Lynn and Jeremiah, an inter-racial couple of Sherman Alexie's imagining, do:

> As a foreign country they occasionally visited, or as an enemy that existed outside their house, as a destructive voice they could fight against as a couple, as a family. But race was also a constant presence, a houseguest and permanent tenant who crept around all the rooms in their shared lives, opening drawers, stealing utensils and small articles of clothing, changing the temperature. (2000: 14)

South Africa is a country where race does not need to explicitly be spoken about to change the temperature in a room. In Walker's research among students at Northern University, she found that "race seemed to be nowhere and everywhere" (2005: 50). She notes that, "Black students in particular are likely to be making strategic decisions about when to comply, when to ignore and when to resist racialized hierarchies" (Walker 2005: 50). However:

> The issue was to try to understand what was going on where the setting of the institution had only recently embraced transformation, where the situated activity element included both public complaints about and denials of racist behaviour and, contextually, the 'rainbow nation' still carried scars of its brutal past. (Walker 2005: 50)

The unique demographics of the space I worked in yielded discourses about race, even though my explicit object of study was language.

Additionally, here I would like to note the language used to describe racial groups in my work. As has been put eloquently by Ta-Nehisi Coates, "the process of naming 'the people' has never been a matter of genealogy and physiognomy so much as one of hierarchy" (2015: 7). Language is a living iteration of how the present haunts the past. I struggled with what words to use to describe people in this work. I have read Steve Biko, who argued calling oneself "black" was the first step toward emancipation because it pushed people to "hold their heads high in defiance rather than willingly surrender their souls to the white man" (1978: 49); that "non-white" would never be an empowering term because "If one's aspiration is whiteness but his pigmentation makes attainment of this impossible, then, that person is non-white" (1978: 49).

I had an instinct to want to push back against apartheid categories. I wanted to call White people Pink people as a way of decentering whiteness, as Salman Rushdie does in Midnight's Children. In the North American context, 'people of colour' or BIPOC (Black, Indigenous and people of colour) are commonly used by racialized people (another sometimes used category). People of colour did not quite sit right with me because White people have a colour too, theirs is the colour of privilege. I was reminded of my South African history professor during my undergraduate studies who explained the irony of needing to use the same racial categories as apartheid to be able to track the extent to which things have changed since apartheid. For the same class I had the opportunity to intern with South African History Online (SAHO) who use the rule of capitalizing racial groups to denote the legal definitions of them in South African law. After conferring with my supervisor, he strongly favoured using the standard racial groups of South African law capitalized.

Literature, History, and the Plurivocality of Race

In this section, I look at how the expansiveness of race sometimes requires additional tools, like literature and creative non-fiction, to capture its nuances. There is a debate around the usefulness of literature and ethnography, and the extent to which disciplinary boundaries can be blurred for the sake of research. The particular mutability of race is why I advocate for every tool at our disposal in its examination. The ability for race to operate discursively without even the need to mention it is also inspected. One of the functions of race is to homogenize diverse groups of people thereby invalidating the individuality of the members within. Another discourse that is explored in this section about homogenisation is remembering the diversity of opinion that existed within both the Afrikaner and English White communities during Apartheid. This historical detour is to remind readers of the mutability of English to strategically be positioned as "anti-apartheid" and "decolonial".

The purity of disciplinary boundaries and hierarchies is one that disproportionately benefits their Eurocentric creators, as Nyamnjoh argues: "Under [the logic of the neoliberal political economy of knowledge] production shaped by and in turn shaping a hierarchy of purity, anthropologists at the centre enjoy a glorification that licenses them to ignore with impunity the work of their colleagues at the periphery" (2017: 91-92). Vincent Crapanzano structured his ethnography of White-South Africans during apartheid in a way that was similar to that of a novel due to the plurivocality of his South African experience. That is, "the cacophony […] of social reality is often sacrificed in ethnographic and sociological description to a theoretically inspired classism", to "call attention to the fact that symmetry, simplicity, and consistency are often list to the social actor through the baroque texture of [their] everyday life" (1985, xiii-xiv). I was surprised at how much his work resonated with me. I also felt apprehensive about this as it was criticized, particularly for his unethical behaviour. He promised anonymity to his participants without being able to deliver that, especially regarding anonymity between community members. Additionally, he used the United States and experiences of White-middle-class Americans, as a barometer for "normal" to measure South Africans against. I strived to ensure to not reproduce similar ethical problems and do not mean to understate these valid reservations. However, also, I do not want to throw the baby out with the bathwater and leave out his work entirely as it is in many ways one of the first attempts to study the powerful in South Africa.

Literature in this work is used to disrupt traditional anthropological assumptions about knowledge production in an attempt to help anthropology become more inclusive of the kinds of knowledges it looks to validate. Throughout my book I weave examples from literature and history, including creative non-fiction based on my fieldnotes[7]. This is somewhat unconventional in anthropology but is done purposefully to situate my study. I agree with Nyamnjoh that "it is possible to marry ethnography and fiction" (2017: 91). There are benefits to "connecting fiction and ethnography can help bring out the perspectives of those neglected by mainstream scholarship" (Nyamnjoh 2012c: 266). Especially in contexts like Africa, as "fiction is one of the most common vehicles used by African intellectuals to document and share 'insider' accounts of their subjectivities and societies" (2017: 88). This is because the goal of anthropology itself is to ascertain an insider account of one's field. Particularly, given that my positionality as an outsider – not being South African, being White, not speaking Afrikaans – leaning on the accounts of insiders who have given me a peek into their world, this seems like one of the most responsible things to do. There were topics and aspects of Stellenbosch which I would have wanted to explore, like the cultures and traditions within men's residences that were not available to me due to my gender. The way I observed that when I, as a white presenting woman, approached a group of men it was as though a volume dial was being turned down on a stereo as a particular set of training kicked in. I once was judging a debate a Bishop's College– a historically Whites-Only, private all-boys school in Cape Town, one of the most expensive schools in the country– where as I walked down the lawn towards the school buildings I was approached by a student who said, "Hello ma'am, do you need any help finding something?". I accepted his help. On my way out, I was approached by probably three other young men asking the same thing. This set of rote manners is the software that kicks back in when a White woman approaches a group of White men (particularly of that social group). I did make attempts

---

[7] See chapter 3.

to go to events organized by men's residences but it would be excellent further research for an anthropologist who is a man to undertake such a study.

Arguing for the recognition of the knowledge created by fiction author Amos Tutuola, Nyamnjoh writes: "what is recognised as knowledge is very much a function of the power to prescribe. And should it surprise anyone that disciplinary debates are markedly uneven across physical and social geographies, and across gender, class, generational, ethnic, and racial divides?" (2017: 92). Though debates around anthropology's colonial history may have quieted elsewhere since "African scholars have yet to find enough ethnographic evidence to confirm the end of colonial anthropology and the logic of a world bounded by hierarchies of race, place, culture, class, gender and generation" (Nyamnjoh 2017: 92), I believe it important to be part of the disruptions of the colonial hangover of knowledge hierarchies; especially considering that "ethnographic research by Africans" and I would argue, other politically disenfranchised peoples who have been disproportionately studied by anthropologists (such as indigenous North Americans), "has been channelled through the outlets of other purportedly less tainted [by racism] disciplines such as African literature, African history, African religion and theology, and African philosophy" (Nyamnjoh 2017: 88). In the context of postapartheid history, scholars like Premesh Lalu are advocating for similarly expansive understandings of evidence (2009).

When I first moved to South Africa, I was overwhelmed by the multi-layered nature of the interactions around me. As Mark Solms, a sixth generation White-South African put it: "everything about South Africa is just excruciatingly painful, in layers, upon, layers" (Brown 2017)[8]. For example, my classes at the University of Cape Town (UCT) were very White, my friends from the UCT Debating Union were very White, yet in some ways being surrounded by whiteness made me feel guilty when I interacted with my Black peers. I felt as though by wanting to befriend them, I was tokenizing them: I felt guilty about not having any Black friends. However, systematic failures to transform UCT was one of the reasons

---

[8] Podcast

why there were so many White people to begin with and why it was difficult for me to make Black friends. If I had studied engineering, any of the applied sciences, or even other 'more practical' humanities, I would have had more Black peers. Many first-generation university students (which in the South African context tend to be Black, Indian or Coloured) are encouraged to take degrees that have clear career paths, because many of their families expect to be supported financially (Theron 2017: 148)[9].

Another example of the multi-layered nature of interactions in South Africa: I mentioned to one of my White women South African friends the issue of catcalling by men who looked as though they were homeless. She concurred it was difficult to know what to do because they as people were so often dehumanized, they are generally people who were Black, Coloured or Indian, and of a much lower class-standing. Hence, not acknowledging them contributes to their dehumanization, but by catcalling us, they were contributing to *our* dehumanization. While this might be an issue in parts of the West as well, the level of tension in South Africa feels much higher due to the extremity of the inequality. With many of the issues facing South Africa, I have concluded that tensions of racial and financial inequality do not exist uniquely there but are much more on the surface, though sometimes still coded.

People have found creative ways to remove racialized people by the use of 'they' and 'these people' which as Ross notes is usually racially inflected and patronising in the South African context (2010: 21). A friend of mine was in the queue at a garage to buy some snacks. She is half-Persian and half-White-British and is White-presenting. The garage was busy and only one attendant was working the cash register while the other was stocking shelves. Both of the attendants were Black. The queue was growing long and a White woman standing in front of her, said, to no one in particular, "Ugh, these people. They just don't know how to prioritize." She then looked around for validation for what she had just said, probably expecting a nod of understanding or a sympathetic smile from someone like her. She looked at my friend who

---

[9] This is known colloquially as "Black tax". Mkhonto 2018, Birnbaum 2015, Ngwadla 2018.

asked, "why are you looking at me?" By doing so she was disrupting the acceptance of the woman's racially-inflected patronising statement, which is quite a normal way for a White-South African to belittle Black people and reinforce their own racial superiority. However, as has been noted widely Afrikaners (and White-South Africans more generally) "complain that outsiders depict them monochromatically, as [...] racists" (Goodwin and Schiff 1995: 21). My intention is to present a more nuanced view than this, as I believe the racism seen in South Africa is as racism is in all places - socially and contextually constructed and taught.

By way of illustrating what I mean about issues being more on the surface in South Africa, I will share an anecdote from Canada. While visiting my hometown, I attended a concert in a church. In front of me sat a woman wearing a hijab. An older White-woman approached her and said "As-Salaam-Alaikum! I'm sponsoring a Syrian family, they're teaching me Arabic, and I'm teaching them English. Their English is much better than my Arabic now! So where are you from?" I did not hear the response of the woman wearing the hijab, it is important to analyse what was said and done by the White woman. She approached an unknown person because she presumed they had a connection because that person had marked themselves as Muslim and the White woman also knew some Muslim people. Not that she was also Muslim in a predominantly Christian space but that she knows other people who are Muslim. Furthermore, by asking the question "where are you from?" she demonstrated the presumption that people *from* Newfoundland do not wear hijabs, hence, this woman clearly was not from Newfoundland. There is a presumption of whiteness created by conceptions of Newfoundlanders as exclusively being people who are descendants of European settlers. Thus, settlers in Canada come with their own assumptions and racially inflected ways of talking about Others.

This example illustrates the "racism without races" Balibar wrestled with. The older white woman is able to make assumptions about the hijab wearing woman without ever mentioning her race. Shortly after the "Scarf Affair" of 1989 wherein students in French public schools were barred from wearing hijabs, Balibar meditated on how it was possible for racism to continue to exist without reference to race:

> The difference between cultures considered as separate entities or separate symbolic structures […] refers on to cultural inequality within the 'European' space itself or, more precisely, to 'culture' […] as a structured of inequalities tendentially reproduced in an industrialized, formally educated, society that is increasingly internationalised and open to the world. The 'different' culture are those which constitute obstacles, or which are established as obstacles […] to the acquisition of culture (1991, 25).

Participants in my research often named a benefit of English as it being an "international language", thus in the characterisation of Balibar as a preferential or "good" association to have. Afrikaans isn't seen as opening these "internationalised" doors, and has some heavy historical baggage. In the political climate of South Africa post-apartheid it is not unusual for Afrikaners to be constructed as the culture which constitutes the obstacle to progress. This is likely due to the conflation between Afrikaners and Apartheid. The National Party is conceived of as an ethnically Afrikaner party, though plenty of English South Africans also voted for them during Apartheid. As of 1980, 57 percent of White South Africans spoke Afrikaans as a home language, about 39 percent of White South Africans spoke English (the rest spoke Portuguese or other languages) (O'Malley). If the vote was purely along ethnic lines then the majority of the National Party would have never increased past 57 percent. Yet, the majority of the National Party increased during Apartheid: it started from 73 seats in 1948 and by 1977 held 134 seats. Their 1977 result had them capturing 81 percent of the seats in parliament – an increase of 54 percent from their initial 1948 election.

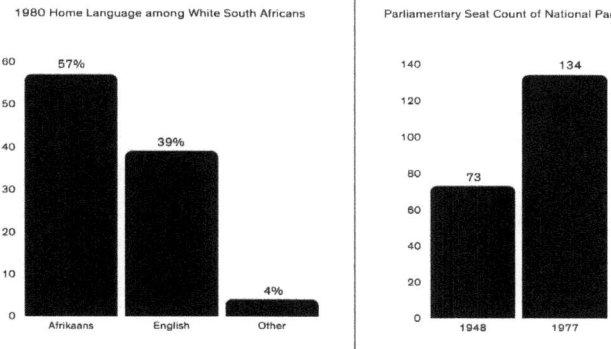

Graph 1: 1980 Home Language among White South Africans (L), Parliamentary Seat Count of the National Party (R) (Designed by Amy Norman)

It is difficult to find an English South African who would admit to voting for the National Party, I certainly never met one and no one I knew who was a born-free English South African admitted to their parents having voted for the National Party. I did have Afrikaner friends, however, admitted to me of their family ties to and participation in the Apartheid regime. Furthermore, we can be sure that not every Afrikaner voted for the National Party as no ethnicity is a monolith. English is extremely slippery in this context. White English South Africans are implicitly able to put more distance between themselves and Apartheid due to its conflation with Afrikaners. Beyond this, English–the language of the largest colonial empire– has been touted by some as a language of "decolonization". This is yet another reason to use English as an entry point for my work.

Though it is related to my interest in concepts of race and racial coding, the topic of this project was not what I imagined myself studying. I took a class during my undergraduate degree in Canada on the Indian Ocean Slave Trade which piqued my interest in the development of Afrikaans as a language. Initially, I was interested in the racial coding of Afrikaans. Some used my positionality as a White-passing non-South African to invalidate my ability to understand nuances in South Africa. I received pushback from people, some peers and some academics. Specifically, I was told that I would not succeed at understanding the nuances of Afrikaans code-shifting. People commonly told me in passing to say: "oh, there are things you won't understand because you weren't born here". This work contains a long history chapter to demonstrate the extent to which I do understand the historical context that created my field site, both at Stellenbosch as a place and Afrikaners as a people.

The other reason I have a thorough history chapter is that there were many times while I was writing, when my supervisor pointed out that I was making assumptions, so the chapter establishes premises for later chapters. In other works I had seen the quick assertions made about the history of Afrikaners, which —though they were not far off the mark— seemed harsh without the historical background. My intention was to write a more fully fleshed out work that includes a historical background because language in Stellenbosch cannot be understood without the history and history in Stellenbosch is deeply entwined with language.

It was important to me to study horizontally or upward, rather than downward as anthropology has done historically. As a student at a South African university, I thought I could make some observations and tie together the knowledge of my peers. The act of attending a university, on some level, makes one an elite, as there is such a finite number of places of study and universities are so expensive to attend. Similarly, Crapanzano's aim was to study the discourse of people who are privileged by power, who are paradoxically victims of their privilege (1985: xiii) thereby studying the effect of domination on the dominated" (1985: 20). Crapanzano argued that "to be dominant in a system is not to dominate the system. Both the dominant and the dominated are equally caught in it. One has the advantage; the other does not" (1985: 20). He argued that apartheid was also oppressive, in a way, to White people. Apartheid attempted to train White people to deny the humanity of those they lived in the closest contact with. Many argued that there was a *swartgevaar,* a deep fear of Black people, with acts like the prohibition of mixed marriages, as evidence of the fear of miscegenation. Crapanzano argued that it was rather "an unspoken, pervasive fear that has its sources in apartheid and that maintains the apartheid in all its virulence" (1985: 20). He goes so far as to say, "it is a fear that informs much, though by no means all, that I heard in South Africa" (1985: 20.). In the post-apartheid (or as some call the period in which I write the post-post-apartheid era), much of what Crapanzano wrote rang true to me.

I was overwhelmed by my move to South Africa. The third chapter of this book is written as vignettes based on my experiences, to attempt to demonstrate the noise I heard during my fieldwork. It is also an attempt to begin to weave together and create a foundational understanding of Stellenbosch for my readers. This is in line with many North American indigenous storytelling practices, which do not prioritise linear retellings, as exemplified by the scholar Thomas King. King weaves together creation stories, personal anecdotes, contemporary works, stories of history and legislation, to probe the importance of storytelling in North American Indigenous cultures and to make a subtle argument that stories are the foundations from which we build ourselves. Indigenous North Americans (and anyone the world over) have been and are shaped by stories, because "the truth about stories is that that's all that we are". Using repetition at the end of each of the five lectures, King reminds his audience that stories carry knowledge and that knowledge creates an onus of moral responsibility as once they are heard, they can never be unheard: "Don't say in years to come that you would have lived your life differently if only you had heard this story. You've heard it now" (2003: 29). In South Africa, where horrific stories of inequality are told every day, it is disheartening how little action is taken, particularly by those who could make the most impact. This book is my attempt to add a chapter to South Africa's story.

The Haunted Consequences of the Synonymity between Stellenbosch and Stellenbosch University

The circumstances of my fieldwork differ from Crapanzano as he was in a village that was majority Coloured[10] with a minority of White people owning the land and businesses. My fieldwork was at Stellenbosch University,

---

[10] In other parts of South Africa this could have been people who were Black or Indian, or some combination thereof.

a formerly exclusively (and presently predominantly) White and Afrikaans university. The demographics and spatiality of Stellenbosch remains similar to other South African towns. The University is still majority White and it is deeply embedded in the town so the town itself needs to be considered to understand the University.

The University is in the central part of the town near a large mall, next to a major road, Merriment. On the side of town closer to Kayamandi and Cloetesville—the Apartheid-era Black and Coloured areas which have respectively remained as such post-Apartheid—, there are not many sit-down restaurants or shopping areas. Most services in Stellenbosch are in central (formerly "White" Stellenbosch). When I searched on Google Maps for "Stellenbosch" without a specific address: the pin is dropped directly next to the University. Zooming out, the University continues to remain in the centre.

Googling "Stellenbosch", the website of Stellenbosch University is a top result. The synonymy of the University and the Town on the internet leads me to believe I must analyse the Town itself to appropriately situate and contextualize the University.

Figure 1: Location of University of Stellenbosch (L) and Location of University of Stellenbosch (R)

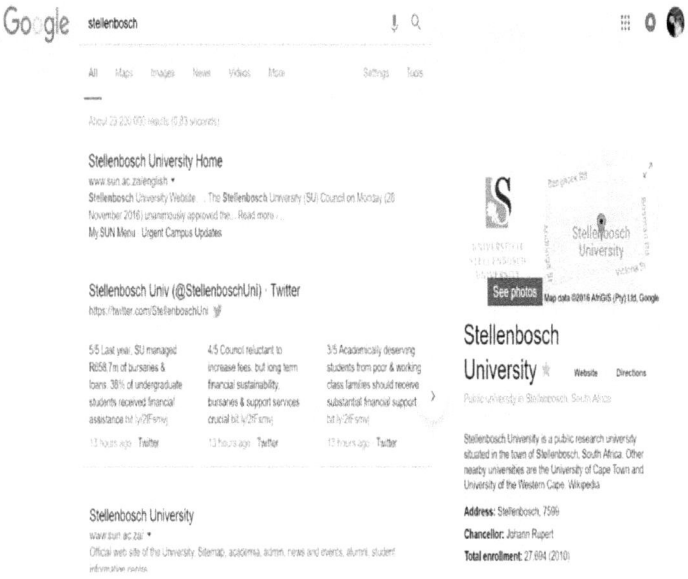

Figure 2: The Synonymy of the University and the Town on the Internet

Considering the demographic distribution of Stellenbosch, we can see that the town centres on whiteness:

Figure 3: Demographic Distribution Of Stellenbosch

While the centre of the community has different colour dots, there is no doubt that purple dots (White people) clusters in the centre of Stellenbosch. There is a lower population density for the purple dots near central Stellenbosch, which means that the properties are more spacious than in Kayamandi or Cloetesville. The purple dots are those with greatest proximity to the services offered in central Stellenbosch. The exception is that the area within Cloetesville where purple dots cluster without mixing, is a gated community called "Welgevonden Estate".

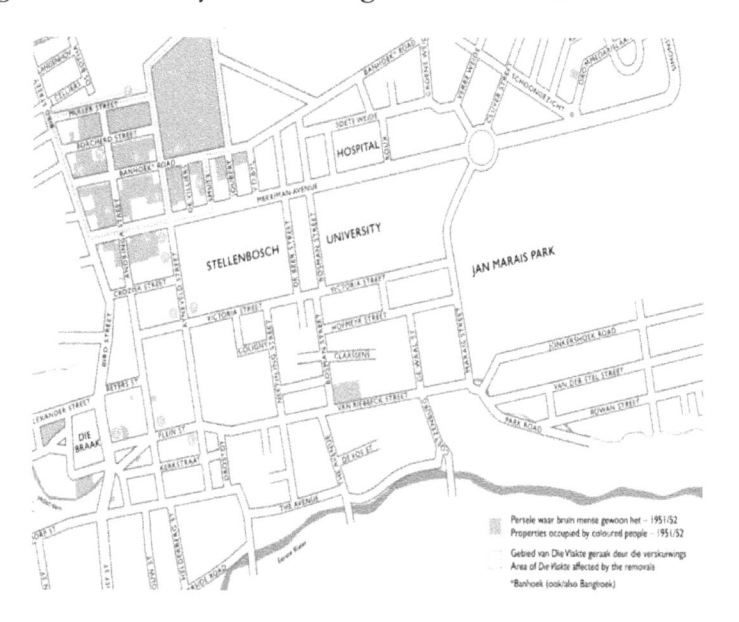

Figure 4: Europe

It was common for friends of mine who were Black students at the University to refer to the area above Bird Street and between Plein Street and Dorp Street as "Europe". This Europe was about a ten-minute walk from the University (in the opposite direction from Cloetesville and Kayamandi). "Europe" has many sit-down restaurants, with dishes that cost R50 or more, bars, and art galleries. Minimum wage at a grocery store at the time was R30 an hour. Parts of the sidewalks were bricked rather than concrete (as is most typical in areas of the Western Cape that have sidewalks) and around the roundabouts on Plein Street had flowerbeds. It was rare to see litter there. One cannot doubt the European ambitions there.

One day when I was walking to "Europe" from the University, I noticed that almost all the clientele at the restaurants there were White. The first two restaurants I walked past were full. The first restaurant had no patrons of colour, while the second one had one person of colour. The waitstaff at these restaurants appeared to be mostly Black or Coloured. I was surprised when a White-Capetonian acquaintance who had visited Stellenbosch, remarked that the diversity she saw surprised. She expected it to be all White-Afrikaans people. I made the distinction that the centring on whiteness does not mean only having White people somewhere, but also how places were being *taken up* by White people. For example, there was a restaurant called Java that had White waiters and White clientele and people who were Black or Coloured working in the kitchen, thus were on the periphery. This was a consequence of Apartheid. Apartheid pushed people in South Africa who were Black, Indian, or Coloured towards the periphery based on their proximity to whiteness on the morphological ranking system. This thesis will use conceptualizations of race as posited by whiteness studies because it "offers a vocabulary that challenges the unmarked and normative nature of racial hegemony, thus rendering its racial politics analytically tangible" (van Zyl-Hermann and Boersema, 2017: 652).

I deploy Jacques Derrida's concept of "hauntology" in contemporary Stellenbosch due to the layered nature of the town.. Derrida rehabilitated "ghosts as a respectable subject of enquiry" (Davis 2005: 373). Derrida tells that us:

> The point is right away to go beyond [...] the first glance and thus to see there where this glance is blind, to open one's eyes wide there where one does not see what one sees. One must see, at first sight, what does not let itself be seen. And this is invisibility itself. For what first sight misses is the invisible. The flaw, the error of first sight is to see, and not to notice the invisible (1994: 149).

Derrida is encouraging us to look for the seemingly invisible – like the normalcy by which White people eat in cafes and people who are Black serve them. De Vos' argued that the Stellenbosch language policy at the time made the needs of the marginalized invisible by prioritizing the needs of "a small but economically privileged group" (2015). At first glance, English seems like an obvious compromise to many who have already had to learn it as their second language and do not want to be forced to learn Afrikaans as an additional language to succeed. In classes taught in Afrikaans, these students might be haunted by the knowledge that if the class were in English they would be able to understand it. On the other hand, if it is not language capability necessarily that dissuades people from wanting to learn in English, it could be that people may not know Afrikaans any better than they know English, but they wish to politically align themselves away from what they perceive to be the interests of Afrikaner elites (see Tinyiko Maluleke July 2016). In many ways, English is a strange compromise for South Africans given that demographically English is a second, third or fourth language for many South Africans. The top six languages spoken as home-languages in South Africa are: isiZulu (22.7%), isiXhosa (16%), Afrikaans (13.5%), English (9.6%), Setswana (8%), and Sesetho (7.6%) (Fihlani 2017). When asked about why English was used at Stellenbosch or if English was important, many of my informants spoke about how English is an international language and it is the language of business in South Africa when, as of 2005, 49% of the population of South Africa struggled to understand English while around 70% of people can understand isiZulu (Steyn 2005: 128).[11]

Additionally, here I would like to note the language used to describe racial groups in my thesis. As has been put eloquently by Ta-Nehisi Coates, "the process of naming 'the people' has never been a matter of genealogy and physiognomy so much as one of hierarchy" (2015: 7). Language is a living iteration of how the present haunts the past. I struggled with what words to use to describe people. I have read Steve Biko, who argued calling oneself "black" was the first step toward emancipation because it pushed people to "hold their heads high in defiance rather than willingly surrender their souls to the white man" (1978: 49); that "non-white" would never be an empowering term because "If

---

[11] Though this is contested by how mutually intelligible languages like isiXhosa and Sepedi are with isiZulu.

one's aspiration is whiteness but his pigmentation makes attainment of this impossible, then, that person is non-white" (1978: 49).

I had an instinct to want to push back against Apartheid categories. I wanted to call White people Pink people as a way of decentring whiteness, as Salman Rushdie does in *Midnight's Children*. In the North American context, 'people of colour' or BIPOC (Black, Indigenous and people of colour) are commonly used by racialized people (another sometimes used category). People of colour did not quite sit right with me because White people have a colour too, theirs is the colour of privilege. I was reminded of my South African history professor during my undergraduate studies who explained the irony of needing to use the same racial categories as Apartheid to be able to track the extent to which things have changed since Apartheid. For the same class I had the opportunity to intern with South African History Online (SAHO) who use the rule of capitalizing racial groups to denote the legal definitions of them in South African law. After conferring with my supervisor, he strongly favoured using the standard racial groups of South African law capitalized.

The considerations of identity and belonging, including my own identity and belonging, coupled with the historical context of my field site, are what has shaped my methods. It was important for me to approach my participants with an informed openness to be able to access the different perspectives that are rooted in the lived experiences of my informants. It is possible that I would not have been able to act ethically without these considerations. Methodology and ethics inform one another.

Ethical Considerations

I acknowledge that I was an inexperienced researcher, thus I paid close attention to the Anthropology Southern Africa ethical guidelines as well as those of the Humanities Department at UCT[12]. The first priority of my research was

---

[12] UCT Humanities Ethical Guidelines: http://www.humanities.uct.ac.za/hum/research/ethics. Accessed 10

to do no harm. This involved informing the people with whom I interacted about the nature of my research and letting them choose to opt out or not be part of it. I offered people pseudonyms for confidentiality purposes because language is an incredibly politically charged issue. This allowed them to protect their identity and opinions from scrutiny and retaliation against them.

Participant observation builds relationships of trust between anthropologists and our informants, so genuine informed consent is highly contested. In the field, it was my responsibility to remind participants I was a researcher. I was responsible for using my judgement to protect sensitive information they chose to share with me. This included asking permission to use their knowledge that they shared with me, more than once. During the process of writing, I gave interested participants the opportunity to look over my work. I saw participants as my co-producers, not just the means to the ends of my research. This is an example of consent in my research. Their ability to control information about their lives in the public sphere was more important than my research. I made certain that my participants understood that they were able to withhold their support for my research, or refuse to participate, or withdraw their consent at any time. I reinforced that it was their right to do so, and that they would not be penalized if that was their choice (for example, by me speaking badly about them to mutual acquaintances or anything else that could be seen as penalization).

In his history of White farming discourse in Zimbabwe/Rhodesia, Pilossof reminds his readers that there is an "importance of disaggregating the White farming community so as to avoid treating them as a homogenous, monolithic whole", though "there *are* continuities and points of connection in the way experience has been related and talked about" (2012: 4). Thus, I have taken care to do my best not to treat the students at Stellenbosch as a homogenous whole, but as an aggregation of individuals who have had unique experiences at the University. There are assumptions held by many about fieldwork and data that imply that it is

---

May 2016. ASA Ethical Guidelines: https://www.asnahome.org/about-the-asna/ethical-guidelines, Accessed 10 May 2016.

timeless; like, when researchers return to old fieldnotes to mine for data sometimes more than a decade old to make comments about the present. This is problematic especially when data itself is often incredibly time-bound to the specific period when it was collected. People's ideas are not immobilized and their thinking on given issues can change dramatically even in short periods.

Yet, we hold onto our printed texts expecting that they be gospel truths. I am aware of the shifting nature of the opinions of individuals that can change through time and experience. Achebe's analogy of the dancing masquerade that begins this chapter is powerful because social reality unfolds and changes with time. During fieldwork, what was a truth can become in time pure fiction; as people may have moved on from the initial snapshot, research might have captured them. In the initial stages of my research when I met Catherine and somewhat clumsily interviewed her, she had the good sense to mention to me how much her opinion evolved from auditing a sociology class which allowed me to suggest we do a second interview. I also did a second interview with Du Toit and in the final chapter, so I reflect on how these second interviews helped me consider the flexibility of people.

As a researcher, I endeavoured to be cognizant of how power moved. Not everyone had the experiences I had at Stellenbosch, so I tried to allow people's conclusions or ideas to come out on their own terms without rushing to my own conclusions. In some cases, I disagreed with the opinions of people I worked with. It was my role to listen to them carefully and without judgement. For example, when some informants called Open Stellenbosch "radical", which I did not think they were not; or when informants who were White spoke about emigrating, something which made me uncomfortable because it is ethically dubious. I chose to use the Gadamerian hermeneutic circle to foreground my biases because I was aware of my own limitations of being able to sway my biases. The Gadamerian circle meant reminding myself that my biases exist and thus I need to listen even more carefully when informants say things I disagreed with, to be able to try harder to understand where they were coming from.

My experience of South Africa and my own education in South African history has made me prejudiced against the White-Afrikaans community. It is impossible not to witness the violences of Apartheid that continue into the present and Apartheid is framed as an intervention of Afrikaners. Through my research and fieldwork I learned about and considered the complicity of English South Africans who benefitted just as much but do not carry the same historical baggage as Afrikaners. Beyond benefitting, the majorities of the National Party — who implemented Apartheid— grew so mathematically English South Africans voted to Apartheid as well. My positionality as an outsider/foreigner was also not a complete immunization against bias. An informant confronted me about possibly being voyeuristic, of my position as being from the global north, and speaking on behalf of South Africans. The undertaking of this study challenged me to unearth assumptions I made about people based on their language and race. While the primary focus of the study was on the English language's ability to chameleon itself away from its colonial past (as Stellenbosch was often described by my participants as an "Afrikaans place" or "Afrikaner space"), I concurrently felt that I needed to make an effort to fairly represent Stellenbosch.

    Before I started my fieldwork, I felt that the experiences I had in Stellenbosch were atypical of the general experience of most White people at the University because the vast majority of my friends were Black, Indian and Coloured who I met at Open Stellenbosch. Given the demographics of Stellenbosch, and the soft norms of social segregation[13] at the time of my fieldwork, it was unusual for a White presenting person to be friends with people from other racial groups. This does not invalidate those experiences as not being part of Stellenbosch but made me feel that I had to make a greater effort to take part in events that were viewed as more traditional such as parties hosted residences and events by the Student Representative Council. One of the reasons this was such a challenge was because I suffer from anxiety and as such, I often had quite intense anticipatory anxiety before going to events where I knew there would be many White Afrikaans people. This anxiety was not unique to

---

[13] As will be discussed in Chapter 4.

Stellenbosch but was heightened there. I pushed through these moments, to be a thorough researcher, I brought friends along for support and to help me meet people I might not have gravitated towards. I asked my participants for suggestions of events I could attend. Anneke accompanied me to a big daytime party hosted by a men's residence, where I met many informants. This is a good example of how participants are co-producers of knowledge. When I met informants for interviews I suggested we meet on the rooiplein or in the Neelsie so it did not require money (as eating together at a restaurant would).

In Stellenbosch, I was one legged when it came to my language abilities, though I did have crutches (a moderate French proficiency and rudimentary German). Studying English made sense because it is my most proficient language. Since Open Stellenbosch[14], a movement to which I have associated myself, is seen as being "anti-Afrikaans" by many, studying the politics of English avoids negative implications if I were to study Afrikaans.

Beyond this, to be able to be properly reflexive, the central role that anthropology played in the categorisation of humans must be acknowledged as it allowed for the development of policies like Bantu Education. The development of biological determinism in the 19th century was entrenched by the rise of practices like craniology, ethnology, and psychiatry. These beliefs were premised on the correlation of "bones, bodies, and behaviour" (Reilly 2016: 9). These practices worked together to form discourses such as using race and gender to explain class differences (Reilly 2016). Thus, I was careful to do my best to disrupt and deconstruct some of the harmful discourses this discipline has contributed to in the past through the writing of this thesis.

The thesis itself consists of: Chapter Two, considers the extent to which settler colonialism is a useful concept in the context of South Africa by examining additional ethnographies of White South Africans; Chapter Three, which presents an in-depth historical analysis of the battles between English and Afrikaans in South Africa, put in

---

[14] See their Facebook Page: https://www.facebook.com/openstellenbosch/?ref=br_rs Accessed 1 September 2016.

conversation with broader African questions of language; Chapter Four, which offers creative non-fiction vignettes based on my experiences and fieldnotes; Chapter Five, which analyses interracial friendships and the lack thereof at the University; and finally, Chapter Six, which discusses English as a springboard for Afrikaners to emigration and the historical obligation of Afrikaners to South Africa.

Chapter 2

Settling on Settler-Colonialism?

Introduction

This chapter focuses on ethnographic representations of whiteness in Southern Africa to situate this work in the broader anthropology of whiteness in Africa. It also considers what those works represent in the history of anthropology. By considering representations of whiteness as a shift from the traditional focus of anthropology to new(ish) angles, I highlight that these calls to diversify the focus of anthropology are not as new and shiny as they may seem. Additionally, given the focus on White South African I thought it was necessary to consider to what extent settler colonialism was a useful framework in a South African context, since South Africa was/is the largest settlement and colonization by White people in Africa.

Historically the works of White, upper-class Anthropologists have represented the "Other": economically destitute brown and Black-bodied people. There have been attempts to broaden the scope and focus of anthropological discipline, for example through the work of "Native Anthropologists": people who look like those they are anthropologising (Narayan 1993). The framing of this development, however, had its problems. As Narayan (1993) pointed out, such anthropologists are defined in relation to the standard of whiteness: an anthropologist from Trinidad working in Trinidad is different to a White anthropologist working in Trinidad. This does not consider the perspectives of those being anthropologised. Trinidad is a racially and culturally complex society created through colonization, slavery, and endured servitude from India and China. Trinidad also has a considerable diaspora. Is someone born to Trinidadian parents in Toronto, Canada going to be accepted as a "Native Anthropologist" in Trinidad? While the "Native anthropologist" is seen as such in the eyes of the White academy, often does not seem so Native to the people with whom they are collaborating. Sometimes the Native

Anthropologist might only have surface area things in common with their subjects. In the case of Narayan who is from India: the subcontinent has incredible diversity, even if someone was from the same religion and linguistic group there could still be class or caste divisions that are known to the participants who think of the "Native Anthropologist" as Other to themselves.

There are attempts by anthropologists to study up or to study horizontally as a means of disrupting the perpetuation of the image of "the Other". By "studying up" here, I mean attempts to study those with comparatively more power than the anthropologist; and "studying horizontally" being attempts to study those from similar socio-economic backgrounds to the anthropologist. Studying up has proven difficult as anthropology requires access and a willingness on the part of the participant to share. For example, two of Laura Nader's students attempted to do an ethnography of a law firm in Washington, DC in the 1970s wherein some individual members were willing to cooperate in limited ways, but the law firm as a whole did not want to be studied. The fact that this study took place in the 70s demonstrates that these concepts are not brand new, rather that they have been more popularized and accepted. This attempt made Nader ask: "How could they participant-observe if the firm wouldn't let them in the door, and if they could participant-observe, how could they do anthropology?" (1972: 22). When participants hold more power than the anthropologist, as is theoretically the case in studying up, it becomes difficult to be able to gain insight because participants are more able to feel empowered to withhold information and practice refusal by directly saying no or by excluding the anthropologist from field sites and interviews. Works that study up can provide understanding on "routes to power – in medicine, in politics, in the NGO world, and elsewhere" and bring forward these practical implications of access as well as theoretical implications (Peters and Wendland 2016, 12). These routes to beyond exist everywhere, they are not isolated to an African context. In the West, Nader probes this point, asking:

> What shapes and functions do the networks of law firms have in an organization where at mid-career the majority of firm members fan out into positions about Washington, yet still

maintain relations with the law firm even after they are no longer on the payroll. What kind of reciprocity is involved here? (1972: 17)

It will be interesting to see the extent to which the field develops, given that calls like Nader's to study up and horizontally have been coming since the 1970s. Though ethnographies of whiteness are growing, it is worth noting that I found in my research a relatively small selection of works, thereby illustrating the limited success that the diversification of anthropological subjects has had. However, most works were published since 2010 so hopefully this trend will ramp up considerably into the future. Though, it is also interesting that the publication of these ethnographies overlaps with a considerable decrease in the number of White South Africans remaining in the country (Business Tech 2018).

The number of White settlers in Africa is small when compared to the footprints of settlers elsewhere in the world. Cases of colonialism by Europeans in much of Africa and Asia tended only to have limited settlers from the metropole: colonial administrators, missionaries, and some business people. In these instances, colonialism can be understood "as a set of social phenomena that is characterised by the ability to reproduce itself by maintaining difference and inequality between coloniser and colonised" but without needing to overwhelm the native population with settlers (Chatterjee in Cavanagh and Veracini 2017, 2-3). Franz Fanon demonstrates that this approach is maintained through threats of violence and the enactment of violence (1965: 35). Colonialism in contexts where settlers remained the minority meant it was necessary to acknowledge the existence Indigenous peoples. Colonisers therefore needed to justify the dispossession of Indigenous people by emphasising their inferiority and while reinforcing the superiority of the colonisers. Permanent settlers in these minority contexts still needed to negotiate their identities in their new settlements. David Hughes argued settlers either negotiated their identities through social forms via integration to the already existing populations there, or through land: its use and maintenance (2010).

First, this chapter examines the concept of settler-colonialism, its usefulness and limitations in an African context. Secondly, it examines the use of language by White-settlers in Africa as a tool in some cases to refuse engaging with Black Africans on their terms, and in others to strategically position themselves as locals who belong. The third section of the chapter examines land and some of the ways in which White-settlers lay claim to it, as their tie to belonging. Finally, I briefly point out that within White-settlers in Africa there are class differences that are worth noting.

Africa, Colonialism, and Settler-Colonialism

Both anthropology and settlers arrived in Africa through colonialism. The use of anthropologists in Africa was intimately connected to the imperial desire to control African territory with the bare minimum settlers possible. For example, the work of EE Evans-Pritchard in Sudanese communities in the 1920s and 1930s was supported by the colonial government so they could find more efficient ways to infiltrate and control those groups (Johnson, 1982). Black people have been (and are) the subjects of the vast majority of anthropological study in Africa. The turn to White subjects in Africa for anthropology is a notable change in perspective. It is almost as though the photographer has turned the camera around on themself. This change in perspective, however, creates new challenges for anthropology. This section focuses primarily on British and to a lesser extent French colonialism as those metropoles controlled most of the African continent as well as having controlled most of the colonies that are prime examples of settler colonialism: Canada (Britain/France), the United States (Britain), Australia (Britain), and Aotearoa[15] (Britain).

It is difficult to generalise coloniality given the vast diversity of experiences. Coloniality was (and is) experienced uniquely based on the context, struggles, and life in colonised places. At the core, colonialism is about power which is dependent on the material, social, and cultural resources of those involved (Cooper 2005: 17). There are many different

---

[15] Aotearoa is the Maori name for New Zealand

iterations of colonialism but most broadly, colonialism is a form of domination that subjugates Indigenous peoples and lands for the benefit of the colonizer (Cavanagh and Veracini 2017, 4). While I focus on colonialism by European countries it is important to note that within Asia particularly Japan and China have or are maintaining colonial projects. Japan colonized the Korean peninsula and parts of Northern China in the first half of the twentieth-century, while China has and is colonizing Tibet.

Though White South Africans never constituted a majority population as White colonisers/invaders in British North America, Australia, and Aotearoa, it is applicable to the wider South African context due to the significant amassing of wealth and power that the White minority population gained through the Apartheid system. In his seminal article, "Settler colonialism and the elimination of the Native", Patrick Wolfe argues that settler-colonial societies are built on a logic of elimination of "the Native" for the purpose of control over land, regardless of what rhetoric is used: "the primary motive for elimination is not race (or religion, ethnicity, grade of civilization, etc.) but access to territory. Territoriality is settler colonialism's specific, irreducible element" (2006, 388). In the South African context some of the building blocks of the Apartheid system were legislation like the Glen Grey Act (1894) and the Native Lands Act (1913) which both severely limited the ability for Africans to hold title to land.

Enacted by Prime Minister Cecil Rhodes, the Glen Grey Act (1894) abolished communal land title and instead established individual title, thereby undermining Indigenous-African systems of land organization (SAHO 2019). There is an analogous piece of legislation in the United States called the Dawes Act (1887) which aimed to treat Native Americans as individuals rather than members of tribes particularly through the individualization of land holdings. Specifically, the Dawes Act (1887) "authorized the President to break up reservation land, which was held in common by the members of a tribe, into small allotments to be parcelled out to individuals" (National Archives 2022). While politicians justified the act as one seeking to improve the independence of Native American individuals, in reality the purpose of the

Act was to undermine tribal sovereignty. Native American tribes are considered sovereign within the United States as "domestic dependent nations" with the right to occupy land and maintain tribal autonomy over affairs that concern their members (considered citizens of these domestic dependent nations)[16]. The Dawes Act allocated the patriarch of each Native American family–in complete disregard to Native American Nations which were matriarchal– 160 acres of land, with each single individual over 18 receiving 80 acres, and orphaned children receiving 40 acres. All Native Americans had four years to select land for their allotment after which "lands that remained unclaimed by tribal members after allotment would revert to federal control and be sold to American settlers" (Locke and Wright 2019, 45). The Act severely undermined the land base of many Native American tribes as only 38 percent of the original land-base was allocated to Native American individuals, while 62 percent of the land was reverted to federal control and sold to White settlers (Citizen Potawatomi Nation 2021). This demonstrates similar tactics were used by the South African and American governments to dispossess those they were colonizing from their lands.

The other provision of the Glen Grey Act was that it created a labour tax to force Xhosa men into employment on commercial farms or in industry (SAHO 2019). There is frequently a preoccupation in settler-colonial countries with disrupting Indigenous economies and attempting to assimilate Indigenous people into a capitalist-market economy. Indigenous economies are based on economic activities that are deeply tied to place and season. For pastoral cultures in Southern Africa, this necessitates access to sufficient land for their animals to graze. This can quickly clash with settler desires for fenced plots of individual ownership which disrupt dynamic herding and grazing practices. With less access to land for pastoralists, there are risks of overgrazing and therefore disruptions to what had been a sustainable Indigenous economy before invasion. Through taxing Xhosa men and requiring them to pay their

---

[16] This is developed through the Supreme Court cases *Johnson v. McIntosh* (1823), *Cherokee Nation v. Georgia* (1831), and *Worchester v. Georgia* (1832) all overseen by Chief Justice John Marshall.

tax in currency, the Glen Grey Act coerced them into taking up jobs in the market economy, thereby clearing their claims to the plains. If they are working and not herding then there is no need for large undisrupted grazing areas so the land can now easily be turned into individualized plots for white settlers. Well before the Glen Grey Act, Mandisi Majavu notes that as "White settlers extended their settlement from the Cape to the Eastern Cape in the eighteenth century, many of these White farmers "merely laid claim to 'grazing place' or 'grazing farm'" without negotiating with Black people for the land" (2022). The resistance to the colonization of their land culminated in what is known as the Third Frontier War (1799-1803) (Majavu 2022). In his speech justifying the Glen Grey Act, Rhodes notes that:

> The natives have had in the past an interesting employment for their minds in going to war and in consulting in their councils as to war. […] At present we give [Africans] nothing to do, because we have taken away their power of making war [...] which once employed their minds (1894, 2).

Rhodes suggests that in the past, war was the main occupation of Africans. It builds on the discourse constructed by White settlers from events like the Frontier Wars who believed they were entitled to take the land of Africans and framed themselves as the victims of a violent, simple-minded, inferior race. This creates a circular logic that justifies why these White settlers are entitled to the land because of their superiority of having minds occupied with things other than "going to war and in consulting in their councils as to war" (Rhodes 1894, 2). In this context, Rhodes is also justifying the need to intervene in the lives of Africans to give them productive occupations. By saying "because we have taken away their power of making war", Rhodes creates a framing that White people have saved Africans from themselves from stopping them from going to war with each other but goes go to observe that there is still work to do for the White Saviour Settlers: "We do not teach them the dignity of labour, and they simply loaf about in sloth and laziness. They never go out and work. This is what we have failed to consider with reference to our native population" (1894, 3). Through taxing them and functionally forcing them to participate in the market economy the colonial government gained a new form of control. The settler-colonial government in South Africa needed to pivot since "The old diminutions by war and pestilence do not occur. Our good government prevents them from fighting, and the result is an enormous increase in numbers" (Rhodes 1894, 2).

Even when settler-colonial governments did successfully coerce Indigenous people to work for wages, this was still sometimes not enough for their logic of elimination. In the Canadian context, the Government had already limited the land base of Indigenous people by relegating them to reserves through the 1876 Indian Act. First Nation Reserves in Canada were significantly smaller than reservations[17] in the United States making it nearly impossible for most First Nations to continue to practice their traditional economy. One of the differences between the settler-colonial context in Canada is that in contexts where White people are the majority but Indigenous people continue to exist, the state works to assimilate Indigenous people with the hope that someday, when assimilation is successful, there will no longer be any Indigenous people. One strategy to do this is to undermine the authenticity Indigenous Canadians. If an Indigenous person is working for wages, are they really Indigenous anymore? In the late nineteenth century, many Indigenous people began to work in salmon canneries, in forestry, or whatever industries were proximal to their reserves. The Government imposed an additional layer of control on Indigenous people who were participating in the market economy when they realized Indigenous people were spending their wages on the "wrong things". Many Indigenous people used the wages earned in their market economy jobs to support socio-economic traditions within their communities. The potlatch ceremony was common among First Nations on the West Coast of Canada "marked important occasions as well as served a crucial role in distribution of wealth" (Hanson 2009). Indian Agents who oversaw the running of reserves initially thought they were making progress when Indigenous people showed interest in

---

[17] Reserves and reservations are functionally the same thing but are called "reserves" in Canada and "reservations" in the United States. "Rez" is common slang across both countries for them.

participating in the market economy but realized that the wages earned were being used to buy supplies and reinvest their wages in the potlatch system (Raibmon 2005, 20): "Instead of supplanting the potlatch economy, the wage economy stimulated it, even as the potlatch encouraged increasing Aboriginal involvement in wage labor, a supposedly modern activity" (Raibmon 2005, 27). The Indian Act was amended in 1884 explicitly to ban the potlatch ceremony. The ceremony was framed as "excessive and wasteful" because colonists had the motive to "shift from an economic system of redistribution to one of private property ownership" (Hanson 2009). This parallel shows how both White governments in Canada and South Africa were preoccupied with controlling Indigenous labour.

The Native Land Act (1913) went beyond the Glen Gray Act's abolition of communal title to "the prohibition from buying or hiring land in 93% of South Africa" (SAHO). Thus, it expropriated land from Black South Africans as it allocated 7% of arable land to Africans, and left the other 93% of land which was more fertile for White people. At the time White people accounted for less than 20% of the population (SAHO). The privatisation of land is a key tactic of settler-colonialism. Many cultures do not believe that land could not be a private possession, through contact and European colonisation leveraged *"Terra nullius"* to dispossess local people of their land. *Terra nullius* originated in Roman law's concept of res nullius ("a thing without an owner"). *Terra nullius* described all the lands outside the boundaries of the Roman Empire, lands that were not owned by a Roman owner (Geisler 2012, 18). This concept was expanded by William Blackstone who asserted that land ought to be gained in conquest, ceded to Britain, or in instances where "the lands are claimed by right of occupancy only, by finding them desert and uncultivated" entitled the right for them to be annexed to be put to better use (Geisler 2012, 18), such as White settlers in South Africa farming the land, or White settlers in British Columbia, Canada logging old-growth forests.

The construction of race and its weaponization were key to the Apartheid regime. Wolfe notes that "different racial regimes encode and reproduce the unequal relationships into which Europeans coerced the populations concerned" (2006, 387). To illustrate he examines how racialisation standards were applied differently by European settlers in the United States between Indigenous peoples and African-Americans. African-Americans, who constituted an enslaved workforce upon whose bodies colonists/invaders created wealth, were treated with the infamous "one drop" rule: one drop of African blood was enough to constitute a person as "black" and therefore enslavable. When it comes to Indigenous peoples, their continued existence constituted a threat to the settler/invader's claims to property as well as that if Indigenous people cease to exist would quickly increase the availability of land for settlers/invaders. Thus, settler governments created the notion of blood quantum: that if an Indigenous person marries a non-Indigenous person that their children become less Indigenous.[18] Effectively, Indigenous people are racialised in a mathematically opposite way to African-Americans because the racialisation of each group serves a different purpose to the economy of the settlers/invaders (2006, 387). Similarly, in South Africa during Apartheid different communities were racialised in ways that served settler/invader communities differently. Wolfe explicitly notes that settler colonialism or genocide cannot be limited to any particular racial group "since a race cannot be taken as given" but rather race is constructed "in the targeting" (2006, 388).

Settler colonialism in Wolfe's characterization has both negative and positive dimensions. The positive dimension is more particularly relevant to the settler colonial configuration in South Africa as the negative dimension of settler colonialism "strives for the dissolution of native societies" (2006, 388). In the settler colonies of the British empire this goal seemed more attainable due to the ravaging of Indigenous societies by diseases like smallpox and tuberculosis, and the highly stressful and sometimes war-like

---

[18] If a person is considered "100%" Indigenous and marries a non-Indigenous person and this happens for two more generations, then the resulting grandchild would be "25%" Indigenous. Many treaties between North American Indigenous nations and the governments of the United States or Canada contain a cut off of 25% "blood" minimum to be considered as legal beneficiaries of the treaty.

conditions of colonization. For example, the population of Iwi Maoli (Indigenous Hawaiians) at the time of initial contact with Europeans in 1778 was estimated to be 300,000 and decreased by 90% because of disease (McKeague 2022, 124-125). Dakota historian Nick Estes argues that lack of immunity to disease alone doesn't explain the extent to which Indigenous people were affected by disease during the colonization of the Americas. If lack of immunity alone was a reason for the utter and complete decimation of a population then Europe would have never recovered from the bubonic plague. Making an analogy to the contemporary Saudi assault against Yemen, he notes most people in Yemen are not dying from the bombs dropped on them but of the conditions that war creates (lack of fresh water, dysentery, typhus, etc). Similarly, the stresses caused to Indigenous communities by invading settlers meant that when Indigenous people got sick they were not in conditions where it was easy to get better. He implied that the narrative about immunity when not put in context implies that Native people are somehow more feeble than settlers (i.e., physically inferior) (Hakamaki, Husain, and O'Shea 2021).

The negative dimension of settler colonialism is most apparent on the Western Coast of the country where the numbers Khoikhoi and San[19] societies were decimated by contact with Europeans by disease and war-like conditions. Land enclosure for farms by Dutch settlers disrupted Khoikhoi from their pastoral grazing areas and San from their hunting-gathering practices. Mohamed Adhikari points out that "stock farmers move frontiers rapidly but their herds consumed large amounts of grazing and water, damaging the ecosystem" (2010, 20). As we saw during the COVID-19 pandemic in North America, communities – like Indigenous peoples– that experience structural violence in the form of food insecurity contributed to higher risk factors for the virus. In addition to the disruption of their food system, Khoisan experienced substantial violence by the Dutch

---

[19]The Indigenous peoples of the Western Cape Sometimes referred to as the Khoisan. Contemporary descendants of San have a preference of using the autonym "bushman". However, within academic discourse San continues to be used. "Bushman" carries racist connotations from the Afrikaans word "bosmaan".

settlers "as afflicted indigenous peoples resisted encroachment, and settlers in turn retaliated, usually with excessive and indiscriminate force" (Adhikari 2010, 20). Settlers "branded, thrashed, and chained Khoikhoi whom they suspected of theft and placed them on Rob-ben Island[20]" (Thompson 2000, 38). The intense pressure of colonization created conditions where as a means of survival Khoikhoi began to attach themselves to colonial farming households, working as farm labourers and herders (Thompson 2000, 38) (La Croix 2016, 1). Those who refused servitude pushed beyond the expanding boundaries of the Dutch settlement. However, by being pushed outside their traditional territory "faced competition with the San, other Khoi groups and Bantu peoples who were already occupying and using these lands" (La Croix 2016, 1). Though "set apart by appearance and culture from both the Whites and the slaves;" Khoikhoi were "technically free, but treated no better than the slaves" (Thompson 2000, 38). One estimate of the Khoikhoi population between 1652 and 1713 is a 36.3 decline (from 50,000 to 31,875) and another a 53.7% decline (from 50,000 to 23,151) (La Croix 2016, 19). Though how Khoisan people coped with colonial invasion differs significantly from Indigenous peoples in North America, the structural quality of invasion is the same. In the rest of what became the country of South Africa, there was not the same kind of population drop off.

The positive dimension of settler colonialism is what is most obviously applicable to the South African context:

> Positively, it erects a new colonial society on the expropriated land base—as I put it, settler colonizers come to stay: invasion is a structure not an event. In its positive aspect, elimination is an organizing principal of settler-colonial society rather than a one-off (and superseded) occurrence. The positive outcomes of the logic of elimination can include officially encouraged miscegenation, the breaking-down of native title into alienable individual freeholds, native citizenship, child abduction, religious conversion, resocialization in total institutions such as missions or boarding schools, and a whole range of cognate

---

[20] Which later went on to house political prisoners like Nelson Mandela during the Apartheid era.

biocultural assimilations. All these strategies, including frontier homicide, are characteristic of settler colonialism (Wolfe 2006, 288).

Put another way:

> A settler colonial relationship is one characterized by a particular platform of *domination*; that is, it is a relationship where power– in this case interrelated discursive and nondiscursive facets of economic, gendered, racial, and state power– has been structured into a relatively secure or sedimented set of hierarchical social relations that continue to facilitate the *dispossession* of Indigenous peoples of their lands and self-determining authority (Coulthard 2014, 7; emphasis original).

To return to our Hawaiian illustration: as the population of Kanaka Iwi plummeted concurrently as American missionaries and businessmen arrived, each with their own agenda. Plantation businessmen scooped up land emphasizing cash crops like pineapple, macadamia nuts, sugar cane, and sandalwood– their practices supplanted subsistence-based agricultural practices practised by Kanaka (McKeague 2022, 125-126). These businessmen "purposefully created significant economic disparities and racial divides as a ploy to secure political and economic power" which eventually led to their takeover of the Hawaiian kingdom out of the hands of their traditional royalty and eventually to the illegal annexation of Hawaii by the United States (McKeague 2022, 126). The destabilisation of Kanaka Iwi cultural practices created an opening where Christian tenets quickly filled the void (McKeague 2022, 125). In the South African context particularly legislation like the Glen Grey Act (1894) and the Native Lands Act (1913) which both severely limited the ability for Africans to hold title to land in any sense at all resonates with settler colonial tactics as it disrupted subsistence agricultural production and prevented Africans from participating the settler/invader economy thereby impoverishing and marginalising them.

Though settler-colonialism is most heavily associated with countries which now have predominantly settler populations (Canada, New Zealand, Australia, and the United States), the conceptions of domination and dispossession of lands and self-determining authority can apply more broadly. Though post-Apartheid South Africa now has the state power in the hands of Black, Indian, and Coloured South Africans (as well as White South Africans), White South Africans continue to own 73.3% of farmland in the country (Crowley 2017), 3% of the biggest firms on the Johannesburg stock exchange are controlled by black South Africans (Reality Check Team 2019), and 70% of managers in the private sector in South Africa are white, thus their remains economic domination of South Africa by White South Africans.

In the United States, Native Americans are recognized citizens of "domestic dependent nations" as was established in the legal case of *Cherokee Nation v. Georgia* (1831). The somewhat contradictory logic of Chief Justice John Marshall set out that:

> Though the Indians are acknowledged to have an unquestionable, and heretofore, unquestioned right to the lands they occupy, until that right shall be extinguished by a voluntary cession to our government; yet it may well be doubted whether those tribes which reside within the acknowledged boundaries of the United States can, with strict accuracy, be denominated foreign nations. They may, more correctly, perhaps, be denominated domestic dependent nations…Their relation to the United States resembles that of a ward to his guardian (*Cherokee Nation v. Georgia*, 1831).

This case recognises the nationhood of Indigenous nations somehow not quite as nation-ish as "foreign nations" – while simultaneously as wards. Wards are a legal category that decidedly has very little self-determination, a foundational characteristic of sovereign nations. This formulation created the category of tribes as "domestic dependent nations": subject to the authority of the United States and under its custodial care as "wards" (Flaherty 2017, 19). This configuration will likely bring to mind the homelands or "Bantustans" for those readers familiar with South African Apartheid history. Bantustans were established by the Apartheid regime for the permanent removal of the Black population from areas deemed to be "White South Africa". The majority of the Black population were moved by the government according to tribal affiliation[21] to very rurally located areas to prevent them from living in the urban areas of South Africa. This was a significant administrative tool to remove Black people from the South African political system by "giving Blacks the responsibility of running their own independent governments, thus denying them protection and any remaining rights a Black could have in South Africa" (SAHO). However, due pre-existing legislation like the Native Lands Act, the remaining land for the Bantustans were poorly suited to agricultural use, and the concentration of people on the land led to overgrazing by the existing cattle (SAHO). Many Indigenous peoples in North America subject to the reservation system voice similar complaints to the present day. Thus, Bantustans were never economically independent from the White South African economy, which could be framed by the government as failure of self-government thereby further justifying their domination as the "superior" White race. The Apartheid regime did not have the "benefit" of disease to wipe out Indigenous populations as settlers/invaders of other colonies did so they instead used innovative legal strategies to become the majority population by "deporting" Black South Africans to Bantustans.

Most colonialism was external colonialism, when an external power expropriates and exploits "fragments of Indigenous worlds, animals, plants, and human beings, extracting them in order to transport them – and build the wealth, privilege, or feed the appetites of – the colonisers, who get marked as the first world" (Tuck and Yang 2012, 4). Ubiquitous goods today like spices, tea, sugar, and tobacco fuelled some of the most horrific colonial missions (Tuck and Yang 2012, 4).[22] Colonising nations were, and are, fed and

---

[21] This is not to endorse the Apartheid configurations of Black South Africans. The Mfecane, Great Trek, Frontier Wars and other conflicts played a significant role in smaller groups being absorbed through one function of disruption or another into larger communities. The delineation of these changes would make excellent historical research projects.

[22] Colonialism began with first venture capitalists: the British East India Company and the Dutch East India Company. In the North American context through ventures like the Hudson's Bay Company (UK), and the Northwest Company (Fr).Many of these missions continue

seasoned through the exploitation of the areas they have colonised. The periods of British and Dutch rule of South Africa easily conform to this definition. Colonialism is not always external, it can also happen within a nation, when "the biopolitical and geopolitical management of people, land, flora and fauna" occurs "within the 'domestic' borders of the imperial nation" through the use of institutions like prisons, ghettos, minoritizing, schooling, policing, to ensure the dominance of (most often) white elite, or an elite who conforms to whiteness (Tuck and Yang 2012, 4-5). Examples include the relationship of Tibet to China, Labrador to Newfoundland in Canada, among others. This kind of colonial domination is known as 'internal colonialism' which, in the South African context, reflects many of the policies of the Apartheid regime, but particularly the administration of Bantustans.

A characteristic that differentiates colonialism from settler-colonialism is that, while both colonialism and settler-colonialism sought control over land, colonialism tended to be dependent on the labour of local peoples, while settler-colonialism tended to be more focused on gaining control over land and less over controlling the labour of Indigenous peoples (Cavanagh and Veracini 2017, 3). Here I am making a rough comparison as settler-colonialism also sought to control and restrain the labour of Indigenous people (see Mawani 2009) but it was not entirely dependent on local people for labour. Additionally, while colonies tend to experience a formal decolonization which hands over power to Indigenous people and an exodus of settlers, settler-colonialism resisted formal decolonization because often there were many more settlers than Indigenous people. While postcolonial theory is suitable in those conditions, it fails to capture the ongoing dynamics of settler-colonialism, as Australian Aboriginal activist and poet Bobby Sikes says "What? Postcolonialism? Have they left?" (in Cavanagh and Veracini 2017, 3).

In colonial Zimbabwe the White-settler population never exceeded five percent of the total population, thus ninety-five percent of the population was Black, Indigenous peoples

---

into the present, coming full circle as now many extractive, colonial-esq efforts occur through Multinational Corporations.

(Hughes 2005, 4). The Indigenous populations of other settler-colonies became proportionally smaller, even if they did not start that way. In the United States and Canada, for example, Indigenous people were decimated by diseases, it is thought that their populations have declined by as much as ninety percent (Ostler, 2015). The present population of the Indigenous peoples of the United States is just under 1.5 percent of the population (US Census Bureau, 2015). The Indigenous population in Canada is 4.9 percent, behind New Zealand's 14.9 percent, but ahead of Australia's 3.3 percent (Stats Canada 2017)(World Population Review)(Biddle & Markham 2017). Transfer of disease and use of genocidal tactics as a means of gaining demographic superiority, Europeans in 'successful' 'neo-Europes' at creating themselves at the norm. A "normal" American, Australian and so on would be by default considered White. Rhodes' speech on the Glen Grey Act implied the hopes of past ancestors that war and pestilence would occur, thereby allowing their "neo-Europe" to be created with greater ease. Strategies of settlers in Africa had to be different because they never gained the demographic upper hand. In places like Zimbabwe, White-settlers monopolized land, political and economic power but they were never able to completely naturalise their presence (Hughes 2010, xii).

Though the differences in settler populations are significant (to the point of being as dramatic) the category of 'settler-colonialism', is still fruitful because the doctrine of *terra nulles* was consistently used as philosophical justification for Europeans to dispossess local peoples of their lands the world over where settlement occurred. They believe the land was being wasted and farming it would be *more productive*. These ghosts of *terra nulles* haunt the present as among the participants of Jenny Josefsson the perception that settlers arrived on "empty land" was still used as a claim to the farms they lived on in KwaZulu-Natal (2014). In Zimbabwe, when it was known as Rhodesia, early land titles required that owners improve it, without being able to prove "beneficial occupation" settlers could be forced to forfeit their land (Hughes 2010, 51). At its most basic, all settler-colonialisms always leave people of European descent far from origin. All settler colonies are left with the following paradox, as outlined Thomas Goldie:

> The White Canadian looks at the Indian[23]. The Indian is the other and therefore alien. But the Indian is indigenous and therefore cannot be alien. So the Canadian must be alien. But how can the Canadian be alien within Canada (1989, 12).

Goldie says there are only two possible answers: either White culture can attempt to incorporate the Other, superficially; through appropriation of parts of their culture material like clothing or food items, or naming of things like businesses; or through more sophisticated representation of the Indigenous experience through art like novels or film. For example, the use of Inuksuit as a logo for the Vancouver Olympics when there is no Inuit territory in British Columbia, and there are less than 2000 Inuit living in the whole province (Stats Canada 2021). Or rejecting the acknowledgement of Indigeneity all together: "this country really began with the arrival of Whites" (Goldie 1989, 12-13). Goldie limits his argument to Australia, New Zealand, and Canada, I believe it rings true in African settler colonies also. Whereas in North America and Australia and New Zealand, the strategy is predominantly to incorporate the Other, in Southern Africa it has been rejecting the Other and is now in a period of transition. Goldie argues that settlers have a "need to become 'native', to belong here" (Goldie 1989, 13), this chapter examines the strategies used in Southern Africa.

I illustrate how anthropologists have represented the mechanisms that settlers have used to create a sense of belonging in southern Africa, namely language and land, and examine the extent to which they are analogous to the experience of settler-colonialism in New Zealand. My central argument is cautionary: since the representation of the powerful through ethnography is a moderately new area for anthropologists, it should become standard to foreground the history of domination by White-settlers and White governments to Africa and Africans.

---

[23] Outdated term for Indigenous North Americans.

White Settlers and Language in Southern Africa

This section focuses on the strategic use of language by White-settlers. It will also examine some of the ethical tension of doing ethnography of colonisers. As part of the imaginative project of colonisation many White-settlers do not learn any local, Indigenous languages. When I moved to South Africa, I was quite astounded at how few White South Africans I met that were fluent in a Black South African language. In grade school, the dialect of Afrikaans that is taught is "standard" Afrikaans, used predominantly by White Afrikaans speakers. The small number of White South Africans who fluently speak African languages makes sense within the logic of the imaginative project of colonisation: learning a Black African language would be conceding to the indigeneity of the Black Africans and therefore the exoticness of White-settlers, as described by Goldie's paradox. In Namibia, where Stasja Koot observed an ethno-tourism business, the White-settler Namibians working with the Ju/'hoansi and Hai//om did not communicate to them in their native language (Koot 2015). In Zimbabwe, David Hughes noted that even among 'liberal' White-settlers who were willing to invite Black people to their clubs or restaurants, very few of them would learn Shona, Ndebele or any of native languages spoken by Black people (2010, 6).

However, relationality of language is not always clear: learning a language could be making an effort in a positive way but it can also be more ambiguous. It is common for White farmers to know some of the predominant language spoken among the workers on their farms. Friendships between children of White-settlers and children of Black people were highlighted both in *Waiting: the Whites of South Africa* by Vincent Crapanzano and Sylvia Seldon's monograph *Orania and the Reinvention of Afrikanerdom*.

During 1980 and 1981, Crapanzano embedded himself in a village given the pseudonym "Wyndall" in the Winelands region which was at his time of fieldwork – in the early 80s– the Cape Province, and would now be the Western Cape. The village he describes as having South Africans of both Afrikaner and British descent, a Coloured population who worked in people's homes and on the wine farms, and a minimal Black population. Though coming from different histories as Afrikaners and English South Africans, Crapanzano describes them all as being caught in "the paralytic time of waiting, waiting compounded by fear, waiting for something, anything to happen" (1985, xxii).

Peter Cooke of Crapanzano's Wyndall speaks of his dearest childhood friend as being a Xhosa boy whose father worked on the Cookes' farm. Cooke laments of the wonderful childhood they shared but when just after his friend's initiation, Cooke's grandfather died and the farm was sold their friendship broke down, though Cooke had met him again in adulthood "He speaks just a little Afrikaans, and I have forgotten my Xhosa, so we can't really communicate" (1985, 95). Similarly, another of his informants, Zachary, describes his earliest memories were "not having any White friends, only Black ones. I spoke their language fluently" (1985, 188). Zachary, like Cooke, describes space coming between him and his Black friends as he aged (1985, 190). My informant Jason also learned isiXhosa from having grown up on a farm. He described being young and "very open to language around you" while being surrounded by Xhosa neighbours and workers meant that he learned Xhosa and English bilingually.[24] Thus, it seems that children tend to be more open to the world and the people in it but as those children age and become more socially and culturally conditioned to see race and make attributions to it.

Seldon's work observes the everyday lives of the occupants of Orania, an all-White settlement in the Northern Cape. The relatively unique nature of the town warrants extra context. The history of the physical space in Orania resonates with aspects of this book including Apartheid ghosts, disruptions to people of colour through removal, and considering the ethics of working with historically powerful minorities– rather than disempowered people as anthropology has done historically. Orania is what is known as a *volkstaat*. "Volk" has an significance in Afrikaner politics beyond its direct translation of "people". It connotes a type of nationalism and community of the Afrikaners. "Staat" translates to "state". Volkstaats were attempts to create enclaved homelands within South Africa for Afrikaners.

---

[24] Interviewed 1 March 2017

Another volkstaat, Kleinfontein, will be examined in the next section. As Apartheid began to crumble, the more "mainstream" the Afrikaner nationalists in the Nation Party were working to protect Afrikaner identity within a broader South African nation while smaller, more right-wing Afrikaners "wanted to protect Afrikaner identity by isolating Afrikaners from other population groups" (Ramutsindela 1998, 182).

Residents of Orania frequently focused on their distinctiveness as Afrikaners – as they also do in media interviews. Seldon represents her participants as fearing the demise of Afrikaners as an ethnic group thus supporting Orania as a guarantee to having a recognisable future (2014). Carel Boshoff Jr explained the purpose of the town as: "We [Afrikaners] do not fit in easily in the new South Africa. It [Orania] was an answer to not dominating others and not being dominated by others" (Fihlani 2015). This quote creates a false binary where domination is inevitable– rather than collaboration and change as is suggested by terms like "transformation". The term transformation makes sense as it implies the need for the complete overhaul of institutions in order to work towards creating a country that lives up to the goals set out in the constitution of human dignity, achievement of equality, and the advancement of human rights and freedoms (SA Constitution 1996, 3). In order to not violate the constitution, the town maintains itself as an Afrikaners-only (and therefore Whites-only) town through a corporate structure:

> [Orania] is privately owned by the Vluytjeskraal Share Block Company (VSBC). Ownership of plots and houses is in the form of shares in the company, in terms of a share block scheme. No title deeds are provided, except for agricultural land. Share blocks are linked to portions of the company's real estate, and the shareholder acquires the right to use the property linked to the share block that they have purchased or acquired (Frandsen 2019).

The ability to buy shares in and of itself is not enough to move to Orania. There is also an interview and vetting process. Prospective shareholders/residents must demonstrate "their fidelity to Afrikaans language and culture, a commitment to employing only white Afrikaners, and a string of conservative Christian undertakings. Unmarried couples, for instance, cannot live together" (Webster 2019).

Orania is perhaps the site of the most successful settler-colonial project in South Africa since it is a "neo-Europe" that has isolated itself almost entirely from the original occupants of the land and its fellow South African citizens, eighty percent of whom are Black. The townsite was previously owned by the Department of Water Affairs (DWA) under the Apartheid regime where a canal and two major dams were planned for the Orange River starting from the mid-1960s. Historian Edward Cavanagh has done excellent work to demonstrate the colonial continuities of Orania beyond the immediate surface level analysis that it is an Apartheid town in a post-Apartheid country. The amount of labour needed for the construction and maintenance of the DWA projects lead to the need to build functionally a company town— similar to many mining projects of the era— including schools, church, town hall, recreational facilities. And so, this site began a life as a place called "Orania". Considering the era, however, the facilities built by DWA were not built equally: with segregated areas for Coloured workers and migrant Black workers (Cavanagh 2013, 396). Though it was possible to purchase the rich irrigable land near the town, the zones carved out as residential were different: "people lived in houses and shacks as guests of the DWA rather than homeowners" (Cavanagh 2013, 396).

The need for extensive construction and maintenance decreased rapidly by the early 1980s so many of the engineers and semi-skilled labourers (who were almost certainly White) left Orania for other work with the DWA. The black residential area was functionally abandoned but the slightly nicer Coloured housing had attracted a mix of Coloured and Black families who moved in as squatters. Only a few White families continued to live there as the DWA maintenance team with a crew of Coloured labourers (Cavanagh 2013, 396). Though residents lacked written rights to the land, they settled permanently, built a community where they raised their children and buried their loved ones (Cavanagh 2013, 397). This choice of uncertain land tenure is less surprising when we consider the context of uncertainty of land tenure for people of colour during Apartheid even when they did have deeds to their lands. Pre-Apartheid legislation like the Native Lands Act (1913) severely limited what land could be owned by Black people and Apartheid Legislation like the Group Areas Act (1950) empowered the Government to evict Black, Coloured, or Indian people from housing and land if they decided it should belong to White South Africans, or one of the other racial groups. Between 1960 and 1983 more than 860,000 people were removed from their homes to implement the Group Areas Act (Overcoming Apartheid). Probably most famously, the removals District Six– a multiracial neighbourhood in the City Bowl of Cape Town– had begun in 1968. This was less than twenty years before Black and Coloured families began to build their community Orania. Concurrently with their settlement, in 1985 Africans resisted being moved from Crossroads to the new Khayelitsha township further away; 18 people were killed and 230 were injured (Overcoming Apartheid). Why not settle somewhere that seemed less likely to be disturbed by White greed like a rural area abandoned by the DWA?

This community were technically squatters but understood themselves – rather than the DWA– as the rightful owners of their dwellings. As Cavanagh describes, "They had become attached to the land on which these dwellings sat" (2013, 398). Due to conversations with staff from the DWA who had told workers that residents would be allowed to keep their home after the project was finished, some believed they *did* own their homes. As it was put by a resident during testimony to the Commission about the evictions at Orania: "Do you really believe that all of us who lived in Orania were so stupid to not build our own houses?" (Cavanagh 2013, 398). These oral contracts were not honoured by the DWA, though former labourers testified under oath to this effect. Cavanagh pauses on the language used by one of the principle DWA engineers who had worked on the canalisation project to consider it as possible evidence that there was knowledge of the understanding that the Coloured and Black people who remained at Orania should at least be left undisturbed. The DWA was seeking to sell their assets around the Orange River canalisation project but in his report AD Brown observed, 'the township is still in use', so he "recommended that the whole 2,769 hectares originally required for the Vluytjeskraal project, 'with the exception of the land occupied by the Township Orania, be allowed to revert back to private ownership'" (Cavanagh 2013, 398). Cavanagh argues that Brown's use of the word township is significant due to its specific connotation in South Africa. The word "dorp" tends to be reserved for villages that contain White residents, while townships then and to this day are known as communities that are underserviced, overpopulated and which tend to have Black, Coloured, and/or Indian residents. Now that the White residents had left, Orania was no longer a "dorp". Furthermore, "his insistence that it be left undisturbed and only the surrounding land be sold" is compelling evidence because why wouldn't Brown just describe the properties of the land so that the DWA could create an accurate bill of sale for their asset? Brown provided no reasoning for why only the agricultural land should be privatized but the township/dorp should be left undisturbed. Cavanagh believes this could have been an attempt at activism by Brown (2013, 398).

In August 1990, Orania was bought by Professor Carel Boshoff III for a private shareholding entity that sequestered land and offered it to Afrikaner settlers as shares. Another private buyer had originally bought the land but did not develop it and forfeited the property (Cavanagh 2013, 399). This became important when the evicted Black and Coloured residents sought restitution. Boshoff gave the residents of Orania until 31 March 1991 to leave Orania as he "did not buy a bus with passengers" (Cavanagh 2013, 400). One of the reasons the Northern Cape had been an appealing location was the hope of:

> mobilizing Afrikaners to settle in the area with little or no need for removing other population groups. The logic behind avoiding possibilities for forced removals is that any kind of forced removal of African communities from areas earmarked for a volkstaat would be tantamount to apartheid (Ramutsindela 1998, 187).

Yet, this "tantamount to apartheid" did happen to the occupants of Orania and it has begun to fade from historical memory except for the work of Cavanagh. This is part of why its history is receiving such attention here.

Newspapers began investigating the situation in Orania and left a record quite sympathetic to residents, who were panicking:

> In the houses, on the street corners and in the single quarters in which families are now staying, this situation is the only subject which everyone speaks about. 'Carel Boshoff is going to shoot us', says a woman who is breastfeeding her infant. 'We are not supposed to say anything about it' says a 16- year-old Gertruida Louw, 'we need to say to Carel Boshoff that we would like to live with him in peace in this beautiful birthplace of ours. The television said that this is the new South Africa and if the television says so then it is so'. 'Ha!', says Mieta Rittels, 'he speaks of Christianity and he says that he is a Christian. How can you be a Christian when you are so ignorant? (Cavanagh 2013, 400)

This might seem extreme but the reactions of the residents should be considered under Luis White's argument for the need to consider rumours as historical evidence seriously (2000). Rumours give us insight into what is believable within a given community. During Apartheid many peaceful protesters were shot, hit by police vehicles, attacked by police dogs; while known activists were disappeared and tortured by the military or police. None of the accusations seem that far out of the realm of possibility given the level of violence experienced by Black, Coloured, and Indian South Africans at the hands of the White Apartheid state barely years before.

It is difficult to prove to what extent residents of Orania at the time of the purchase by Boshoff knew that evictions were coming. Cavanagh tracked down a report of the Commission on Restitution of Land Rights from 2005 with testimony from the residents. The report contradicts itself at times but broadly Cavanagh summarizes that there were two main understandings among residents:

> One group was informally told of the sale and forthcoming eviction. Houses were secured for some of them in Luckhoff. Those who did not secure accommodation found accommodation for themselves in towns nearby. Several of

these remain as DWA employees today. Another group were [sic] not informed of the sale and forthcoming evictions. They were removed forcefully by the Orania settlers. No arrangements were made for their transportation or accommodation by DWA. Many of these moved either to friends and [sic] relatives nearby. Others ended up in Warrenton. Many of these were retrenched by the DWA soon after the forced removals (Cavanagh 2013, 400).

From his appraisal, Cavanagh believes the first group were the majority considering the retrenchments and offers for relocation of employees by the DWA starting from the mid-1980s. The minimal economic activity in the surrounding areas meant those who stayed generally did not have the means to pay rent to the DWA. There were advertisements for the sale of Orania in the *Government Gazette* (likely not read widely by the remaining residents of Orania), potential buyers did at times tour the townsite (possibly alarming inhabitants and creating rumours), but there does not seem to be an earnest effort made by the DWA to communicate with residents about their legal standing, or lack thereof (Cavanagh 2013, 400).

The reports of residents who remained in Orania after its sale to Boshoff are shocking. About six months after the sale to Boshoff in early 1991, residents experienced frightening encounters with the shareholders who were looking forward to the foundation of their volkstaat. On an autumn Friday evening, men "with dogs 'told [the residents] that they would have to leave in three days', and then 'locked the entrance gate to the "coloured location" preventing them from going to other areas within Vluykieskraal [sic] Farm including the grocery store'" (Cavanagh 2013, 401). This escalated as 'shots were fired throughout the nights' that weekend to threaten and intimidate residents, and 'beatings, pistol whippings and harassment with dogs' were carried out by the newcomers on those remaining behind on the Saturday (Cavanagh 2013, 401). A former resident who had moved to Hopetown at the time of the inquiry by Commission on Restitution of Land Rights 'We were removed in a very painful manner', testified to this effect:

It was in the evening of one Friday when Carel Boschoff [sic] and his friends came on bakkies[25] to order everyone out of the area. They fired guns throughout the night [. . .] we were forcefully removed at gunpoint. We did not have transport to transport our goods [. . .] we also did not know where to go. We lost a lot of our properties because we were not given enough time to pack (Cavanagh 2013, 401).

After this traumatic experience, the former community at Orania were able to file a restitution claim because "they enjoyed 'beneficial occupation' for ten years or more, which made up for their lack of any written rights" (Cavanagh 2013, 402). However, it ended up being the Government rather than the VSBC which paid the community compensation as the VSBC argued that it was a failure of the DWA to communicate with residents and thus it was a failure of government. The commission agreed (Cavanagh 2013, 402). It is heartbreaking to think of the descendants of the Black and Coloured community of Orania who, while perhaps not legally barred from visiting the graves of their ancestors, are unlikely to be welcomed in open arms by the current residents of Orania to do so. The command over the narrative spin by the volkstaat residents likely still causes former community members headaches if they have continued to follow the fate of their former home.

Seldon's work about Orania (somewhat surprisingly) also contains evidence of the normalcy of bonds of language between young White-settlers and Black South Africans. Seldon is told by Wynand that his father, Carel IV, "spoke Tswana as well as he spoke Afrikaans" (2014, 132). Command of an African language most closely associated with people who are Black is leveraged by her participant to demonstrate a form of belonging to place. Wynand represents White people speaking African languages as a generational phenomenon, especially among settlers who grew up in rural South Africa:

Before the Afrikaner nationalism became the dominant political outlook, and before the widespread school attendance for Africans, it was easier for White people to learn the language

---

[25] Pick-up trucks

that most of the people in the area spoke, rather than expecting them to speak a minority language like Afrikaans or English (2014, 132).

This quote implies that there was a negative impact on the extent to which Afrikaners learned African languages most closely associated with people who are Black both from Afrikaner nationalism and that the fact that Africans began attending learning English and Afrikaans. It places blame on two systemic factors and in other ways points to a past belonging, possibly deeper than the one that exists now because more White people used to know African languages. While Seldon asserts that "many of the people in Orania could speak other African languages", she does not cite any other examples of individuals that can. Furthermore, in the very next paragraph she speaks of a conflict that arose between a nearby farm owner and temporary workers because "neither they nor their regular workers understand the language the temporary workers spoke, making it difficult to assess their trustworthiness" (2014, 132). This does not make Seldon's assertion about "many" people in Orania knowing African languages seem very credible. However, as Seldon's aim is explicitly not to dismiss the people of Orania as racists (2014, 18) then it is logical to want to claim their fluency in African languages as it implies a form of recognition to the "Other" since speaking a language is an acknowledgement validation of speaking to someone on their own terms. This kind of recognition of the "Other" that seems incongruence with being racist. Yet, this seems fundamentally at odds with what other visitors to Orania have experienced. A journal spoke with a resident who stated, "I see nothing wrong with apartheid," (Fihlani 2014). I struggle to imagine someone who sees nothing wrong with Apartheid as being someone who is not racist.

Seldon is a good example to consider the ethical quandaries working horizontally. In my mind, her work fell short as she did not make enough effort to foreground the historical injustices which the Afrikaners in her work benefitted from. Seldon says that "people who are too similar to ourselves can be read through our existing frameworks and be regarded as deviant, instead of trying to understand their frameworks" as she is arguing that we must apply the same logic of relativism to groups who are comparatively powerful that anthropology seeks to study now as it has to the disempowered it has previously studied (and continues to study) (2014, 17). The frameworks of residents of Orania are manifestations of White-settlers attempting to resolve their feelings of out-of-place-ness. There seem to be two strategies of resolution. Some attempt to erase historical injustices perpetrated by their ancestors which created the systems which supported the accumulation of opportunities and wealth for them. Like Yolandie Jonk who claimed "It [apartheid] didn't affect me" to journalist Pumza Fihlani in 2014. By virtue of being White during Apartheid, the wages of Jonk's parents and grandparents were significantly higher than Black, Coloured, or Indian people. Opportunities like higher education were significantly more plentiful for White South Africans. The other way to resolve this out-of-placed-ness is justifying, in some way, the system that advantaged them and oppressed others. Crapanzano's work offers clear examples of this:

> "The Blacks are barbarians, uncivilized, raw," one Afrikaner woman in Wyndal told me. "They can become professors and doctors, but there is always something lacking. Just a few days ago a Black man who had been educated in Europe said that he found something lacking in his own people. It was on TV. It is in the blood. [...] My son is in the permanent forces, in South West Africa. He says, 'You can take a Black man from the bush but you can't take the bush from the Black man.' (1985, 20)

This kind of racism has been denunciated enough publicly that few Afrikaner leaders would make such appeals in the present because they would be politically counterproductive. Though it does still happen occasionally. Other strategies that result in similar outcomes are used instead.

Carel IV attempted to justify Orania's existence by arguing the advances in the human rights of Black, Coloured, and Indian South Africans: "has also been accompanied by an unfair marginalization and victimization of the Afrikaner community. Textbooks, for instance, are biased to showcase Afrikaners as a brutal people without highlighting their positive contributions to the country's history" (Brulliard 2010). In Orania, there is a sculpture garden that contains busts of Hans Strijdom, D. F. Malan, HF Verwoerd, J. B. M. Hertzog and Paul Kruger– all prominent Afrikaner political leaders. Mavaju argues that the garden "commemorates White supremacists who were either the overseers of or served as midwives to the birth of one of the most egregious crimes against humanity–the apartheid system" whose "anti-Black racist world-views were unbending" (2022). It is difficult to square the circle on how a community that venerates those who caused so much suffering to Black, Coloured, and Indian South Africans can truly respect people of other races as truly human.

The leaders of contemporary Afrikaner movements are very clever negotiators with national and international governmental organizations as well as with the media. They have embraced the language of "minority rights" and "self-determination", language which in other settler-colonies is most closely associated with Indigenous peoples or other oppressed minorities. Afriforum is a prominent example of this. They describe themselves as an organization to protect "the rights of cultural minorities and aggrieved citizens. Often, these cultural minorities are white Afrikaners, but they also include members of the Afrikaner-speaking brown community and other citizens" (Immigration and Refugee Board of Canada 2024). Very few people who are Coloured or Black and speak Afrikaans as a first language would identify as an Afrikaner due to the term's association with White nationalism. Even White people who speak Afrikaans as a first language often distance themselves from the identity of an "Afrikaner" because they want to put space between themselves and White nationalism. During my time in Stellenbosch, it was more common than not for a White-Afrikaans speaking person to correct me if I called them an Afrikaner. However, there are important legal reasons why Afriforum emphasizes the possibility that they can offer support to people other than Afrikaners because as, as it pointed out by the Head of the Human Rights Advocacy Unit at the South African Human Rights Commission, "one will be hard pressed to find an organization that focuses exclusively on whites as such an organization runs the risk of being viewed as exclusive and possibly discriminatory, on the basis of race" (Immigration and Refugee Board of Canada

2024). Afriforum CEO Kallie Kriel insisted it was wrong for the United Nations to call Apartheid a crime against humanity because there were not enough people killed by the regime to warrant such a label (Modjadji and Goba 2018).

Afriforum consistently participates at the United Nations Forum on Minority Issues. In 2023, the stated purpose for their participation was that:

> Through international actions like these, AfriForum raises awareness on the international stage about issues such as racially discriminatory laws, as well as incitement of violence, against minorities in South Africa. The organisation also puts the South African government's negative, and even hostile, positions, statements, and policies towards minorities on record (Afriforum)

Whereas minorities in predominantly White countries tend to be politically disempowered, White South Africans hold significant economic power which easily translates formally and informally into political power. Though the proportion of the hyperwealthy becoming black has grown, whiteness is still a significant indicator of economic security (Sguazzin 2021). Only 10% of households are headed by a Black person who can afford medical aid as compared to 70% of white-headed households under the same circumstances (Mlaba 2020). The average monthly income of White households (R117,249) is still more than ten-times that of Black South African households (R10,554) (Gradín 2014). White people still occupy 62.9 percent of top management jobs while being less than 10 percent of the population (Commission for Employment Equity 2023). In mid-level positions, around 35 percent of those jobs are occupied by White people (Reality Check Team 2019). The way Afriforum conducts themselves, it is as though the possibility of White people to experience life as it is for the majority of Black South Africans is itself a form of oppression. Yet, what does it mean for millions of Black South Africans to live in those conditions everyday?

The work of Afriforum and Solidariteit– a trade union primarily for Afrikaner workers– is a historical continuation of older forms of social organizing within the Afrikaner community. During Apartheid, there was a semi-secret organization called Die Afrikaner Broederbond (The Afrikaner Brother Bond) where members conspired, among other things, to ensure Afrikaners were frontrunners for economic opportunities. The ethic of keeping power and money within the "volk" clearly continues in the present as well. The economy of Orania is deeply intertwined with institutions like Afriforum that seek to maintain the dominance of White South Africans. The business clients call-centre based in the community, which employs about 55 people, are Afriforum and Solidariteit. Workers make calls to recruit and retain members for the organizations (Webster 2019). Both organizations prey on, and fan fears within the Afrikaner community. Doing so pushes individual Afrikaners to continue to turn inward within the volk, making other forms of non-racial forms of consciousness and solidarity – like class or geography– more difficult to gain a foothold within the White, Afrikaans speaking community.

Carel Boshoff IV frequently turns to the language of "self-determination" to justify the need for Orania to exist in his interviews with media:

> It was 30 years ago, at a time when the minority government of that era was not yet ended. We foresaw that it should be. And we thought the concept of self-determination for a people like the Afrikaner people being one way of facilitating peaceful and orderly transformation (Smith and Pitts 2019).

His command over language is impressive. Rather than calling the Apartheid government by its name, he uses the word "minority" which has extremely different connotations to a Western audience. Next, he calls upon "self-determination" as a "peaceful" solution towards "transformation". The converse of his statement implies that if Afrikaners are not allowed to live separately from Black, Coloured, and Indian people there could be violent consequences (as violence is the opposite of peace). Alternatively, if we return to Cecil Rhodes' speech for the Glen Grey Act where he asserts that historically war was the main occupation of Africans, Boshoff's statement could also be implying that if Afrikaners do not live separately then they could be at risk of attack by violent Africans.

If Afrikaners are living lives segregated from Black, Coloured, and Indian people there has not been any transformation from the Apartheid status quo. When Indigenous people in settler-colonies like Canada advocate for our rights to self-determination it is because the colonial government has taken away or ignored our community autonomy. This happens most frequently related to natural resource development where governments do not give us a say. For example, my home territory –Nunatsiavut– is downstream from a white-elephant hydroelectric dam built by the Province of Newfoundland and Labrador that is going to significantly elevate levels of methylmercury in fish and other marine wildlife because the Province refused to clear the trees and other brush from the basin before flooding it (Crocker 2019). Fish, seals, seabirds and their eggs, mussels, and other marine life are staples of Inuit traditional foods and are still integral for Inuit food security. Even as a region with better self-determination than most, Nunatsiavut Inuit were failed by the Canadian legal system. The project itself is outside the borders of the modern treaty between Nunatsiavut Inuit, the Government of Canada, and the Government of Newfoundland and Labrador so through a technicality there was no need to consult with the Nunatsiavut Government even though Nunatsiavut Inuit will bear a disproportionate human and cultural cost of the project. The interventions in Indigenous communities through legislation like the Indian Act (1876) were justified on the paternalistic basis that Indigenous people were backward and needed to be civilized. Indigenous communities need self-determination to protect ourselves from further colonialism by the Canadian state and to reconstitute our societies after genocidal policies like residential schools which attempt to "take the Indian out of the child"[26]. It is alarming to see the language of self-determination leveraged by those who have used their power towards settler-colonial ends.

There are ethical questions in relation to how people from minorities with significant social power can be represented.

---

[26] Attributed to Canada's First Prime Minister John A. MacDonald who also served as the Minister for Indian Affairs whose purpose was to assimilate Indigenous peoples in Canada.

During oral history interviews with White-settler farmers in Zimbabwe, Rory Pilossof was in somewhat of an analogous position to Seldon as he is also working with a group of people who have historically held an incredible amount of privilege. He thought very carefully about how to engage in analysis on the information from the oral history interviews so as not to write "simply an apologist account of White farmers in Zimbabwe, or a tirade against an unchanged group of racist neo-colonialists who deserved exactly what they had coming for them" (2012, 187). The balance he struck was an attempt to portray what happened to farmers in their own words and to engage with "the factual inaccuracies, prejudices, and faults contained" in them while showing how they echo the past (2012, 187).

However, Pilossof's position as an interviewer partnering with a local NGO is quite different to an anthropologist who has become embedded in a community and is required to build relationships of trust with their informants to be accepted by them. Pilossof, as a historian, does not have contact with these farmers again as he received permission to use the interviews from Justice for Agriculture. Furthermore, it is unlikely that farmers were given the option to veto or have input into his characterization. The ability for anthropologists to represent their informants, then, is hung on the ethical framework particular anthropologists use to hold themselves to account and how stringent their adherence to them is. For example, during the final publication of her PhD thesis, Joy Owen had to make a number of revisions and resubmissions as she was in a romantic relationship with one of her informants who changed his mind a number of times on what he was comfortable with her including (Personal Communication, 2017). Though there can be a case made for moments where anthropologist should burn their bridges with their informants, as with Ilana van Wyk's work with the Universal Church of the Kingdom of God where van Wyk openly calls the leaders of the community in which she worked "repugnant" as she felt they preyed on the financially disempowered and socially vulnerable (Doran 2017, 118).

In this instance Seldon –it appears– has decided not to burn bridges with her informants. She seemed to want to be better in the eyes of people from Orania than the journalists frequently publish accounts of Orania which are harshly negative "in contrast to how the journalists appeared to enjoy their visit" (2014, 45). There is a particular danger in contexts like this to be too gentle with one's participants if one does not also represent the privilege that was begotten by the systems that have supported Seldon's participants. The possibility of Orania existing at all is because the founders of the town could afford to purchase the entire town as a corporation (92-93). Given that Apartheid gave ample opportunities to White South Africans to get university educations and access to capital to start businesses, at the expense of the dispossession and exclusion of the vast majority of the country, as is noted by Jenny Josefsson (2014, 264). If, for some reason the tables were turned, the likelihood of Black, Indian, or Coloured South Africans being able to set up the same kind of structure as Orania would be near impossible as their access to capital and education (which is a signalling mechanism for reliability from the perspective of financial institutions) was limited by Apartheid. This point can also be applied to her discussion of the costs of moving to Orania Seldon where she omits that:

> To purchase a property in Orania requires having existing savings from previous employment outside Orania, or saving from two salaries: it is impossible for a single person or even two people on average salaries to buy a house in Orania. It is only two salaries of around R6000 that will provide enough to cover living expenses and a loan [...]. (2014, 96)

While I agree that Afrikaners and settlers more generally must find ways to come to terms with the atrocities committed by their ancestors, by representing Orania as a method of coping with the transition to democracy in such a seemingly neutral way erases those atrocities.

In field sites less contentious and controversial than Orania, language can also be used strategically by White-settlers to prove their authenticity and connection to place. For example, in Botswana, White-settlers used language to distinguish themselves from other White-settlers in southern Africa (Gressier 2011, 358). The history of Botswana being quite different to that of South Africa is pointed to by Cate Gressier's informants: it was a protectorate and then independent so local Black people have been in control since the 1960s. The internal politics of Botswana are critiqued by representatives of minority tribes as the national language puts them at a disadvantage in terms for schooling, for example. For the White-settler minority this policy helps as it allows them to maintain a sense of cultural integrity and belonging through feeling comfortable in English and Setswana (Gressier 2011, 363). One of Gressier's informants, Richard, got into a confrontation with a visiting African-American tourist who questioned his ability to 'belong' in Africa: Richard responded by saying "I was born here, and I live here, and I grew up here, and I speak the language, and I know the people, and they all know me" (2011, 369). Gressier's analysis demonstrates how her White informants have had advantages from policies that have disadvantaged others in Botswana.

Language can be used as a strategy of symbolic ownership. Hughes observed how White-settlers claimed the Kariba dam by naming its features. "Names filled a landscape with meaning- or, even more profoundly, made it possible for them to hold meaning at all" (2010, 58) so White authors, rather than naming features using descriptions indigenous to Zimbabwe used language to displace Black people and allow Whites to occupy the indigenous position (Hughes 2010, 60). He does note that in other instances in southern Africa Bantu-language or Afrikaans terms are deployed for features of the bush unknown in Europe. This borrowing and improvisation, in a way, is a concession to the foreignness of Europeans and their language in Africa (Hughes 2010, 59). While Crapanzano does not focus on names in the same amount of detail as Hughes, he does mention that the streets in Wyndal are "named after Afrikaner heroes as the Boer generals Botha and De Wet, the Great Trek leader Piet Retief, and Dirkie Uys, the fourteen-year-old boy who preferred to die alongside his father during a Zulu war than flee" which, borrowing from Huges' logic, implies to creates a sense of Afrikaner ownership over the town (Crapanzano 1985, 5).

White Settlers and Land in (Mostly) Southern Africa

Land has always been key to colonialism. As articulated by Wolfe, "Land is life—or, at least, land is necessary for life. Thus, contests for land can be—indeed, often are—contests for life" (2001, 387). This section examines the ethnographic representations of the connection between White-settlers and land, with respect to how it roots White people in Africa. In *Whiteness in Zimbabwe* (2010), Hughes sketches the metaphysical landscape of Zimbabwe through intensive reading of literature and historical narratives, in addition to interviews, to contextualise his ethnographic project. The more hands-on ethnographic portion of his work took place with commercial farmers in the Virginia region of Zimbabwe. He seeks to make sense of these farmers' understanding of their 'belonging' in Zimbabwe. Hughes argues that there are two means colonialists can use to negotiate their identities in their new settlements: either through social forms via integration to the already existing populations there or through land (2010). An example of negotiating a settler identity through social form can be observed through the widespread intermarriage between Portuguese settlers and Africans from settlement in the 17th and 18th century until 19th "Enlightenment" ideologies created firmer demarcated boundaries by race and religion, namely Christianity (Mark 2002, 29). Hughes found in Zimbabwe that farmers represented their belonging as occurring primarily through their relationship with land rather than intermarriage like the Portuguese.

While White-settlers in North Americans and Australians used violence to empty their land, the White-settlers of Africa had to "*imagine* the natives away" in what Hughes calls "the imaginative project of colonisation": insulating themselves away from Indigenous peoples so as to imagine themselves as having a larger, more 'natural' presence (2010, xii-xiii). Representations of White-settlers in southern Africa generally tend to corroborate this argument, though it does have some limitations. For example, Crapanzano explains that from the perspective of the White-settlers Bantustans are meant to "control the influx of Blacks into 'White' South Africa [...] they 'solve' the Black problem by declaring Blacks to be citizens of homelands" (1985, xiv). Bantustans are an example of a policy of internal colonialism that aimed to control the geopolitics of Africans in South Africa. As was the Natives Land Act of 1913. It allowed settlers to imagine themselves as a more 'natural' presence. The creation of reservations through treaty and land cessation in Canada functioned in a similar way. Canada began negotiating treaties– a starting point for limiting Indigenous land occupation– West of Southern Ontario starting in 1871, only four years after its Confederation. In 1876, the government passed "the Indian Act" which created reserves and a pass system wherein residents needed a pass to leave the reserve. This meant new settlers to the Canadian West did not feel demographically overwhelmed even when they often were. Similarly, the White-settlers in Africa legislated the Indigenous people away to confirm their imaginative desire of belonging.

Kleinfontein, the community where Stephan van Wyk's fieldwork took place, exemplifies settler attachment to land. During the transition to democracy in the early 1990s, the *Boere Vryheidsbeweging* (BVB)[27] (the organisation which eventually founded Kleinfontein) argued for the creation of a *volkstaat* in the old Boer Republics of the *Zuid Afrikaansche Republiek* (ZAR) and the *Oranje-Vrystaat* (OVS). Van Wyk characterises their argument as "[since] the *Boere-Afrikaners'* republics and freedom had been taken from them unjustly, and that the strain left by the death of approximately 30 000 women and children in concentration camps during the Anglo-Boer War remained" (2014, 1). Several members of BVB bought a property located east of Pretoria that had historic significance to them. It was a site where the Boer had managed to win a skirmish against the British forces, killing a number of them in the process, toward the end of the Anglo-Boer war (van Wyk 2014, 2). Furthermore, by doing so they were able to slow down the progress of the British while they were trying to capture Paul Kruger (president of ZAR) as he fled Pretoria. His flight was successful because of their battle (van Wyk 2014, 30). The planning Maritz Rebellion was also done at the site. The Rebellion was planned by veterans of the South African War during WWI against the government

---

[27] Translation: Afrikaner Resistance Movement

of South Africa(van Wyk 2014, 30). Van Wyk says the BVB symbolically identified with the people involved in those projects, as was articulated by one of his participants:

> We are the descendants of the Boers. We are tied to this area historically and in a spiritual sense, not just a physical sense; we are continuing the very same struggle started with them. [...] The Boer Republics were ours and they were taken away from us by unjust means. We have a rightful claim to them and most Afrikaners until today still reside in their borders (van Wyk 2014, 30).

This is corroborated by the research of Crapanzano who represents the Great Trek 1836-1854 as being the centre piece of historical consciousness for Afrikaners from the northern provinces. The Great Trek resulted in the founding of the OVS, ZAR, and other smaller republics. He describes it as "an extraordinary flight of small bands of farmers- in all they numbered 6,000- from British rule into the wild and treacherous regions of the interior" (1985, 65). Not only the ability to have land, but land of their own, unfettered by the British. The ethnographer does not problematize their informants perceived attachment to the land that erases those who were attached to the land before their informants.

The participants in Gressier's work are not represented as exclusively negotiating their relationship to land but she does note that in the Okavango Delta in Botswana "the majority of White citizens who work in the [tourism] industry conducting high-cost safaris" in the framework of the government's "high-cost, low-impact policy", philosophically guided by ideals of conservation, has "encouraged the development of elite lodge-based safaris" which implies, at least, a philosophy conservationism (2011, 355). The role as tourism host and conservationist of White-settlers seems fairly common. Koot argues that some White-settlers in Namibia use tourism as a means of strengthening their own sense of belonging to nature and society through the Bushmen: "they show a strong attachment to the Bushmen, and because Bushmen are positioned in nature, strengthening their own sense of belonging to nature" (2015, 5). In Namibia, as settlers subscribe to the Western culture-nature dichotomy "Bushmen were often equated with the bush and wilderness" thus, even if in the present-day settlers are working in the tourism business with Bushmen and not on the land itself necessary since Bushmen are equated with nature settlers are negotiating their identity through ideals that a principally similar to nature conservation (Koot 2015, 6). She explicitly notes how:

> local White Namibians who are involved in tourism […] identify as people from the bush, show strong conservation values, feel emotionally and sometimes spiritually attached to their surroundings, have lots of detailed knowledge about the environment and tend to gain from it economically (Koot 2015, 11).

This representation of White-settlers as negotiating their identities through the land is present here as well. In this instance as protectors of the land.

These observations hold true in Hughes' analysis in Zimbabwe where White-settlers took ownership of conservation. Hughes traces the positioning of White-settlers as conservationists by examining the change in discourse around the Kariba Dam from an "industrial impoundment" whose "rising water killed all but a fraction of the animals of the Zambezi valley and drowned all plant life" to a reimagined "unspoiled Africa[n]" lake, a picture of "nature restored and enjoyed" which erased the displacement of 57,000 Tonga (2010, 31). By escaping to nature, White-settlers were also escaping "their awkwardness and downright fear amid Black society", going to nature seemed so "natural" that it might obscure this escape's role in the imaginative project of colonialization (2010, 48). After decolonization, Hughes' informants "grumbled nostalgically about the general slide in standards […] especially with respect to conservation" (2010, 102). The removal of the Tonga from the southern shore of the Kariba meant that they lost their physical place in history. In the 1980s and 1990s, authors cast Black fishermen as abusers of the ecology of the Zambezi. These condemnations are reminiscent of nineteenth century notions of civilised and uncivilised hunting: "the moral failure of natives empowers White [settlers] to assume the mantle stewardship" (Hughes 2010, 52). There was a concerted effort to "constrain rural Black users of the Zambezi Valley while supporting or enabling of White-dominated tourism in the valley" (Hughes 2010, 53).

In addition to stewardship of "nature", the rhetoric and actions of White-settler farmers in Zimbabwe is one of a 'need' to improve land required of settlers in Zimbabwe (2010, 51). This philosophy of land improvement has stayed with settlers intergenerationally as Hughes spoke with farmers about the "hydrologic revolution" of the 1990s, wherein commercial farmers blocked natural waterways to irrigate their crops. Some White-settlers still argued that their ancestors settled on 'virgin' land but the larger number admitted their ancestors were trespassing. Instead, they argued that they and their ancestors *understood* the virgin bush better thus know how to nurture it and preserve it. To justify the impounding of rivers and streams they had to flip the criticism on its head: dams and reservoirs, they told Hughes, actually *enhanced* natural waterways. Put another way, this industrialization could be seen as a form of ecological stewardship (Hughes 2010, 75).

Josefsson argues that in the colonial present, discourses around the ethos of nature conservation has made Africa a 'frontier' once again. Coming full-circle from colonial times, conservation is being increasingly enmeshed in the hunting industry and the narratives of game farmers: "Farmers become stewards of nature and endangered animals" thereby maintaining "control of their space" by doing a "greater global good" (Josefsson 2014, 264). Their farms become accessible only to an "international community of people sharing the same ideals" but not the local Black people (Josefsson 2014, 264). She notes the change in the landowner's attitude toward subsistence hunting on one of the participating farms: "After the conversion [from open cattle farm to enclosed game farm] this was no longer allowed and incidents of hunting or outside people found on the farm were treated as 'poaching' and 'unauthorised' access" (2014, 266). The owner of another nearby farm that underwent conversion forcibly removed the tenants, allegedly having said "I bought the land, not the people" (Josefsson 2014, 268). Just like Boshoff in Orania "did not buy a bus with passengers" (Cavanagh 2013, 400). With the help of "other farmers and armed men" "scattered the dwellers' chickens and cattle into the bush, forced [the dwellers] onto a truck and burnt their houses" (Josefsson 2014, 268). In a post-Apartheid era, the conversion of cattle farms to game farms has become a way for White-settlers to continue their "imaginative project of colonisation". There is a perception that game farms are less likely to be subject to land claims than more traditional farms, like cattle farms (Josefsson 2014, 265). Thus, these conversions are being used to detach the Indigenous Black land dwellers from the land White-settlers have come to own.

Connections to land claimed by White-settlers in African ethnographies examined in this chapter is common with those rural White-settlers in New Zealand. This demonstrates a commonality among settlers in settler colonial environments. Michèle Dominy did ethnographic work among high-country sheep farmers on the South Island in New Zealand. After staying with small communities of high-country settlers on the South Island of New Zealand, she was asked to testify at the Waitangi Tribunal as the Ngai Tahu people sought remedies from the Crown for its failure to protect their rights guaranteed by the Treaty of Waitangi. They contested the Crown's denial of their right to lay claim to pastoral land on the same basis and scale as Europeans (Dominy 1995, 361). Dominy represented the testimony given by the three White-settlers before the tribunal as "mutually reinforcing [...] all claim[ing] powerful connections with the land" (1995, 363). Hamish Ensor "asserted social connection to land by measuring the continuity of inheritance patterns, demonstrated by leases passed down through generations of farmers acting as custodians of the land" (Dominy 1995, 363). Ensor "underscored the importance of conservation issues to high country people, citing his own appointment to the Queen Elizabeth II Trust" thereby alluding "to the multiple-use value of high-country lands for production and for scenic and conservation purposes" (Dominy 1995, 364). Finally, the son of a retired farmer presented his family as "caretakers": "we care for the country as a whole, for the next generation as opposed to managing for the day" (Dominy 1995, 365).

Dominy describes the rhetoric of these farmers as being more than just one of ownership and control of resources, it conflates "the continuity of their presence over several generations in the high country with topographic and environmental knowledge" as they speak to "an ongoing and constantly changing relationship to land, rather than of recourse to continuity with the past" (1995, 370). While this ethnography is speaking particularly to the relationship of White-settler farmers to land in New Zealand, who make up a tiny subset of the settler population, it allows a rather neat comparison to be drawn. Both populations of White-settlers clearly do see their relationship with land as grounding their belonging to place both in African settler-colonialism and settler-colonialism in New Zealand.

Dominy was asked by her participants, the White farmers, to testify at the Waitangi Tribunal on their behalf. In her view "[a]nthropologists have responsibilities to their research participants, to their colleagues, and to the discipline" (1990, 12). Balancing those against each other, she decided she could give back to her research participants what she had taken by providing a preliminary report of her field project which explored the relationship of the high country people to the land in a distinctive and isolated environment. A possible tension when studying horizontally is that one's participants might not like what one has to say. Anthropology is dependent on the anthropologist's ability to build and to an extent to maintain relationships with interlocutors. Without these relationships one cannot do participant-observation, only observation. Dominy encourages us to resist overly simplistic understandings of power:

> Certainly, it is the responsibility of the anthropologist to recognize the domination of some discourses by others. It is more typical for us to give voice to the silenced and the Indigenous than the colonial discourse which presumably speaks for itself. But we need to recognize that there are a multiplicity of colonial and indigenous discourses which vary by segment of the population over time[...] the languages of the West, of indigenous peoples, and of anthropology are often mutually interactive; they are not unidirectional, regardless of where we locate power (1990, 12).

Dominy did have stipulations of her appearance at the Tribunal. She would not accept payment, which was offered, and importantly that she would not change the content even if the farmers took exception to her testimony. However, even if Dominy's informants agreed to these terms, that does not remove her from the social constellations that she developed through her fieldwork. Anthropologist studying horizontally must ask themselves how to be respectful of their participants and the knowledge they hold, even if they hold more social, economic, and/or political power than groups who are more frequently anthropologised.

Van Wyk's ethnographic approach more successfully towed the line between being respectful to his participants, and by extension their knowledge, and a healthy scepticism of their goal. He specifically followed the legal mechanisms by which Kleinfontein can exist. He notes the limitations of collective ownership residents have to place upon themselves in order to maintain their Apartheid status quo, which he explicitly calls it (2014, 105). His considerations undermine the reader's assumption that everyone who moves to a *volkstaat*, as he mentions a number of times that the older residents, "were sympathetic to the creation of a *volkstaat* but moved to the settlement primarily for reasons related to affordability and security" (2014, 105).

Whereas as the idea of the *volkstaat* began in response to the end of Apartheid in South Africa, in the context of Zimbabwe, Hughes acknowledges that decolonization dramatically forced the hand of White-settler farmers towards shaking the hands of Africans, but once Hughes shift from historical and literary analysis, with the occasional interview, by way of creating the contextual (literal and metaphysical) landscape I found it interesting that he did not spend much time examining the relationships that White-settlers in Zimbabwe *do* have with Black individuals. For example, Hughes writes:

> Of course, agriculture inevitably brought farm owners into frequent contact with farm workers. "The labour" could facilitate or disrupt farm operations, enriching or infuriating the boss. Even so, these Blacks operated within the confines of Whites' administrative project Euro-Zimbabweans *managed* them but did not construct an identity around them. Commercial farmers, like many other savannah Whites, felt the

primary tension or contradiction as (White) Man against the land- not White against Black (2010: 74)

The issue with this particular kind of characterization is that by foregrounding the understanding of the White-settler, the ethnographer erases the complexity and agency of Africans, just as early anthropology did. To a certain extent Hughes attempts to pre-empt this question by asking his readers "how could I do the research with attention to power and inequality? [...] An ethnographer, however, cannot avoid humanising his or her subjects, some of whom, in this case became genuine friends" (2010, xvii). This is an important question to consider for anthropologists working with White-settlers in Africa: how does one remain accountable to one's informants as well as to those who are disempowered by the consequences of the colonial legacy? How should one balance the worldview of one's participants if their worldview is violent to others? The intimacy of ethnography can lead to awkwardness through the possibility of the final monographs challenging the worldviews of informants. It seems untenable to ask every anthropologist studying up or studying horizontally to be hypercritical to a point of destroying relationships built during fieldwork. Yet, as was pointed out by Gerald Berreman, anthropologists are embedded in global structures of power, thus carrying a duty to analyse our involvement (in Peters and Wendland 2016, 2). If anthropologists are the co-producers of work, as argued by Nyamnjoh (2012), then there is a tension to on the one hand be using the knowledge of informants to illustrate a point and on the other to be causing them a great amount of distress.

There are some instances where ethnographers do burn bridges with their informants. For example, Ilana van Wyk chose to openly call the leaders of the community in which she worked "repugnant" since she saw them as preying on the financially disempowered and socially vulnerable (Doran 2017, 118). The leaders of the Universal Church of the Kingdom of God (UCKD) preached a prosperity gospel while waging a war against demonic and heavenly forces. Parishioners, who were living near or below the poverty line, were constantly asked to give money to the church to a point where their personal bills, the schools fees of their children, etc went unpaid (van de Kamp 2016: 164-165). The UCKG published a press release condemning Ilana van Wyk's work; describing it as "one-sided", "biased", "fraught with incorrect statements and sweeping generalisations". They describe the fact that she disliked her informants as possibly defamatory (UCKG 2015). Thus, van Wyk would not be able to do any follow up work within UCKG, or possibly with other evangelical groups who might be wary of van Wyk if they did research on her before allowing her into their parish. Many anthropologists revisit old field sites to draw on their pre-existing relationship, but van Wyk made the choice to publish a harsh critique of UCKG because she felt it was the morally right thing to do. Contextually, this might be an issue for those studying white settlers in Africa: to publish harsh truths will likely lead to burnt bridges.

Shades of White: Class Politics

By just painting White-settlers with one brush, one can miss nuance. The work of Danelle van Zyl-Heaman reconsiders class politics within Afrikaner history in South Africa, by offering "a historicization of the Afrikaner experience of transformation from a working-class perspective, thereby reinserting white workers into the historiography of the demise of apartheid and the democratization of South African society" (2014, 155). Part of the work of Afrikaner nationalism was to persuade White workers to replace their class-based identity with an ethnic-based one, that "potential competition from cheaper African labour posed a greater threat to [working class Afrikaner] interests than did the bosses" (O'Meara in van Zyl-Heaman 2014, 142). There was a consolidation of power in the form of an alliance between sections of the White working class and the nationalist in the National Party (NP) that made its 1948 victory possible (van Zyl-Heaman 2014, 142).

Van Wyk investigates contemporary White labour issues through the testimony of the White day labourers in Kleinfontein. The workers decried their working conditions and equated the relationship between workers and employers as being the same relationship as in the rest of South Africa. They felt as though they were treated like they are "less human than the shareholders of the cooperative who 'own' the homes and for whom they work. Shareholders who treat workers as people who have feelings are the except rather than the rule" (2014, 98). Seldon, on the other hand, dismisses those who call the Kleingehuk "Orania's White township" (2014, 83) or that workers felt they were being "'treated like *k******' by rich people in Orania" (2014, 101) by pointing out that it's possible for them to earn a higher salary than some of the local teachers thus "it can be argued they are not as financially undervalued as they claim" (2014 101). Furthermore, Seldon does not provide any commentary on the fact that White-workers in Orania expressed their poor treatment by using a racial epithet for Black people. Being paid well can be understood as a signal of respect, however, it does not guarantee that translates into social acceptance. Seldon concedes that "since they do not stay long term, are not individually contextualised by having a family, and occupying an unusual social position" (2014, 101) which implies that they are not being invited to the social events that Seldon writes about elsewhere in her work, so perhaps once again, her goal of recharacterizing Orania more positively than other accounts may have concealed unequal power-relations that were occurring there.

Conclusion

This chapter has examined a selection of anthropological work on whiteness in Africa and explored the new problematiques that arise as anthropology enters (hopefully) more consistently into territory of the anthropology of the powerful. Settler-colonialism in Africa operated differently than in Canada, the United States, New Zealand, and Australia, as diseases like malaria majorly deterred settlement in significant portions of the continent. In places where settlement occurred, settlers never became the majority, unlike other British and French settler colonies.

Anthropologists need to consider to what extent canonical methodologies and frameworks can be used for non-canonical subjects. I argue there cannot be an exact transplanting of the traditional cultural relativism that anthropologists employ onto non-traditional subjects. When anthropologists are studying people in positions of privilege, or relative privilege, cultural relativism can mask suffering of those who are disadvantaged by the advantages informants have received through society. The intimate relationships created through participant observation create a challenge for anthropologists studying the powerful as many informants tend to cope with the darker sides of their privilege by justifying, burying, or obscuring it. All forms of privilege systematically advantage subsets of people at the cost of disadvantaging other subsets. Anthropologists are put in a delicate position when trying to avoid perpetuating the camouflaging or burying the plight of the disadvantaged while studying the advantaged. Informants are unlikely to open up without establishing some form of trust and the challenging of their worldviews could make them quite antagonistic. An antagonistic informant is unlikely to consent to having their voices be published, anonymised or not. The ethics of working with the powerful, then, in addition to the general ethics anthropologists deploy, is complicated by its focus on setting norms of its own (as English as a norm among southern African settlers) and it can obscure the responsibility of the powerful for the plight of a "disadvantaged".

Chapter 3

Afrikaans, English and Africa: A Story of Love and Hate

We know of no better soil, no better water, no purer air, no finer heaven, no more beautiful flowers– no place where one can live and study more healthily, and with God's grace, than in Stellenbosch.
  – Rev. Neethling in Francois Smuts: 1979, 328.

The world, the real one, was civilization secured and ruled by savage means.
  –Ta-Nehisi Coates: 2015, 32.

Introduction

This chapter examines the colonial history of South Africa. How history is remembered and re-presented impacts the discursive structures people where root themselves, as they position themselves or are able to be positioned within narratives of the past (Hall, 1990: 235). History is crucial to investigate the rhetoric of those advocating to keep Afrikaans in Stellenbosch. I use historiography to show the historical revisionism of the town historian of Stellenbosch, Francois Smuts. Historiography evaluates the sources used to write history, analysing the possible biases to consider the historical value of the source. Historical revisionism is the act of writing or rewriting history, in this case omitting or greatly minimizing the importance or centrality of individuals, communities or events from the historical record (Censer, 1995: vii). These kinds of histories are re-presented as (convenient) truths by people within the community. They become key to the discourse about an identity where they can root their identities.

South African language debates need to be understood in a broader African context. All African countries faced decisions about how to prioritize languages. There are over 2000 languages in Africa, each with their own unique histories and nuanced developments. I was not able to do justice to them here, but I sought a cross-section of some. Too often South Africa is discussed without reference to the rest of the continent. This contributes to ideas of South African exceptionalism — that South Africa is somehow different from the rest of the continent. For example, Ngugi wa Thiong'o in his 2017 tour of South Africa[28], argued Africans should continue pushing for their respective governments to include their languages in learning institutions to preserve the social, cultural and linguistic heritage rather than languages like English (Chatora, 2017) (ENCA, 2017)[29].

In July of 2013 when I visited Cape Town, history and the recent past kept being explained to me as context for what I was seeing, like the spatial inequality between townships and the Southern Suburbs (a wealthy, historically white area of Cape Town where the University of Cape Town is located). In my next semester of university in Canada, I studied South African history which continued to contextualize the inequality I witnessed. The power of the "obvious" means that many South Africans are not forced to confront what historical forces shape the present. Christoff, told me he thought many young Afrikaners were quite naïve about how deep anti-English sentiments among their elders is: "it's not just that their parents and grandparents struggle with [the] English [language], but that they really really hate them."[30]

"It's not just that they struggle", I responded, "but it's because they have no motivation to want to learn more". I spoke from experience with my ex-boyfriend's family. I noticed their reluctance to interact with me. His father's family was Afrikaans and I knew he spoke fluent English but I found André's[31] family incredibly quiet. The first time I met them, his friend noted that they were "quieter" than expected. André responded in a huffy tone "maybe if they were able to speak their first language they would have been more engaging". Compounding factors like perhaps that I was an 'outsider' ('uitlander') to them since I was not born in South Africa or the Afrikaner diaspora might have made his

---

[28] On the theme "Secure the base, decolonise the mind"
[29] Online news article.
[30] Interviewed 2 November 2016.
[31] André is a pseudonym.

family shy. Christoff agreed that many Afrikaans people prefer to be reserved than interact in English.[32] Christoff also observed that a significant number of them see the value (even if mostly international) of learning and speaking English, and some would even claim to speak English without an accent, in the purported manner that native speakers are assumed to speak.

Another informant, Du Toit[33], joked that from where he grew up in the Northern Cape, Afrikaners speak English in "self-defence". This expression can be understood innocuously, implying an embarrassment at one's English skills; it can also be interpreted with its legal origin in mind. Self-defence is "the right to defend oneself with whatever force is reasonably necessary against actual or threatened violence" (Webster's Dictionary, 2014). In this instance, it implies the speaking of the English language to an Afrikaner is itself a threat. All good anthropology should be historically contextualized; the feedback from my participants in the field impressed upon me the way that the history of South Africa lives on in the present.

By sketching the history of White-Afrikaans-speaking people, I want readers to understand the common historical narratives to which they tie themselves, to establish what the perception of an "Afrikaner" is. For example, Afrikaners as "a people who historically considered themselves the Christian saviours of heathen Africans" (Goodwin & Schiff 1995: 13), Afrikaners as attached to the land and therefore entitled to hold their ground in South Africa, and as bona fide Africans unlike their fellow White but English-speaking South Africans. Afrikaners, in addition to thinking themselves as needing to be separated and protected from so-called the savagery of the surrounding non-European populations, sought to insulate themselves from European ways with their own competing characterization of what being "civilized" meant. Racial purity was central to Afrikaner nationalism. Interracial sex was both taboo before Apartheid, and was illegal during it (Goodwin & Schiff, 1995: 13). Residential segregation— which prevented economic competition from Black Africans and thereby the retention

---

[32] This will be expanded in detail in a later chapter.
[33] Interviewed 28 October 2016.

of political power for White-South Africans, (also probably to help with the prevention interracial sex)— did not prevent all contact between Black people and White people (Moodie 1975: 260). Residential segregation curated a particular types of contact across racial lines.

In face-to-face interactions, Moodie points out the use of strategies by Whites to maintain their supposed superiority such as "calling them by their first names, speaking authoritatively to and of them in their presence or within earshot, expecting deference and so on" (Moodie, 1975: 260). This kind of behaviour continues in the present day with White people calling adult Black men "boy". The huge gulf of economic inequality between White and Black-South Africans creates the conditions of possibility for White students at Stellenbosch University to have not had Black peers in schools. Formerly "Whites-Only" or "Model-C" schools are public schools but they are allowed to charge tuition– a significant barrier for many economically marginalized people in South Africa. Thus, some White South Africans may have only seen Black people in roles perceived to be subservient to them. For example, an acquaintance of mine who was Black moved a mini-fridge into his residence room. All the White students seemed shocked because if he had the disposable income to have a mini-fridge then he came from a moderately wealthy family.

The South African War[34] looms large in the memory of the Afrikaner community. JK O'Connor wrote, after the end of the South African War, about the resentment and disdain felt by Afrikaners. Afrikaners were forced to give up their freedom and become part of an English controlled and structured state (1915: 6). The feelings which O'Connor was writing about remained present at the time of Crapazano's study. Crapazano's participants put Anglo-Afrikaner history at the forefront of their psyche. When he explained to Afrikaners in the village who he was and why he was in Wyndal, he noted they emphasized their mistreatment by the English and argued that they were misunderstood; while the English made an effort to keep the spotlight away from themselves by speaking about other groups in South Africa

---

[34] Previous referred to as the "Boer War", see SAHO 08-Nov-2011 or Encyclopedia Britannica Online.

(1985: 26). Both tended to cast themselves as a necessary emissary to explain their truth to the outside world (1985: 26).

Crapanzano's observations about the English helped frame my thinking about how the English attempt to alienate themselves from the predicament of South Africa, as if they are not agents whose actions affect the country. Hermann Giliomee's narration of South African history bolsters this view when he speaks of the search for identity of Dutch-settlers during British colonization: "the burghers had to be loyal British subjects, but also identify with their particular history and cultural distinctiveness" (Giliomee, 2003: 195). Giliomee is a former president of South African Institute of Race Relations while also having been a professor of Political Science at UCT and of History at Stellenbosch. He argues the English intelligentsia reinforced the image of Afrikaners as unprogressive and parochial, which was the light with which they characterized the concerns of the survival of the Dutch language (Giliomee, 2003: 196). The British-settlers, unlike the Dutch-settlers, commonly retained emotional ties with Britain. They remained isolated from Afrikaners, attending their own churches, playing their own games: "they did little to get to know the Afrikaners and their ways, preferring to keep their own company or occasionally that of an anglicized Afrikaner" (Giliomee 2003: 196).

Crapanzano's writing was criticized as over-generalizing the views of White-South Africans, as the community he studied was "a relatively insulated rural community (with all the attendant conservative attitudinal implications) in the Western Province of a country in which the centre of political gravity has moved to the cities" (1985: 60). Furthermore, the conflict between the English and Afrikaners that Crapanzano describes is an "overdrawn picture of the alleged contemporary 'hostility' of relations between English and Afrikaans-speaking South Africans" (Hugo 1985: 60). I shared Crapanzano's characterization of English-South Africans with Christoff who pushed back against it. In his view, it was not that English-South Africans retained emotional ties with Britain but rather that English-South Africans were sometimes seen as less sentimental about South Africa.

Patriotism is not informed by rational behaviour but by sentiment or emotional attachment to a country – this could mean that with the English South Africans, their patriotism is elsewhere if they remained attached to a real or imagined homeland elsewhere, making South Africa appear more secondary in their hierarchy of patriotism. At this point, Christoff, based on his experience, stated that few have maintained strong 'British' identities. After reading my initial description of the distinctions between White Afrikaans- and English-speaking South Africans, Christoff noted that for both of the major subsets of White-South Africans, the strong distinctions caused by the South African War have petered out across generations and were replaced to lesser or greater degrees with a new mixture of identities.[35] Charney notes that the 'new' Afrikaner middle-class formed by the growth of White-owned business and parastatals during Apartheid more than doubled the amount of Afrikaners in White-collar jobs and led to the greater integration between Afrikaners and English-South Africans (1984, 269-270). In Christoff's words:

> Every successive generation has integrated more fully into the English-speaking economy and, consequently, become, their Anglophobia would wane and become more superficial. I think, to the great dismay of more serious Afrikaner nationalists, economic forces gradually replaced separate ethnic identities with a broader 'White' identity[36].

The increased integration of Afrikaners with the English was part of the plan of Verwoerd[37] who said (10 years before the beginning of Apartheid):

> Patriotism, fellow-citizenship, friendship, all have become more of importance to us. The English-speaking and the Afrikaans-speaking sections have become like the new bride and bridegroom who enter the new life in love to create

---

[35] The closeness between English and Afrikaners will be visited during later chapters of this thesis.
[36] Interviewed May 28, 2018.
[37] One of the key architects of Apartheid.

together and live together as life mates (quoted in Moodie 1975: 285-286).

This vision from Verwoerd demonstrates the willingness of architects of Apartheid to sacrifice elements of Afrikanerdom (distinction and separation from English-South Africans) to consolidate a broader White identity.

So far in this chapter, I have laid out some of the beginnings of the elements of the story told about English- and Afrikaner-South Africans. Here I want to re-raise King's argument from my first chapter that stories are part of our core identities, that how history is told and internalized influences how people imagine themselves: who they are and where they fit in society. I believe King's argument is congruent with Stuart Hall's conception of identities as relating to "the invention of tradition as much as to tradition itself" which arises from:

> The narrativization of the self, but the necessarily fictional nature of this process in no way undermines its discursive, material or political effectivity, even if the belongingness, the 'suturing into the story' through which identities arise is, partly, in the imaginary (as well as the symbolic) and therefore, always, partly constructed in fantasy, or at least within a fantasmatic field (1996: 4).

Thus, this chapter is an exploration of some of the historical events that play heavily into the imaginary and symbolic indicators of being, becoming and belonging at Stellenbosch University. Rather than a year by year approach it moves between moments of thematic significance.

This chapter is split into four sections: the first is a historical overview of European settlement, highlighting the conflicts and alliances between the British and the Dutch. The second focuses on the history of Stellenbosch, how it came to be a university town and its significance to the wider White-Afrikaans community. The third examines the more contemporary language debates in South Africa. The final section extends beyond the South African borders to put the historical and contemporary South African in conversation with language debates more broadly on the continent.

Struggles in Stellenbosch

From the outset of these sections which centre the Afrikaner experience and history, I foreground Moodie's research questions: who asks what stories have Afrikaners told themselves, and what factors and people have changed those stories (1975: xvii)? He argued that Afrikanerdom can be understood as a form of "civil religion". The characteristics of which he highlights as a sacred history, a civil theology, and a civil ritual.

The Dutch, sent by the Dutch East India Trading Company (VOC), settled the Cape of Good Hope in 1652 to build a base and refilling station to link between the Netherlands and Java (Thompson 2011: 33). There are strong associations of whiteness with the Cape even though most settlers during that period were people who were Black or Brown enslaved from places like Madagascar, Indonesia, Sri Lanka and other parts of the Indian Ocean (Thompson, 2011: 36). When the company released some of its employees from their contracts and gave them land with the status of "free burghers", the settlers began to move further away from the initial settlement (Thompson, 2011: 33). Burghers were expected to produce food. The VOC directors hoped this would be less expensive than food only being produced by enslaved peoples (Thompson 2011: 35). This is the first story Moodie outlines as part of the origin myth of the Afrikaner people: free and hardworking, adventurous farmers (1975: 2). Stellenbosch was settled in 1679, shortly after the "free burgher" policy, and named after Simon van der Stel, the Governor of the Cape at the time (Hanekom, 2013). It was the first of the Dutch settlements outside of Table Bay (Thompson, 2011: 35).

Francois Smuts, commissioned by the town council of Stellenbosch in 1979 as a celebration of the town's 300-year history, wrote a triumphant account of the settlers of Stellenbosch. Though the work of Smuts is historiographically suspect, given it was commissioned, I believe it is valuable beyond its 'objective' historical worth because it speaks to the imaginary in which Stellenbosch sits for Afrikaners. How ideas of the past in Stellenbosch are remembered are "maintained only through the forms in which 'the past' is publicly demarcated and represented" through material representations such as museums, heritage sites and festivals (Hanekom, 2013). Thus, it is "kept alive by those who organise and maintain these material displays" like Smuts' work (Hanekom, 2013). This suggests language, writings and texts are also mobilised in the service of memory and identity construction. For example, there is an irony that if Simon Van der Stel lived in South Africa during Apartheid, that he would have likely been classified as a Coloured person, but in 1979 he was used as a symbol by the hegemonic White Afrikaners, whose political supremacy was reinforced by the hierarchical racial segregation of the Apartheid regime (Hankom, 2013).

Smuts describes Stellenbosch as "the first true farming community in South Africa, where people from another continent were permanently settled and achieved ownership of land which they could leave as an inheritance to their children and their children's children" (Smuts 1979: 64). Achieving this future-focused goal required an investment in community making, at the heart of which were culture and cultivation, especially through the reproduction of shared values in the younger generation. Stellenbosch was also home to the first permanent Christian church in Southern Africa in 1687, just after the completion of courthouse and town hall, which he describes as beyond being the "spiritual and intellectual centres" of the village (1979: 64).

The use of Dutch Calvinism was pivotal to produce and reinforce a shared belief in the common purpose of the presence of settlers in South Africa and to ensure the continuation of their culture. Children and the young were protected from competing values (including the English when they became neighbours). The English considered themselves as more civilized than Dutch-settlers because they maintained close connections to contemporary British culture. From the British perspective, Afrikaners, in developing a distinct identity from their Dutch forefathers, had lost their way (Giliomee 2003: 194). "The *volk*'s existence as a nation was threatened by mixing and intermarriage" and much later this became the logic by which "apartheid was required to preserve the *volk* and their holy mission" (Goodwin & Schiff, 1995: 13). It was a case of double protection: protection from the savagery and barbarism of the surrounding non-European populations; as well as protection from competing ways of fellow Europeans who happened to be non-Afrikaner, and thus had their own competing characterization of what being "civilized" meant.

The best protection from the Brown and Black-bodied locals was guaranteed by seeking to convert[38] them rather than running from them. They plucked them away from what Dutch-settlers saw as their savage cultures through education. Dutch-settlers thought education "gave" them a language: teaching them to read and write in Dutch meant they could better serve the White man, or better help the White man to accomplish the White man's burden. How Afrikaners as a community positioned themselves was rather precariously - in a life of tension: caught in a tense relationship between the savage and the competing civilised European, at the risk of being torn apart by the opposing forces. They were truly betwixt and between – not quite African (this was symbolized as the "savage", the "slave") and not quite European (the "civilized", the "free"). As Smuts describes: "It was a community that developed a spirit of co-operation, particularly as a result of seclusion" (1979: 64). A characterization which sets the settlers as independent, future-focused, and civilized people but disregards the fact that the settlers were actually dependent on the labour of enslaved people.

Smuts acknowledged that there were enslaved peoples in Stellenbosch but whenever enslaved, Black, or Coloured people were mentioned, he references acts done by White settlers on behalf of those people (1979: 279). This reinforces and validates the accomplishment of the "White man's burden". Smuts references the population and demographics of Stellenbosch to speak about the work of a Dutch missionary, who "included religious service for all non-Whites and school teaching for slave and other non-White children" (1979: 279). Smuts fails to explain that the work done by enslaved people in Stellenbosch was crucial to the survival of the settlers. Thompson points out that enslaved peoples were responsible for building the infrastructure for

---

[38] Metaphorically, as it was illegal to baptise enslaved people under Dutch Roman law.

the Cape, including "roads, orchards, vegetable gardens, and arable fields" (2001: 33). The Cape lacked adequate capital and skilled labour to do so (Thompson, 2001: 35) until the arrival of enslaved people.

After 1658, the VOC government, the senior officials and the free burgher community were dependent on the labour of enslaved people (Thompson, 2001: 36). They were the "bedrock of the political econom[y]" (Scully 1990: 1). After the 1838 emancipation, Western Cape farmers organized petitions to demand the closure of mission stations, as they were providing land to the enslaved peoples they formerly owned (Worden, 1985). Therefore, rather than Black- and Brown-bodied people being the White man's burden, the White man was the burden of the Brown- and Black-bodied people he had enslaved.[39] Characterizing the settlers of Stellenbosch as independent, this labour – crucial to the ability of the settlers to live there. This hints that Afrikaners overlook their parasitic relationship with enslaved people and with the local pastoralists who were pushed off their land by the settlers (Thompson, 2001: 33).

This section describes how the narrativization of Afrikaner history undermines the contributions and agency of the enslaved peoples in the building of the Cape Colony and instead foregrounds Dutch-settlers as the key agents. It notes the use of Dutch Calvinism to create a common purpose between Dutch-settlers.

In 1795, when the British captured the Cape from the Dutch, they took over responsibility for a thinly populated, loose-knit territory. The Cape switched hands between the Dutch and the English a number of times at the beginning of the 19th century but after 1814 it stayed under British control (Thompson, 2011: 51). The British regime led to dissatisfaction within the local Dutch community. Resultantly, when British Parliament banned participation in the slave trade in 1807, it deprived the Cape of its fresh influx

---

[39] There is a direct link between the work of enslaved people and Andriaan van der Stel, the son of the namesake of Stellenbosch. Thompson notes that in 1706, Adriaan van der Stel owned a large number of enslaved people in the Cape: 169 people. (Markell, Hall, & Schrire,, 1995).

of labour. The enslaved people brought to the Cape Colony never became a self-sustaining population because of the brutal working conditions. The owners of enslaved people responded to the British ban on participation in the slave trade, by increasing the workload of their current slaves and agitating for more control over Indigenous labour (Thompson, 2011: 57).

In the early part of the 19th century there were regulations aimed at ameliorating the lives of enslaved people. These regulations went mostly unenforced but were still resented by the owners of enslaved peoples (Thompson, 2011: 57). This disruption of the Afrikaner way of life, is an event that is "selected out as a prologue to the Great Trek" (Moodie, 1975: 3) in the story Afrikaners tell about themselves. Life among the non-enslaved people who were Black or Coloured was not much better than their formerly enslaved counterparts. Khoikhoi 'servants' were restricted by law to living at mission stations, licensed kraals or on farms, and could not travel without a certificate (Giliomee, 2003: 95). One of the reforms was a court where complaints by Khoikhoi servants could be heard against their masters. Moodie finds an author who speaks to how these courts were received and understood by Afrikaners. They say: "It was not so much love for the native that underlay the apparent negrophilistic policy as hatred and contempt of the Boer" (Reitz, 1900: 92 in Moodie, 1975: 3).

This understanding points to how Afrikaners found ways to make themselves the main character of the story. Slavery was banned in the British empire in 1833 and by 1838 all slaves were freed (Thompson, 2011: 58). However, due to the intense and intimately exploitative relationship between enslaved peoples and the people who owned them, the "freedom" that the British asserted did not change much about their day to day lives. The White men were still their burden. The emancipation of enslaved peoples is often characterised as a direct cause of the Great Trek[40]. Moodie's examination finds that the interpretation in the sacred history of Afrikaners is "rather it was Britain's failure to keep her promise of full compensation which led to embittered feelings" (1975: 5). He used Reitz again to show how

---

[40] Explored more in-depth in the next section of this chapter.

Afrikaners made themselves the main character of the story of the emancipation of enslaved peoples in South Africa: "greyheads and widows who had lived in ease and comfort went down poverty stricken to the grave" (1900: 8 in Moodie 1975: 5). Rather than the emphasis on the brutal conditions and dehumanisation that now formerly enslaved people were supposed to be freed from, the suffering of their Afrikaner enslavers were foregrounded at every turn.

The VOC's control beyond Cape Town and Stellenbosch was weak. The British gradually pressed to control the entire colony, thereby emphasizing British culture and institutions (Thompson, 2001: 68). A partnership developed between the British rulers and wealthier burghers after the 1806 British takeover. The British controlled military and bureaucratic power while agriculture was controlled by the burghers (Giliomee, 2003: 95). An influx of British settlers also contributed pressure for greater Anglicization (Thompson 2001: 68). Mostly the upper stratum Afrikaners began to Anglicize and were nicknamed the 'Queen's Afrikaners' (Giliomee, 2003: 193). During his reign, Governor Craddock incentivized teachers who instructed in English by paying them an additional allowance. In 1822, Governor Lord Charles Somerset proclaimed English as the official language of the colony (Sigcau, 2004: 241). By the 1830s, only English was used in government offices, law courts, and public schools (Thompson, 2001: 68). The combinations of these events in the 1830 meant that anti-British feelings were beginning to be widespread among Dutch-settlers.

There were early hostilities between Dutch-settlers and the British around the institution of slavery and language.

In Stellenbosch, Smuts narrates a rosy picture of the Landdrost and Heemraden. He dramatically describes its end saying: "The glory was gone. In 1840 a municipal council was established in Stellenbosch, but it has none of the colour, dignity and tradition, or the extensive powers of the old College (1979: 64-65)". Smuts advocates for readers to see the British as villains who unjustly meddled in the affairs of Stellenbosch. Thompson pushes back against Smuts' view. Thomson describes the *landdrost* system as "extremely sketchy" rarely did they have paid staff except in some cases a clerk and one or two soldiers (2001: 46).

The nosy picture painted by Smuts is an explicit example of Afrikaner historical revisionism.

Locals in Stellenbosch founded their own Dutch private-school. However, the policy of Anglicisation meant the opening of free English schools. The teachers were encouraged to learn basic Dutch, though it was not required, as "the speaking of Dutch even on playgrounds would be prohibited at their schools" (Smuts, 1979: 300). The teaching of Dutch was in a poor state. In 1870, only three schools in the Cape Colony offered it. In reaction to the Policy, parents removed their children from the government school and sent them to the Dutch private-school (Smuts 1979: 301). By 1889 there were 146 Dutch private schools in the colony (Giliomee 2003: 211). This demonstrates the resolve of Dutch-settlers to continue their culture at a cost, rather than send their children to a free school where their children could be converted to English culture and distance themselves from their Dutch roots.

While Dutch was the language of instruction at the school "pupils were also taught English, so that this essential part of their education was not neglected" (Smuts 1979: 304). It was perhaps because in the beginning of the nineteenth century, "Afrikaners found the idea of English cultural supremacy difficult to refute" (Giliomee, 2003: 195), as by 1860 the Cape had not made any great economic advances or cultural achievements (no books, paintings, or notable innovations). By his evaluation, they were a "rural, isolated, relatively backward people with only a few who had received more than a rudimentary education" (2003: 195). Giliomee believes "the feelings of inferiority were compounded by what Barrow called 'the reluctance that a vanquished people must feel in mixing with their conquerors" (2003: 195).

The Queen's Afrikaners were willing to sacrifice their culture for greater access to power. This demonstrates there being reasons for Afrikaners to know English well apart from it being imposed on them. Jan Smuts, an early twentieth-century Prime Minister of South Africa, was a clear example: an Anglicized Afrikaner who used his Englishness for social and political capital. He was incredibly successful, as he, among other things, was granted the honour to address the joint British houses of parliament. However, another possibility, perhaps more common amongst those not in the upper stratum of society, could have been that these Afrikaners were using the same strategy taught to learners in Springbok like Du Toit who was taught to speak English "only in self-defence" (Smuts, 1979: 304).

> *Here, the quickness with which the people of Stellenbosch rallied around the use of the Dutch language in schools is the first of the recurring theme of language as a tool of cultural organisation for proto-Afrikaners.*

By the 1860s, Stellenbosch was described as "reflect[ing] ruling class [of settler-farmers] perceptions of the existence of a secure and stable community predicated upon successful regulation and control" (Scully, 1990: 8). The positioning of the Moederkerk, the Drostdy and the gaol in the centre of the village demonstrated the prominence of religion and the maintenance of law and order by the settlers there (Scully, 1990: 8). Settlers feared the possibility of the emancipation of the people they enslaved. FRL Neethling and other Stellenbosch settlers wrote to the Cape Town Burgher Senate and "depicted in apocalyptic terms [their] political and sexual nightmares"; "The flame of devastation will not alone destroy our habitations but will also cause your houses to fall in ruin! Not only our wives and daughters, but also yours will in libidinous manner be prosecuted by our slaves with rape and defloration" (Giliomee, 2003; 111).

As noted earlier, Dutch-settlers were trying to protect themselves both from the threat of conversion to Anglicization but also from the suspected "savagery" of the Black and Brown-bodied people around them. Thus, they attempted to convert those Black and Brown-bodied people to their way of being. These inflammatory predictions by members of the Dutch-settler community clearly testify to a fear that the conversion of Black and Brown-bodied people was based on the institution of slavery. Therefore, if the institution fell, these Brown and Black-bodied people might realise the injustice of the situation they had been placed in and react with vengeance. This in a way mirrors the reaction of the fear that caused White-flight from South Africa at the end of Apartheid when another institution that justified the dehumanization of Black- and Brown-bodied people fell (Johnson, 2009).

However, the abolishment of slavery did not deconstruct the relationship between formerly enslaved peoples and their former masters. The new legislation that governed relations between employers and employees still empowered the employer to punish their employees (Scully, 1990: 9). To such an act there was even resistance from the 'noble' Stellenbosch landdrost who questioned it, saying: "What would become of us and of the whole country if the natives were to feel that they should be free, were to know their power, and then to join together to regain their natural freedom as the original possessors of this country?" (Giliomee, 2003: 95), as he felt the feeling of freedom would be "dangerous and idealistic" (Giliomee, 2003: 95). Thereby, speaking directly to my argument that settlers had founded their supremacy on the ability to treat their Black and Brown-bodied peers with cruelty and contempt rather than as humans. The Master and Servants Acts was retained throughout most of the twentieth century. It was only abolished in 1974. As of 1990, when Scully was writing, farm workers were still not protected by specific labour legislation (1990).[41]

> *The fear of the abolishment of slavery by Dutch-settlers is linked to the possibility of enslaved people enacting revenge on them, not unlike the fear of Afrikaners of Black, Coloured and Indian South Africans enacting revenge on them at the end of apartheid.*

While the people of Stellenbosch resisted Anglicisation through education, other Dutch-settlers had a different form of resistance in mind. By 1840, 9% of the White-settlers left the colony to find a "promised land". They are now known as *voortrekkers* (pioneers) (Thompson, 2011: 70). This was the beginning of many conflicts between the Dutch and English. The *voortrekkers* eventually set up governments of two independent states during the 1850s and 1860s: the Transvaal

---

[41] Though labour is not the focus of this study it has been the question in the public as well as in academia about to what extent are ventures like mining, for example, profitable if they come at the cost of Black-bodies (See Teicher 2014 or McCulloch 2012).

and the Orange Free State. British (and other non-Dutch) settlers continued to settle in the *voortrekker* republics, especially after the discovery of gold on the reef in the Transvaal (SAHO, 2015). Transvalers felt threatened by these settlers that they called *uitlanders* [42]. This term was applied to anyone who was not Dutch and was not naturalised by birth, especially to British settlers (Nyamnjoh, 2016a: 9).

Stellenbosch has been one of the highest ranked academic institutions in South Africa and was built for Afrikaners[43]. An analogy can be made between the fierce defenders of Afrikaans in present-day Stellenbosch to Dutch-settlers of the Transvaal fearing the ability of others to profit from gold in a land they thought of as possessing. Around the same period as the Great Trek, English became the 'Master language' in the Cape (Sigcau, 2004: 241). Afrikaners in the Cape were able to protect themselves from the English threat by becoming rich from gold, thereby more successfully ensuring the survival of their culture in their children and their children's children by sending them to Dutch private-schools.

The move to the interior and the contact with indigenous South Africans people made the Dutch Reformed Church (NG Kerk) want to evangelize on the frontier: to convert the new Black-bodied people they were meeting to their way of being to protect themselves from their influence of the culture and worldview. However, to convert people, ministers were needed. Previously, they were coming from the Netherlands to South Africa or South Africans going to

---

[42] Trans: foreigners

[43] Between 2012 and 2019, Stellenbosch stayed in the Times Higher Education's top 350 universities in the world
(https://www.timeshighereducation.com/world-university-rankings/stellenbosch-university#pane-university-rankings-chart). They rank above UKZN (401-500 in the world)
[https://www.timeshighereducation.com/world-university-rankings/university-kwazulu-natal], University of South Africa (1001+ best universities) [https://www.timeshighereducation.com/world-university-rankings/university-south-africa]. TopUniversities.com puts Stellenbosch as the 4th best university in South Africa, below UCT, University of the Witwatersrand, & University of Pretoria
(https://www.topuniversities.com/university-rankings-articles/brics-rankings/top-10-universities-south-africa-2018).

the Netherlands for training. However, given the drastically increasing need this model was unsustainable. This sparked discussion among the NG Synod to found a seminary in the Cape (Smuts, 1979: 316). Some voices were resistant because it "would not be able to provide the broad education and enlightenment of a European university" and would produce "bigoted theologizers, semi-enlightened and semi-civilized members of the community" (Smuts, 1979: 317). Again, they demonstrate the fear of over-Africanization and a descent into purported barbarism, thus displaying a need to protect themselves through maintaining a connection with their country of origin.

There was much debate about where the seminary should be: Cape Town, Stellenbosch or Paarl. Some feared Anglicization in Cape Town "would soon take a direction inappropriate to the [NG Kerk]" (Smuts, 1979: 319). Stellenbosch was ultimately chosen because community members donated the old Drostdy as the venue for the seminary (Smuts, 1979: 319). Smuts emphasizes the distinctiveness of Stellenbosch, as the Drostdy was "one of the most magnificent examples of Cape-Dutch architecture ever erected and had played an important role in the history of the country" (Smuts, 1979: 319).

A brief explanation of how Stellenbosch came to be the home of the first Afrikaans-medium university.

As one reads through Smuts' narration of Stellenbosch's history, we see that even if Stellenbosch is not actually particularly important in the history of South Africa (which I argue it is), it becomes clear that Stellenbosch is positioned to be important. The place of Stellenbosch in the psyche of the Afrikaners seems as if the town itself is a historical pageant at all times because Stellenbosch has historically occupied "a unique and important position in the minds of many Afrikaner nationalists and in the sphere of Afrikanerdom" (Duffy, 2006: 37). This remained true as Stellenbosch is the oldest and highest ranked university that teaches in Afrikaans. During apartheid majority of universities operated in Afrikaans, but none of them overtook Stellenbosch in prestige.

The University grew quickly in its first forty years.[44] The student population was 96% Afrikaans-speaking. It was described by the *Cape Times* in 1938 as "traditionally rather rabidly nationalist" (Duffy, 2006: 11). It was predominantly male[45]. Many of the academics became local political leaders. Professors also involved themselves as members of government commissions, as well as through their participation in discussion on the issues of the day on the national stage (Duffy, 2006: 11). This demonstrates that professors in Stellenbosch carried on positioning Stellenbosch as an important place through involvement in national public issues.

Stellenbosch is seen as the home of "successful Afrikanerdom": many Afrikaner institutions were founded and housed there (Duffy, 2006: 37). Duffy considers Stellenbosch as having a disproportionately strong influence in Afrikaner Nationalist circles during the late nineteenth and twentieth centuries (Duffy, 2006: 38). Her work finds that:

> nationalist students at Stellenbosch shared many concerns with their elders- a concern with societal issues and the poor White population; a belief in the importance of maintaining an Afrikaans culture; the desire to see a South African Republic free of British control; and a belief in racial segregation (Duffy, 2006: 118).

Given that of the six Apartheid heads of state, four of them were educated at Stellenbosch, many colloquially call Stellenbosch the "birthplace of apartheid", including Open Stellenbosch (see Boynton, 2016 or Claiborne 1989).

The present character of places tends to be shaped by their past. The extent to which Stellenbosch has been historically male and Afrikaans dominated

---

[44] In 1934, there were 1094 students and 91 academic staff members at the University of Stellenbosch. By 1948, these numbers more than doubled to 2262 and 183 respectively. In 1934, there were 1094 students and 91 academic staff members at the University of Stellenbosch. By 1948, these numbers more than doubled to 2262 and 183 respectively (Duffy 2006: 11).

[45] In 1948 there were nine male students for every five female ones (Duffy 2006: 11).

can speak to how those characteristics are easily passed down between generations at the University even if it diminishes slightly with time.

Historical Afrikaans and English Relations in Broader South Africa

After the Great Trek, Afrikaners, even those who did not actually trek, began organising around the use and recognition of Dutch. Institutions like publications[46] and *boereverenigings*[47] created a greater sense of comradery among Dutch-settlers (Giliomee, 2003: 222). The new *Voortrekkers* states were specifically racially hierarchical in their constitutions (Giliomee, 2003: 176). Some Voortrekkers saw themselves as people chosen with a divine mission, like the Biblical people of Israel (Giliomee, 2003: 178). This belief still exists today. I witnessed a protest on the rooiplein, the town square-like area within the University, in October 2017. A young woman in about her 30s read a paragraph from "Die Stem"—the Apartheid national anthem— and went on to say:

> Our God placed the Afrikaner here, when they decided to put us here it wasn't a civilized country didn't make a mistake to put us here by not fighting, we have the right to be here not the privilege, so if Wim [de Villers][48] thinks he knows better than God, a three pronged deity…[49]

In this quote, the young woman on the rooiplein is rationalizing her identity as an Afrikaner through evoking the religious destiny— specifically alluding to the Father, the Son, and the Holy Ghost, the deity of Dutch Calvinism— that was set out in the 'sacred history' of the Afrikaner people by the architects of Afrikanerdom.

There were practical barriers faced by the Voortrekker states, a fact that tends to be erased or de-emphasized in Afrikaner history. Economically, the new states were too weak to bring their new 'Boer' societies together and to

---

[46] Such as *The Patriot* and the older *Zuid-Afrikaan*
[47] Farmers' societies.
[48] Rector and Vice-Chancellor of Stellenbosch University
[49] 21 October 2017

underpin a democratic state: many citizens were reluctant to pay tax and ignored call-ups for commandos. They were far from the British coastal ports and neither had marketable exports (Giliomee, 2003: 179).

Initially in the 1850s[50] the British principally accepted Boer independence north of the Vaal River but their attitude changed to one of aggressive expansion in the 1870s (Worden, 2000: 18). Though divided by physical distance and emotional resentment, British cultural influence remained strong. For example, Bloemfontein, the capital of the Orange Free State, was a predominantly English town as the nineteenth century approached, in private schools and even in rural schools established by farmers (Giliomee, 2003: 186). I was surprised to learn this. Having visited Bloemfontein twice, I had the impression that it was very Afrikaans. Additionally, Christoff mentioned his school (which now has majority Afrikaans-medium classes) started as a British colonial school, he described Bloemfontein in the present as having nine Afrikaans people for each English person that lives there.[51]

By the 1880s, the British, directly and indirectly, exerted control over much of Southern Africa. After the defeat of the Pedi and a successful Boer rebellion in Majuba in 1881, the British agreed to withdraw (Worden, 2000: 27)[52]. This is another moment in what Moodie deems to be the "sacred history" of the Afrikaners. It was seen as "the Transvaal republic [winning] back its freedom by armed force and the might of its God" (1975: 8). The victory against the British led to a strengthening of the presidency of Paul Kruger in the Transvaal as he was more able to coercively control local indigenous peoples without British interference (Worden, 2000: 27).

---

[50] At the Sand River Convention of 1852.
[51] Interview took place November 2nd, 2016 at a picnic table on the Rooiplein at Stellenbosch University
[52] A men's residence at Stellenbosch University named Majuba, presumably the victory won by the Boers there. I always thought its name did not sound very Afrikaans and seemed somewhat out of place. When I understood its historical context, it became clearer: the connotation as a celebration of Afrikaner strength.

The Voortrekkers who left the Cape initially did escape British control, but it did not last long.

There is debate about the causes of the South African War (1899-1902)[53]. Some historians argue economic reasons: the Transvaal became incredibly valuable after the discovery of gold. Others emphasize the political conditions like restriction of voting rights of *uitlanders* in the Transvaal (Worden, 2000: 30)[54]. Most *uitlanders* were fairly unbothered by this but it led to strain between the governments of the Transvaal (headed by Paul Kruger) and Cape Colony (headed by Cecil Rhodes) (SAHO, 2015). The conflicting political ideologies of British imperialism and Boer (*voortrekker*) republicanism were strained by the discovery of gold in the Transvaal (SAHO, 2015). Rhodes wanted to annex the Transvaal for Britain. His plan included the Jameson Raid, wherein Rhodes planned an uprising of *uitlanders* to coincide with an invasion of the Transvaal by Leander Jameson[55] from Bechuanaland[56] which further provoked the War (SAHO, 2015).

Rhodes was an English supremacist, contending that: "we [the British] are the first race in the world, and that more of the world we inhabit the better it is for the human race" (SAHO, 2011). The end of the War led to a unified South Africa under a mantel of British imperialism (SAHO, 2015). The English language in South Africa[57] benefitted from its association to the power of the British Empire, which sat atop the hierarchies of many a global order. Even while always being a minority in the White population in South Africa, the English either were in power themselves or have had close access to the seat of power.

Drawing on Tamarkin's analysis, we can understand how the Cape Afrikaners were effected by their English allegiances. The War was a betrayal for Cape Afrikaners. Rhodes had initially aligned himself with the Afrikaner Bond

---

[53] This war was previous known as the Boer War (SAHO 2017).
[54] That is, only those who had been living in the republic for more than 14 years were given the right to vote (SAHO 2015)
[55] The man who Jameson Hall at UCT is named after.
[56] Now Botswana.
[57] As in many other places.

in the Cape Parliament—one of the many strategic alliances Afrikaners made with the English South Africa's history. Rhodes supported Afrikaners on the 'native' question as a supply of cheap labour – which was a most pressing economic problem among Afrikaans famers (Tamarkin, 1996: 315). Thus, like Giliomee's "Queen's Afrikaner", driven by their economic interests, the Afrikaner Bond aligned itself with Rhodes. Rhodes' support on the 'native' question quelled the fear among Afrikaners of an English-African political alliance leading to the domination of the Afrikaners by Africans (Tamarkin, 1996: 315).

I agree with Tamarkin's characterization that Rhodes created an illusion of convergence of both interests and outlook by arguing that a non-ethnic White colonial nation could be created in South Africa. Afrikaner Bond's wanted greater protection for their economic interests, particularly farms, and a greater symbiotic relationship with English South Africans to improve their prosperity (Tamarkin, 1996: 315). However, there was a major contradiction in this alliance: Rhodes' desire to expand into the Afrikaner republics and the solidarity of the Afrikander Bond with their northerner brethren which formed part of their ethnic consciousness (Tamarkin, 1996: 316). The alliance was broken by the War, but it was characterised not as Rhodes dragging Cape Afrikaners to his ideological and political domain, but rather that Rhodes "invaded and settled in theirs" (Tamarkin, 1996: 319). Perhaps contemporary Stellenbosch can be seen as using the English language as Rhodes' used the Afrikaner Bond at the beginning of the 20th century[58].

> *Some Afrikaners Anglicized to advance economically as some white-Afrikaans-speaking people do in the present. However, Afrikaners who aligned with the British in the Cape were betrayed by Rhodes who instigated the South African War against their brethren.*

The War sits prominently in the psyche of many Afrikaner/White-Afrikaans people. The War was more than a physical fight over land: in the minds of many Afrikaners, it became understood as a war over the future of their

---

[58] See chapter 5.

children and the values those children would live by. During the War, there were accounts of women saying that they would prefer to see their houses burnt down rather than see their husbands surrender. The defeat in the War pushed people to cling harder to their culture: parents considered if they should allow their children to speak English. After the War, an Afrikaner woman in Bloemfontein expressed what separated her people from the English; she said "republicanism, history, the *taal* (language), and hatred of the [British] race" (Giliomee, 2003: 256). Worden says the War was "highly destructive of life, property, and produce, and entrenched a bitterness between Boer and British which was to endure throughout the twentieth century" (2000, 32); and based on my fieldwork and discourse in the media it is alive and well in the present.

Once the War began, the Boer republics were technically conquered in a year, but guerrilla resistance continued for two more. The British adopted a scorched earth tactic, destroying over 30,000 Boer farmsteads. They also used concentration camps: the families and servants of the farmers were imprisoned. About 26,000 women and children and 14,000 Africans were killed (Boer & British, 2000: 33).[59] Benneyworth estimates the number of Africans in the camps was closer to 20,000. Furthermore, African prisoners were not only expected to grow food for themselves and the British army's stores but also to pay for the food they were growing (SAHO, 2011). While the death toll in the Afrikaner camps decreased by the end of the War, this was not the case for interned Africans. The concern raised by the whitstlebowling on the conditions in Afrikaner camps by Emily Hobhouse and Joshua Rowntree did not extend to the camps for Black prisoners of war. In a White supremacist framework not all death are equally grievable or of equal concern (Davenport and Saunders 2000: 227-232).The conditions were horrendous. Malnutrition was common (Giliomee, 2003: 254). There was overcrowding. The lack of sanitation made the inhabitants of the camps particularly vulnerable to diseases such as typhoid and measles, for which they had not built up immunity or been vaccinated (Giliomee,

---

[59] Specifically, just over 4000 women and more than 20000 children (Giliomee 2003: 256).

2003, 255). Even those sympathetic to the War were shocked by the conditions of the camps (Giliomee, 2003: 255).

After the War, schools were restricted to teaching three hours of Dutch. Although shortened, these were more teaching hours than languages like Setswana received. While not connected to an empire like that of the British (which had asserted itself on an unprecedented global scale), the Dutch South African language was soon to be standardized and renamed Afrikaans and very much was still a relative of Dutch. Even if it was seen as its baby brother, it got an advantage over local African languages spoken by Black-bodied people. Even still, a common story told by Afrikaners[60] was that those who exceeded the limit of Dutch speaking at school were forced to wear a placard that read "I'm a donkey, I spoke Dutch" (Swart, 2001: 80). This story mirrors the oppressive experiences of Kenyan children: if students were caught speaking Gikuyu in the vicinity of a school they were given corporal punishment or were made to carry a metal plate around their neck with the inscription "I am stupid" or "I am a donkey" (Ngugi, 1984: 114-15).

After the end of the South African War, the decimated Boer Republics became part of South Africa and their citizens were subjected to policies of Anglicization similar to those in other parts of Africa colonized by the British.

In this era, Dutch-settlers debated the status of Afrikaans and how best it should be formalized (see Hofmeyr or Swart 2001)[61]. In 1912, the British introduced a parliamentary system of government, which formalised English education 1914 (Swart 2001: 4). A strong Afrikaner nationalist elite began emerging in the Western Cape consisting of farmers and professionals who were shareholders and directors of major financial institutions, and intellectuals of the NG Kerk and Stellenbosch University. The solidifying of the Afrikaner community allowed them to gather capital to be able to found the Nasionale Pers Publishing House and the newspaper *De Burger*, and to set up the large trust and insurance companies

---

[60] though thought to perhaps be an exaggeration
[61] In groups like the Afrikaans Language Association (1906) and the Genootskap van Regte Afrikaners

Santam and Sanlam in 1918 (Worden 2000: 100). Afrikaans was recognized by provincial councils as a language, and by parliament in 1925 (Swart 2001: 4). This control of capital continues to exist as noted by my informant Freddie, Afrikaners and Afrikaner firms established during Apartheid or from funds accumulated during Apartheid continue to be dominant economically:

> The other day in class, we spoke about where the economic power lies in terms of White people. It lies overly in the Afrikaners' hands, if you think about the Rupperts for example Koos Becker from Media24, Naspers. Which is basically a multinational corporation scarily, so the Afrikaans buying power is very strong compared to English inputs.[62]

Once the National Party came into power in 1949, Afrikaans was central to public life through legislative policies. Before the passing of the Bantu Education act, "there had already been a strong precedent of unequal education" (Reilly, 2016: 249) between White children (particularly those of elites), and the 90% of Black South Africans who attended state-aided mission schools. Reilly extensively explores the philosophies of racialism that informed education policy in South Africa. It was influenced by policies in Britain and the United States. Officials, missionaries and mission societies; the hierarchy of the Colonial Office in London; anthropologists and others in the 19th century outgrowth of social sciences, came together to "formulate and propagate education politics of differentiation on a massive scale" (Reilly, 2016: 168). Through his historical analysis of those at the forefront of education policies for peoples of African descent, Reilly found that these White supremacists specifically crafted policies that aimed to pacify Black people to ensure the ability of White people to economically exploit them (Reilly, 2016: 170). This included Charles T. Loram, appointed by Jan Smuts, pre-Apartheid (Reilly, 2016: 170).

The premise of education, even before Apartheid, was that "the content, method, and aims of education could not and would not be the same for all peoples, [...] this premise

---

[62] Interviewed 2 March 2017

typically featured race and gender differentiation" (Reilly, 2016: 251). In the early twentieth century, anthropology contributed to the justification for withholding quality education from Africans by "linking social Darwinism with functionalism: the 'original nature' of Africans had been disrupted by 'contact' and would have to be 'preserved' by a protective colonial authority" (Reilly, 2016: 177-178). A study on 'The Poor White Problem in South Africa' (1932) found that inadequate education was a major cause of White poverty and made it clear that changing what was being taught to Black children would be the most important tactic in lifting [White people] out of poverty and separating their material conditions from Africans (Reilly, 2016: 254-255).

The Bantu Act put education under the control of the government, instead of churches who were previously in charge. It was financed the schools through the taxation of Africans themselves: considerably less was spent on them than on White children. Many Black teachers and students protested the curriculum and regulations set down by the Act. The teacher to pupil ratio reached almost 60 to 1 by 1967 (SAHO, 2011). It was part of Verwoerd's plan; he said that when he controlled 'Native' education he wanted to "reform it so that Natives will be taught from childhood to realise that equality with Europeans is not for them" (Tabata, 1980: 6). Rather like their parents and grandparents before them, who converted the Brown and Black-bodied people around to their way of being, Bantu Education was the Apartheid regime's tool to reach the same purpose: a docile Black labour force, justified by the characterization by the Apartheid regime that Black-bodied people were in need of "White Christian guardianship" (Tabata 1980: 6).

> *As with the colonial period, during Apartheid the education of Black people in South Africa was linked to racist social Darwinian assumptions. Though during Apartheid, the specific need for protection from competing ways of fellow Europeans who happened to be non-Afrikaner waned. Apartheid mean Afrikaners controlled the system, thus, their characterization of what being "civilized" was empowered. However, they still needed protection from the savagery and barbarism of the surrounding non-European populations. Education was used by the apartheid regime as a tool to convince Black South Africans of the social superiority of*

whiteness, or at least denying them the ability to access to information that could indicate otherwise.

In 1976, when the Apartheid regime tried to force Black students to take their exams in Afrikaans to pass matric, students organized protests in Soweto, which devolved into riots at the onset of police violence (SAHO, 2016). Colloquially, people made links between the protests of Open Stellenbosch and the 1976 Soweto Uprising. At a protest one person made a sign that read "I thought we had this conversation in 1976 though fam???"[63] Afrikaans itself might be considered an 'African language' but there is no doubt as to its European roots or ambitions and connections. Afrikaans has come to be referred to as 'Baby Dutch' by the sons and daughters of the Netherlands (Nyamnjoh, 2016a: 151). Within Afrikaans there are hierarchies of social visibility that are informed by encounters with Europe, which thereby places *suiwer*[64] Afrikaans, spoken by mostly White and White presenting people, at the top.

This belittles *Kaaps* the variety of Afrikaans spoken mostly by people who are Black or Coloured (Nyamnjoh, 2016a: 151). This hierarchy has a powerful discourse that makes some Brown and Black Afrikaans-speaking people use English even when with a White Afrikaans speaker. For example, Christoff assumed that a girl he worked with who was Coloured, was an Anglophone because she always spoke in English to him. However, after hearing her speak Afrikaans on the phone, Christoff asked her why she spoke English to him. Her answer was that she came from Atlantis (an area known to be Coloured), north of Cape Town, and did not like to speak Afrikaans in public because she sounded – in her words – "very local" when she speaks Afrikaans. As Christoff put it, "it was like she wanted to spare my White ears her accent".[65] The experience of Christoff's friend is not isolated, it has been experienced by generations of Coloured South Africans– as articulated by Wilfred Barett Damon:

---

[63] See https://twitter.com/PhaksPhothinja/status/638800114274971648, accessed 1 February 2016.

[64] *Trans:* pure

[65] Interviewed 28 May 2018

"Afrikaans is my mother tongue. [...] I [...] saw the first light of life as a vassal in the then Cape Colony of the Union of South Africa, and at the age of ten had to transfer my young vassalage to the Republic of South Africa" (2024). Damon is now refusing the subservience of his dialect, refusing to "protect" White ears:

> These days, Afrikaans is my conversational language of choice in the New South Africa. Perhaps I now speak the language with more boldness, a boldness based on the realization that the language also became completely mine with the dawn of broader democracy in the country. And if my dialect sounds come through when I speak in my Vlakte dialect – that careful, apologetic and self-conscious vassal sound that distinguished me and my people in Stellenbosch from the other Afrikaans-speakers of the town – I no longer have to apologize to anyone for that. After all, it was the sound of my Afrikaans for a most important part of my conversational life and remains the basis of my spoken Afrikaans (2024).

In the Dutch hierarchy of today in the Netherlands, young people will excitedly show off their spoken English skills to foreigners and each other. While in South Africa:

> Africans look down upon themselves, they do not want to buy and read books written in African languages, but they buy books written in English even though they are written by African writers [because] for market purposes, [African authors] are writing in English (Seema 2016: 189).

To conclude this section, I return to Moodie's argument. So far this work has centred the Afrikaner narrative of South African history and I highlighted some of the moments Moodie points to as important in what he calls the "sacred history" of the Afrikaner people. The second characteristic that Moodie argues makes Afrikanerdom a "civil religion" is a civil theology, which is "rooted in the belief that God has chosen the Afrikaner people for a special destiny" (1975: 12). Moodie's study is on the history of Afrikanerdom up until the beginning of Apartheid, where he identifies "two cycles of suffering and death—the Great Trek and the Anglo-Boer

War" (1975: 12). He draws parallels between the telling's of these stories and Christian resurrection:

> The agony [of crucifixion] on the Cross is followed by the resurrection, with its implicit promise to the Christian of a life to come [...] even as the resurrection followed Christ's passion, so the foundation of the republic is resolved the suffering of the Great Trek" (1975: 13).

In this cosmology, British imperialism became a supreme evil as it threatened Afrikaners linguistically and was more open to racial egalitarianism[66] thereby equated the British with the threat of the "Black masses" (Moodie, 1975: 15). The third characteristic is that of "civil ritual", which takes "the abstractions of the civil beliefs" and makes them "personified for the ordinary Afrikaner in tales of heroes and martyrs and in emotion-laden symbols that graphically portrayed the most important themes" (Moodie, 1975: 18), which Moodie argues meet the Durkheimian criteria. Moodie points to the Women's Monument (Bloemfontein) and the Voortrekker Monument (Pretoria) as "sacred shrines of civil religion" (Moodie, 1975: 18), as well as events at places like Paardekraal[67] and Blood River[68]. The argument Moodie presents is that civil rituals provide "the civil faith with positive content. It unites Afrikaners in their sense of unique identity and destiny, inspiring the faithful, converting the sceptical, and ever reminding them of their sacred separation from English and Black African" (Moodie, 1975: 21).

South African Language Beyond English and Afrikaans

This chapter until now has focused on the history between the English and Afrikaners. This section provides some context on the discussions facing the 9 other official South

---

[66] The extent to which British policies or policies made by British-South Africans were actually more progressive when it came to the treatment of people of colour is very much debatable.

[67] A place where Afrikaners vowed to regain independence from the British Empire.

[68] A battle between Zulu and Afrikaners where the Afrikaners won by a significant margin.

African languages. Neville Alexander saw the goal of South African language policy as to "facilitate communication between different language groups", working against the effects of the Apartheid language policy but not sacrificing multilingualism to do so (1989:52). This is a challenging balancing act. During transformation in a post-Apartheid, the Language in Education Policy stipulated that individuals have the right to choose their language of learning. This right presently cannot be accessed by most. The current education system had no choice to study in an African language (other than Afrikaans). In the Western Cape, English and Afrikaans pupils can be taught from primary to university level in mother-tongue, while isiXhosa is not used as a medium of instruction past 3rd grade (and only in a tiny number of schools) (1989:52). Sigcau argues that this is discrimination as English and Afrikaans speakers have that opportunity. The outcome of comparative research locally and internationally points towards the benefits of mother-tongue education systems, but the government is hesitant to implement it (Sigcau, 2004).

Contemporarily, African communities in South Africa seem to prefer English as a medium of instruction for their children because English is associated with success, power and social prestige, but they are not the only community which has had a language shift towards English (Sigcau, 2004: 245) (Mutasa, 2000: 220). Dyers argues that this shift to English from other first languages is far more marked in middle-class and upwardly mobile Black and mixed-race families. There are a number of interlocking factors that work against this language shift occurring in lower class families (2008: 49). Sigcau posits that the positive attitudes about English exist because European languages are regarded as "global and universal, and that it is through them that as non-European can achieve development" (Mutasa, 2000: 245). In the 1980s, 96 percent of Black South African pupils were taught with English as the medium of instruction beyond the third grade (Sigcau, 2004: 241). She argues that African languages should be valued much more than they currently are since there is "scientific evidence, showing that pupils perform better in their own mother-tongues but also [that it] violates human rights, as pupils are not educated through the medium they understand best" (Sigcau, 2004: 240).

There is a gap between policy, records and reality here, even in classrooms that are English-medium according to official records. In the Western Cape, medium of instruction in many underprivileged schools is often functionally isiXhosa (with some explanations in English and the textbooks and tests of the learners will all be in English) (Brock-Utne & Holmarsdottir, 2004). Students and teachers who share a mother tongue used code-switching and code-mixing to communicate with one another (Brock-Utne & Holmarsdottir, 2004). Policymakers cite the fact that there are not enough teaching materials in African languages to use it formally as a language of instruction, but this defence of the status quo fails in that if the policy were changed, textbook publishers would have to follow suit (Brock-Utne & Holmarsdottir, 2004). Furthermore, in South Africa there are few books written in African languages (other than Afrikaans). This is at least in part because during Apartheid, an arm of Bantu education were censorship boards who had to approve all books written in African languages (Seema, 2016).[69]

Not all South African languages treated equally, therefore not all South Africans are being treated equally.

African Language Debates: Empire, Achebe, Ngugi and Beyond

The purpose of this section is to contextualize the South African language debates within the broader African context. Generally— regardless of the fact that colonization in other parts of Africa followed a similar recipe to the one used in South Africa— South Africa is treated as exceptional. It is characterised as "exceptional" in Africa, whether because of the level of development achieved in places like Cape Town

---

[69] There has been significant scholarship in the post-Apartheid era by scholars such as Tinyiko Maluleke, Fiona Ross, and contributors to the special issue of the journal of Arts and Humanities in Higher Education, "State of Urgency" eds. Peter Vale & John Higgins. In Chapter 4, Melissa notes some of the issues raised in this section.

and Johannesburg, or because it was by far the largest settler colony in Africa, or because it is the only country where Apartheid happened. This chapter aims to highlight how South African challenges are not as exceptional as they may seem. Only since the early 90s have South Africans been able to have debates that were had thirty years earlier in the rest of Africa. This section examines a few case studies to highlight how other African countries have discussed and implemented language policies.

Most countries in Africa were decolonized in the 1960s and 1970s, well before the end of Apartheid in 1994. South Africa is multilingual, similar to the rest of the continent[70] (Moyo, 2006). During Apartheid, state resources were used to develop Afrikaans. For one, it was institutionalized as a medium of instruction or an additional language class in schools but also through literary and arts festivals, and funding universities to teach in Afrikaans. However, the institutionalization of Afrikaans did not happen equally. As noted by Coloured author Wilfred Barett Damon, it was not his home dialect and melody of his Vlakte dialect of Afrikaans that he heard in school, rather that the Afrikaans-medium of language in school was "unfortunately the exclusive and unwritten cultural property of the Afrikaner, a cultural treasure that they still worked hard on and jealously maintained at that time" (2024). Though Coloured people in the Western Cape were and often are still Afrikaans speakers, it was not their Afrikaans receiving support but rather swuiver or "pure" Afrikaans was "presented as the right way to learn the language" (2019). If "pure" Afrikaans was the "right way" then "[b]y implication, all the other speech variants of the language, especially those of the vassal users, were sub-standard Afrikaans", Damon and his fellow "vassal users of the language had to accept that we only had user rights to it" (2024).

Damon describes how Afrikaans and its dialects were leveraged to create difference between White and Coloured South Africans during Apartheid:

> The language appeared in a political garb when it was hijacked to become a slogan of Afrikaner nationalism. It turned into a

---

[70] There are some exceptions, like Swaziland.

divisive ruling instrument, a shibboleth as powerful as one from the time of the warring Israelite tribes themselves. It was a trigger that not only indicated distinction between people, but could also bring about the physical separation of races in the country along with all the other racial elements such as descent and appearance, hair colour, physique, social status, vocation, the state of health of the teeth in a person's mouth, and all the other nonsense that cast a dark shadow over human tolerance and acceptance and fatally hampered any healthy future people relations between the people of the country. Yes, so the language turned into a conduit that established and helped maintain the other separation mechanisms of the apartheid world, to hinder natural conversational interaction between white and coloured Afrikaans speakers in Stellenbosch and everywhere else in the country, and to shroud spontaneous language contact between people of different races in suspicion and mistrust. And if there is any truth in the idea that man is instinctively, for his own survival, wonderfully adaptable, then it is also true that as a brown boy I experienced, lived through and survived that language divide – that invisible and impenetrable metaphorical concrete wall (2024).

The converse of Damon's analysis is that Afrikaans could have also been a conduit of connection between people, if it had not been hijacked for the purpose of White nationalism. When Stellenbosch University makes rhetoric overtures about the need for Afrikaans language to increase access to post-secondary education among Coloured people, they are gesturing either blind to the concrete wall placed between Afrikaans speakers by the Apartheid government or – more generously– they are gesturing to the fact that they are aware of the concrete wall and are hoping for Afrikaans language to be a sledgehammer to break the wall down. However, failure of the University to make "all the other speech variants of the language" equally at home there then Coloured students could continue to feel as though they only have "user rights" to it.

On the other hand, English is not a politically neutral language, although it has become naturalised in many places as such. English came to Africa as a colonial imposition through the power of the British Empire: "the choice of English was not only for its use as a means for communication, it was also a tool for radiating and maintaining the political, social and cultural superiority of the colonizer" (Seema 2016: 188). The dominance of English firmly placed and still places Cecil Rhodes, with his pasty-pink complexion and those like him, as linguistically superior to the Africans. Given that the British were competing with the French, the Portuguese and other Europeans for supremacy globally, the prevalence of language can be considered as a metric by which to measure the contest.

Chinua Achebe, speaks about the consequences of the imposition of English by emphasizing the ability that colonialism had to unite people:

> It gave them a language with which to talk to one another. If it failed to give them a song, it at least gave them a tongue for singing. There are not many countries in Africa today where you could abolish the language of the erstwhile colonial powers and still retain the facility for mutual communication (1997: 344).

In addition to communication within African nations, given the success of the English in their quest for global domination, speaking English also taps speakers into global conversations in a way their native tongue would not allow. Though Africans cannot shed their Black-bodies for washed-out whiteness, but global hierarchies can be tapped into by speaking the Queen's received English.

Achebe pushes us to consider whether African authors ought to write in English or their native language: "Is it right that a man should abandon his mother tongue for someone else's? It looks like a dreadful betrayal and produces a guilty feeling" (1997: 348). Ngugi wa Thiong'o, haunted by his experience at the *Conference of African Writers of English Expression* in 1962, challenged Achebe's view of English as occupying an "unassailable position of English in [African] literature" (Achebe in Ngugi, 1984: 112). Ngugi says rather than wondering "how best to make the borrowed tongues carry the weight of our African experience", we should instead ask "how [African writers] can enrich [their] languages?" Furthermore, that it ought to be questioned "[w]hy […] should an African writer […] become so obsessed in taking from his mother-tongue to enrich other tongues?" (Ngugi, 1984: 112).

> *The usefulness of colonial languages has been contested: they can unite people by giving them a common language; however, colonial languages separate African people from the knowledge laden in African languages.*

In recent years, Ngugi's attitude towards languages of colonisers has softened. For example, at a lecture hosted at UCT in 2017, Ngugi pointed to Kwame Nkrumah's example that while he valued African languages and saw them as vital for the development of African studies and African scholarship, "he did not call for linguistic self-isolation, for he also saw the role of other languages like Arabic, English, French, and Portuguese" (2017). Ngugi explicates his interpretation of Nkrumah's beliefs as "clearly for him, African languages were not a lower rung on the ladder to an English heaven but rather as equal partners in the construction of a common, multilingual heaven" (2017). Though Ngugi has historically made quite radical calls, he has also translated his books into English, implicitly conceding to the usefulness it brings in expanding the audiences of his works. The act of translating is an act of world-building. As articulated by Naòmi Morgan:

> I started translating literary texts as a means of recreating the French and Francophone world where I had furthered my French studies, and as a way of sharing my favourite texts with other readers in an environment removed from the academic world which has been my home for almost 40 years (2024).

Translation is an opportunity for non-language speakers to experience the worlds of other languages.

Nyamnjoh and Shoro argue that:

> the debate about a writer's choice in language […] is really a debate about a writer's attitude with regards to the European language; the value the writer assigns to the European language, how the writer uses the language and to what ends (Gyasi 1999: 75). This attitude, in turn, speaks to the writer's attitude toward their own language and perhaps more specifically their own identity (2011: 42).

People's identities have often been deeply touched by their experiences in education. For example, Eugene Achike, the patriarch in Chimamanda Ngozi Adichie's *Purple Hibiscus*, is a product of colonial education who avoids speaking Igbo, his mother tongue. Kambili, Adichie's narrator, describes her father's attitude saying:

> [Eugene] hardly spoke Igbo, and although Jaja and I spoke it with Mama at home, he did not like us to speak it in public. We had to sound civilized in public, he told us; we had to speak English. Papa's sister, Aunty Ifeoma, said once that Papa was too much of a colonial product.

European colonialism paid little attention to pre-existing forms of education in Africa, as is reflected by the lack of documentation from that period. However, there is a contemporary revival of local knowledge (White, 1996: 10). If we consider the history of European education among Black Africans, it was most often introduced by missionaries with the aim of training converts to proselytize and spread Christianity as taught in mission schools, often in partnership with colonial regimes (Dlamini, 2008: 6). For example, Achebe's father converted to Christianity and was educated by an Anglican mission, thereafter going on to teach and spread the gospel (2012). He describes the Bible as playing an important role in his own education (2012). However, the linking of Christianity to education meant that the Bible was translated in many Indigenous languages for teaching purposes whereas subjects like geography, history, mathematics and the natural sciences were often neglected or were taught in the colonial language (Dlamini, 2008: 6). Colonial powers developed more formal policies around education that were nominally more removed from the complete control by missionaries, but there were often huge discrepancies between policy and practice (White, 1996: 9).

In the 1960s, there were a succession of British conferences held to "assist" colonies in organizing their education systems when they became independent states (Skutnabb-Kangas & Philipson, 1996). Through this and other means, post-colonially much of the colonial infrastructure for things like education remained intact. Brock-Utne argues that "when it comes to bilateral donors both the British and the French seem to use development aid to strengthen the use of their own languages as languages of instruction" (2001: 122). For example, Madagascar had taught elementary and secondary school in Malagasy, reintroduced French as the language of instruction in secondary schools because the French government supplied them with textbooks as a type of educational aid (Skutnabb-Kangas & Philipson, 1996: 123).

As countries decolonized, they were left to reckon with the many-headed monster that is the question of language. Malawi, like South Africa, has about twelve spoken languages, though only English is an official language and Chichewa is a recognised national language (Moyo, 2002). In Malawi, English became the language of higher education, documentation in government, commerce and industry, and for international communication such as diplomacy and in the procurement of loans. Chinyanja and Chitumbuka (two local languages) were languages of instruction in early education and for mass communication at the national level, on the radio and in print-media (Moyo, 2002). This implies that the other nine spoken languages in Malawi were not used in official capacities. The language policy involved elevating Chinyanja which he decreed "as the sole national language for mass communication on the radio and in printed media" and "came to symbolize his project of national unification and integration, linguistically and culturally" (Moyo, 2002: 265). Furthermore, Banda (the president) renamed 'Chinyania' Chichewa because the dialect of Chinyania that he promoted was that spoken by the Chewa ethnic group.

In Kenya, Kiswahili, a local *lingua franca* was encouraged by the British colonizing forces because it facilitated local administration. It was given a new function during the independence movement where it was used to facilitate unity between different ethnic groups in a common political project - giving them a common consciousness. Ironically, English, the language of former rulers, was also given the same role. Post-independence Kenya, however, witnessed a devaluing of African indigenous languages, including Kiswahili, and the rise of English (Dlamini 2008). Bunyi traces how that the dominance of English and Kiswahili in Kenyan education is linked to government goals of 'development', noting that English dominated education has had little use to the majority of Kenyans, particularly those that live in rural areas who continue to draw on their indigenous knowledge for survival (2008: 25). She demonstrates this by pointing to the continued low enrolment in communities that are culturally far removed from the Eurocentric culture of the Kenyan elite and English even after the elimination of primary school fees, as a means to encourage 'development' through greater access to education (Bunyi 2008: 26). Even for children who do enrol in primary education, there are significant rates of repeating grades and drop outs, which Bunyi attributes to the structure of the curriculum which, for example, requires children in Standard 1 to simultaneously be literate in their indigenous language, Kiswahili and English (2008: 27). Given the much higher likelihood that children from elite backgrounds will have had exposure to Kiswahili and English, the educational deck has already been stacked in their favour.

Even in countries where some vernacular languages are used as lingua francas or used in official capacities, other local languages are neglected.

These observations by Bunyi give weight to the claim by Kamwanganmalu that there is a widening socio-economic divide between African elites who have access to material resources and employment opportunities because they are proficient in former colonial languages; and the masses, who have no access to those opportunities because they are illiterate in both the colonial languages and their native languages (2016: ix). Making the acquisition of foreign languages a requirement to be able to finish secondary school or attend university, in a way, perpetuates the core idea behind the policy in African French where Écoles Rurales colonies based their curriculum on manual labour and vocational training. That is, if rural people (the lowest form of 'native') are incapable of intellect (because, in the eyes of White supremacists like the French Colonial Regime, intellect is only possible in a colonial language), one should just cut to the chase and only educate them for their highest possible place in society (Clingnet & Foster, 1964: 193). This attitude completely disregards the epistemic richness of African languages and the Africans who speak them, because it hangs success on one's ability to learn a second language to a fluent proficiency. Something many contemporary and historical Anglophones seem incapable of.

Nyamnjoh argues that the colonial education in Africa has led to a "real or attempted epistemicide - the decimation or near complete killing and replacement of endogenous epistemologies with the epistemological paradigm of the conqueror" (2012b: 129). This is because institutions in Africa have made "infinite concessions to the outside- mainly western world", and that this "education has tended to emphasize mimicry over creativity, and the idea that little worth learning about, even by Africans, can come from Africa" (2012: 129.). The concessions made by Africans has occurred because of the success of the propagation of colonial languages, like English; as the greater the success of a colonial (generally European) empire, then the greater the advantage it is to speak their language. Even if within a person's own context in Africa, a colonial language could be unnecessary for local success. Language acquisition has become a marker for intelligence and power. For example, if a Chinese person has no ambition of leaving China, there would be no reason to learn English. But since English has become a signifier for competence that might help someone get a job or a promotion even if their job does not actually require English.

Fanon argued colonialism was more than a system of physical oppression. It colonized the minds of Africans. He highlighted universities as a method that "deeply implanted in the minds of the colonized intellectuals that essential qualities" were those of "the West, of course" (1961: 46). In contemporary education and socio-linguistics, this sentiment is still present. Research demonstrates that a core reason mother-tongue instruction is often not advanced in the African context is due to "an emotional learning from the colonial times that may breed contempt for one's own culture and admiration of the culture of the colonisers- equating knowledge of the colonizer as *the* education" (Brock-Utne 2001: 119). In Namibia, Harlech-Jones (1998) found that people who strongly favour the use of non-vernacular languages[71] tend to emphasize the financial, political, and

---

[71] Like English or French.

socio-economic advantages of European languages and minimize the psychological factors (such as pride in one's culture), educational factors (like ease of learning literacy and abstract concepts), and linguistic factors (like language preservation) (Harlech-Jones in Brock-Utne 2001: 116). Many studies in the African context identify language as an important resource that influences chances of economic development and success (Dlamini 2008: 3).

> *The use of language important impacts like the disregarding knowledge from African languages (to the point of epistemicide of that knowledge) as well as people's self-esteem.*

Dlamini has argued that contemporary African education is in crisis due to concerns about language and related pedagogy (2008: 1). She roots this crisis in the efforts of postcolonial African leaders to attempt to mediate the colonial past using Indigenous knowledge while simultaneously "working to create a common sense that suits their personal and often corrupt economic interest, thereby suppressing political consciousness that might result in exposing their corruption and hegemonic tendencies" (Dlamini, 2008: 2-3). In other words, the failure of African leaders to meaningfully change "the malfunctioning policies and practices inherited from colonial regimes" except in a few instances which were "shaped by commercial and capitalist interests" (Dlamini, 2008: 2-3). Thus, there has been calls for the review of the failed policies and an exploration of alternative strategies and approaches (Bamgbose in Kamwanganmalu 2016, vii).

Dlamini also notes the multilingual lives of Africans as a marked departure from the globally popularized "English as a second language" conception, as many children learn the language of their parents but as they grow begin to learn the languages spoken by children around them, who often come from at least one other ethnic group. Consequentially, even after years of schooling, English or other colonial languages are rarely spoken fluently after many years of study as students do not typically speak English to one another or with their teachers outside the classroom (Dlamini 2008: 6). Generally, post-colonial African states have addressed issues of language by giving official recognition to selected regional languages, though these languages tend to only receive symbolic equality to the former colonial languages. Kamwanganmalu says "those countries have hardly considered what it means for an African language (or for any language for that matter) to be recognized as an official language" (2016, x) as their application of official-ness tend to be haphazard. In the 1990s, it was noted that "there is a general feeling that language problems are not urgent and hence solutions to them can wait. Language policies in African countries are characterized by one or more of the following problems: avoidance, vagueness, arbitrariness, and declaration without implementation" (Bamgbose in Philipson 1996: 161).

Even in this context of lacking institutional power, it is not to say that all is lost for African languages. Ndhlovu pushes us to remember that "the dominated have other means by which they can pothole, ridicule, demean and ultimately resist the forces of domination. This means conformity is calculated, not unthinking, and beneath the surface of symbolic and ritual compliance but there is an undercurrent of ideological resistance" (2010: 176). Therefore, whatever the outcomes of debates on official language policies: "speakers of minority languages still have some choices for the use of their languages, no matter how limited these choices might be" (Ndhlovu, 2010: 177).

Kamwanganmalu argues to increase demand for African languages in the Bourdieuian "linguistic marketplace" requires meeting some intertwined conditions: giving vernacular languages privilege and prestige historically associated with former colonial languages like teaching the entirety of school in local languages and requiring certified knowledge of local languages to work in the public sector. This would increase the demand for and the prestige associated with these languages in the marketplace. (2016: xi-xii). However, there are significant financial costs associated with the production of local language learning materials. The unit cost of a textbook produced in French is much lower than the unit cost of one produced in any of Senegal's national languages, for example, due to the small market for which the book would be produced (Vawda & Patrinos, 1999).

Few African languages have had the government support that Kamwanganmalu advocates for, except Afrikaans. As an African language, it is an anomalous case that meets Kamwanganmalu's requirements through its upliftment during Apartheid. It received almost exactly this treatment. However, the version of Afrikaans that became standardized and institutionalized was *suiwer*-Afrikaans which acts as a marker of White-Afrikaner identity and political ideology; and the marginalization of Coloured Afrikaans-speakers (Deumert, 2005: 116).

> *There is dissonance between the ever-present nature of African language in day-to-day use in Africa and the absence of African languages from official use in places like government and education.*

Nyamnjoh argues that "[t]he production, positioning and consumption of knowledge is far from a neutral, objective, and disinterested process" as "[i]t is socially and politically mediated by hierarchies of humanity and human agency imposed by particular relations of power" (2012b: 130). I believe there is no question as to the need to invest in African languages in the South African context. Apartheid financially enriched not only the Afrikaans people but also their language, as it developed into an academic language. Indeed, Mahmood Mamdani argues that the development of Afrikaans would not have been possible without a vast institutional network: ranging from schools and universities to newspapers, magazines, publishing houses and more, all resourced through public funds. He foregrounded this argument by saying that colonizers made their languages that of the scholarly, the scientific, global affairs while local languages became home languages whose growth was truncated – and that colonialism cut short the possibility of an intellectual tradition in the language of the colonized.

As a result, African home languages remain "folkloric" - shut out of the world of science and learning, high culture, law and government. Afrikaans, Mamdani suggests, is an example of a well-established African language. The vast affirmative action program of Apartheid lifted Afrikaans from a folkloric language to a language of science and scholarship, high culture, and legal discourse, in the short span of half a century: "It is no exaggeration to say that

Afrikaans represents the most successful decolonizing initiative on the African continent" (Mamdani, 2017). Further, he emphasizes "Not only did this happen under apartheid, the great irony is that it was not emulated by the government of independent South Africa" (Mamdani, 2017). Mamdani's new found love for Afrikaans signals how languages are able to change their spots more effectively than leopards can. Today, as a White person in South Africa, knowing a Black South African language is arguably an effective way to demonstrate that one is "woke"[72].

Conclusion

The purpose of this chapter was to place my fieldwork in its historical context. This chapter was firstly a summary of the history of the settlement of Stellenbosch. I illustrated how Stellenbosch came to be a historically significant place, particularly in the imaginary of Afrikaners. Stellenbosch University is alive with almost pageant-like symbolism. This chapter demonstrated how Stellenbosch was set up as a place of their own for Afrikaners, such that Afrikaners wanting to pursue higher education need not do it on the terms of the English.

The reasons why Afrikaners were so determined to seek independence and separation from the English, is rooted in the events of the suppression of the Dutch language after the English takeover of the Cape which itself led to the Great Trek and eventually the South African War. The history that has brought us to the present at Stellenbosch University is very complex and tragic in many ways. However, as Moodie indicates, the idea of "Afrikanerdom" was crafted and built by leaders of an ethnic group— those like Paul Kruger, Verwoerd, Herzog, etc.— trying to establish their identity as a body politic ended up becoming crucial to the system of logic used to justify the oppression of other groups (1975: 281).

---

[72] A slang term from African-American Vernacular English which denotes "parts of the Black community for those who were self-aware, questioning the dominant paradigm and striving for something better" (Merriam-Webster: n.d.).

The history of Afrikaners is one of feeling under threat. First, of being subsumed by the Indigenous people in South Africa. Second, by the threat of assimilation to the English way of being. The methods by which languages can be used to unite people are the same ones which have the ability to divide them or perpetuate established divides. For example, in colonial Zimbabwe, settlers were encouraged to learn the local vernacular so as to be better able to control and convert the locals (Makoni, Dube & Mashiri, 2006: 396). In many ways, language acts like Coyote, the trickster from many North American Indigenous folktales. Coyote can be trying to act for good and cause bad results or try to act badly and cause good results. While in the present, many Black South Africans seemed to be bemused and somewhat pleasantly surprised when I would make attempts to learn their languages, Black Zimbabweans did not like settlers knowing their languages as they felt that it threatened "their sense of security because [it meant] the dominant group could intrude into their social world" (Makoni, Dube & Mashiri, 2006: 396). Like Ndhlovu, I would like to highlight that "hegemony is never total and complete, but rather porous, leaving room for different kinds of resistance" (2010: 177). In Stellenbosch, hegemony is at once direct and diffuse, depending on one's positionality there are different relationships people have to Afrikaner and English hegemonies, thus strategies are needed.

Understandings of collective history is also important to the identity framework of Stuart Hall, as set out in the introduction. There is certainly a cannon of Afrikaner history that has been curated towards an end of Afrikaner nationalism. However, there were Afrikaners who broke that mold. The stories of those who didn't fit the project of that historiography were not celebrated or maintained within their ethnic history. We can look to examples like Reverend Beyers Naudé and Professor Albert Geyser to demonstrate during Apartheid there were Afrikaners who made great sacrifices in their personal and professional lives to oppose Apartheid. Reverend Naudé was from a well-connected Afrikaner family: his father was a founding member of the Broederbond. Naudé became the youngest member of the Broederbond when he was only 25 (SAHO). By attending

Stellenbosch for graduate school, Naudé mixed with other Afrikaner elites like Hendrik Verwoerd and John Vorster, who would later both become prime ministers of the Apartheid regime (Soggot 2004). Naudé began a career as a minister in the NG Kerk, initially towing the line for the biblical justification of Apartheid offered by the church. In an obituary Margot Soggot emphasised that

> the 1960 Sharpeville massacre, in which government troops killed 69 black demonstrators, was to be one of the events that triggered Naudé's move away from the Afrikaner establishment and towards the liberation movements. His political awareness had already been sharpened in the university town of Potchefstroom, where he was exposed to clerics and Broederbonders who questioned aspects of the apartheid policies (2004).

After Sharpeville, Naudé was a founding member of the Christian Institute. It was a nonracial ecumenical organisation that challenged aspects considered traditional to the NG Kerk which also provided humanitarian relief. The Christian Institute's publication Pro Veritate was edited by Naudé. After wrestling with questions related to Apartheid he eventually resigned from the Broederbond after 22 years of membership in 1963. From his pulpit in September 1963, Naudé condemned Apartheid from his pulpit– a huge risk of further ostracisation due to his already controversial status from having quit the Broederbond (SAHO). He was stripped of his position within the NG Kerk and due to his anti-apartheid activism he was banned by the regime between 1977 and 1985 (Soggot 2004).[73] Once he was unbanned, Naudé succeeded Archbishop Tutu as the secretary-general of the South African Council of Churches in 1985. A couple years later, in 1987 he formed part of the Afrikaner group that met with ANC representatives in Senegal (SAHO). Naudé did not attend the meetings in Senegal alone, showing that there were other Afrikaners supporting the ANC. This book is being published near the 20th anniversary of Naudé's

---

[73] Banning was a punishment tactic of the Apartheid government. Functionally, it was a form of house arrest with further restrictions like restricting people from talking to more than one person at a time.

passing. I wonder if Stellenbosch University will do anything to mark this esteemed alumnus…

One can find other resistances in other places that people assume are synonymous with conservatism during Apartheid. There were dissenters of Apartheid at the University of Pretoria, like Profs. Adrianus van Selms, Cas Labuschagne, Berend Gemser and Albert Geyser in the Theology Department who could not agree with the theological and biblical justification for Apartheid by another Afrikaner church, the Nederduitsch Hervormde Kerk van Afrika. Geyser left the University of Pretoria over this matter and took a post at the University of the Witwatersrand. Lectureship of Labuschagne– one of his supporters– in the Faculty of Humanities at Pretoria was terminated without notice. His other supporters were often ostracized and struggled to find work (van Aarde et al 2014). The censorship of the Apartheid regime and its domineering ideology sometimes make these stories of descent difficult to find. Sometimes, however, they're not hiding but are discursively "unthinkable" so we don't think to look. To return to Hall's 'roots' and 'routes', this time for Afrikaans-speaking White South Africans. Their Afrikaner roots embeds them in a context of recognition– moments of history marked by . When young people think of what route they are going to take in their lives some people need the assurance of examples like Reverend Naudé and Professor Albert Geyser for examples of routes taken by other Afrikaners. This could have transformative potential individually and collectively (Hall, 1997).

Within the Afrikaner community there are high profile moments that border on Apartheid denialism, such as an interview by FW de Klerk where he would not agree with the statement that Apartheid was a crime against humanity. De Klerk later retracted his statement, at the request of Archbishop Desmond Tutu (Swart 2020). The significance here is that if de Klerk felt a level of confidence to deny Apartheid as a crime against humanity in the first place then in my extrapolation similar denialism is likely in the quiet thoughts of many White South Africans. Including English South Africans as well. In considering the neo-Nazi skinhead trend in Germany in the 1980s, Balibar is "one of the ways in which collective memory contributes to drawing the parameters of present racism – which also means we cannot hope to eliminate it either by simple repression or by mere preaching" (1991, 41). High schools in South Africa teach about Apartheid, so it is not the repression at hand which is the issue. However, there is a current of attempting to negate the levels of cruelty and dehumanization of Apartheid as is observed by Mugabe Ratshikuni when people argue that Apartheid "didn't kill as many black people as Nazism killed Jews, hence it can't be put into the same bracket as a crime against humanity" (2020). To disrupt attempts to minimize the atrocities of Apartheid clearly needs a third strategy. Emphasizing Afrikaners who resisted the pressure to conform to the expectations of ethnic unity in favour of Apartheid disrupts simplistic narratives which uniformly paint Afrikaners as backwards racists and simultaneously offers a signpost to help future generations of Afrikaner examples of resistance to tyranny from their own culture.

Chapter 4

Routes to Stellenbosch

> *We especially tried to impress on them that Afrikaans, like all languages, can make the reader suspect certain unheard of dimensions of reality. We tried to cultivate a taste for the effects of alterity in certain writerly (scriptible) texts and to show that even in this language a writer could undermine identity, totality and closure, could subvert state power, could demolish stereotypes and could address the reasons for oppression and suffering in the world.*
> – Marlene van Niekerk

> *A good snapshot stops a moment from running away.*
> – Eudora Welty

Introduction

The town of Stellenbosch, like much of South Africa, remains divided along the lines set by Apartheid. Though it is only about 50 kilometres east of Cape Town, taking the train to Stellenbosch (if it runs on time) takes about an hour and fifteen minutes. If one were to take a taxi from Cape Town Station, one would first have to go to Belleville or Khayelitsha and then transfer to a second taxi to Stellenbosch. Yet, driving in a personal or rented car usually takes about forty-five minutes. In his work on postmodernism, David Harvey argues that the "persistent pressure of capital circulation and accumulation" has culminated in "disconcerting and disruptive bouts of time-space compression" (1989: 327). In South Africa: those who have been able to accumulate capital are able to live a life where time and space are compressed, but those who have not been able to access that capital accumulation are still on trains and taxis which stop and start and never run on schedule.

Aesthetics and cultural practices, David Harvey argues, are "peculiarly susceptible to the changing experience of space and time precisely because they entail the construction of spatial representations and artefacts out of the flow of human experience" because aesthetics and cultural practices "always broker between Being and Becoming" (1989: 327). His observation is that "in periods of confusion and uncertainty, the turn to aesthetics (of whatever form) becomes more pronounced" (1989: 328). This can be seen in Stellenbosch's charge of keeping the aesthetics of the area of the town where most White people live to be rigidly tidy. This over-focus on the aesthetic appearances in Stellenbosch, at a time when Afrikaners are experiencing many pulls and pushes on the contours of their identity, is in-line with Harvey's observations. In the psyche of many (perhaps more elite) Afrikaners, Stellenbosch is an important place in which their identity is rooted to and routed through. Thus, there can be political consequences of this compression is a triumph of aesthetics over ethics, as a prime focus of social and intellectual concern (1989: 328)

At its most simplistic, our idea of 'place' is "a locality with a distinct character – physical, economic and cultural" (Massey 1995: 46). Places fill the need to feel settled in a place, which carries with it a feeling of continuity and coherence. However, Harvey argues that the darker side of fulfilling this need is exclusivist nationalisms, regionalisms and localisms (Harvey in Massey 1995: 48). An identity being place-bound means that those 'locals' will feel disrupted by new people of different cultures, classes or ethnicities coming in (1995: 46). This explains how Stellenbosch became a battleground at the time of my fieldwork: between people who saw themselves as the saviours of their language (namely, Afriforum and their supporters), and those who saw Afrikaans as a barrier to entry, keeping people who were Black, Coloured or Indian out of Stellenbosch entirely (or at the very least, very uncomfortable there).

This chapter contains vignettes based on my fieldnotes. It illustrates the kinds of inequalities that are present in everyday life including how long it takes to arrive in Stellenbosch from Cape Town. People with access to different levels of capital accumulation will have dramatically different experiences arriving in Stellenbosch from Cape Town. For instance, the cost of a ride-sharing platform[74] is more than R300 between

---

[74] Like Uber or Taxify.

Cape Town and Stellenbosch and cars in South Africa are quite expensive[75] while the train costs R12 or R20.

Setting the Scene at Stellenbosch University

André showed me around Stellenbosch in his White Citi-Golf. With the windows rolled down, he smoked a cigarette. We drove past walled-off houses; little green lawns peeked out from them and floral trees over them.

"This is where the rich people live."

He wove through small streets lined with White buildings. As we came through the area with restaurants and storefronts, he said: "See the flowers?"

The car whipped around a bricked roundabout, the dividers of the intersection and the edges by the sidewalk had flowerbeds.

"They're replaced all the time. Must be every six weeks or something. Meanwhile, people in Kayamandi are still using communal toilets."

Figure 5: Replanting of Flowers in Stellenbosch

When I looked up the intersection on GoogleEarth, workers were replanting the flowers.

---

[75] Often costing R50,000 or more, plus monthly insurance and maintenance and petrol.

There is continuity between apartheid city planning, apartheid municipal spending priorities, and the present priorities of the Stellenbosch municipality.

The almost-summer sun lost its afternoon heat. I sat on a picnic table at the University, in a quasi-quad, surrounded by rectangular cream buildings with red tiled roofs, almost uniform in height. The ground was red brick, hence its name: "the rooiplein"[76].It had the feeling of a town square. In the centre was a white statue of Jan Marais with a grey plinth. Marais was understood to be the founder of the University. He used his mining fortune to open an Afrikaans university so Afrikaners didn't have to attend the University of Cape Town to attend university (Giliomee, 2003: 363). I never knew what the word for a plinth was until I moved to South Africa. I learned because of RhodesMustFall. "The thing he [the Rhodes statue] sat on is still there." "You mean the plinth?" Funny, the unexpected things one learns from activists.

Figure 6: Jan Marais On His Plinth

---

[76] *Trans* red plain

The library was sunk into the plein between the statue and the buildings that edge the quad. The stairs down to the library had an amphitheatre-effect. Many public meetings were held, like interrogations for SRC or FeesMustFall mass-meetings. Architecturally, this scene could be found in the Netherlands. It looked like the Netherlands from my high school history books. Its Western European character was corroborated by the many bike racks and the White-bodied people around. Wanijuk, who grew up in Kenya, said Black-Kenyans assume "all the White people are visitors, or not all of them are visitors but if you see a White person you just assume they're a tourist"[77]. Though there are White Kenyans, they are so few that the chances of a White person being a tourist is much higher than being a Kenyan.[78] Hugo, from Mozambique, noted that "coming to Stellenbosch from Maputo where you mostly see Black people as a norm and then here you see a lot of White people with few Coloured people. It is very different, and then you go back to Maputo and you are like, so many Black people."[79] Within South Africa, Siphe who grew up in Johannesburg noticed huge differences between Stellenbosch and her hometown: "the biggest were the demographics; Johannesburg is very diverse especially when it comes to the races and the different languages. For the first time I came here there were so many White people and this side you pick up that you are Black and that you are different".[80]

---

[77] Interviewed December 16th, 2016
[78] Interviewed December 16th, 2016
[79] Interviewed November 10th, 2017
[80] Interviewed March 2nd, 2017

Figure 7: The Sunken Entrance To The Library

Much of the flora were invaders from the northern hemisphere, but some of it hinted I was in South Africa like succulents that grew at the base of trees. One of Rhodes' projects was the importation of plants from far-flung places that suited his tastes (Nyamnjoh, 2016a: 124). These flora expats, not unlike their human counterparts, "burn more readily and fiercely than do native flora" (Comaroff & Comaroff 2001: 235). Recent migrants to the Cape, human and flora, could be found to be allies. At the turn of the millennia, when Africans– who had been kept out of Cape Town by apartheid– came to the Western Cape to seek better economic opportunities. Many aspects of their lives were provisioned by alien timber like Australian rooikrans (*acacia cyclops*). Rooikrans was used to build their homes, for their own fuel, to sell on the roadside to the White-middle class for *braai*[81] wood (Comaroff & Comaroff, 2001: 247-248). Fynbos wouldn't make very nice houses or braai wood… Unfortunately rooikrans doesn't make very safe houses because it burns so well– a wood of last resort. Many of the

---

[81] South Africanism for "barbeque".

houses where the rooikrans is being burned to braai are not very safe either. Wealthy people want to build their homes high up on the hills to have views of the ocean or valley below. Building those homes up in the hills make it near impossible to use Indigenous knowledge of small preventative fires to avoid much larger more destructive fires. One of the many ironies of the Western Cape is people at both ends of the economic spectrum are at risk of their homes burning down… though for very different reasons.

There were people hanging-out on the lawns in groups of two or three. Everyone who sat there was White. There were a few scattered people that walked past me that were Black, Indian or Coloured, but it was clear that unlike South Africa— which is 80 percent Black (CIA World Factbook 2018) — this university did not reflect the demographics of the country.

Two Black men who were wearing black uniforms— private security guards nicknamed "the men in Black"— stood opposite the entrance of the library. Metal grills lined both sides and lead to the door of the library. I remember when there were neither the security guards nor metal grills around there. I guessed it was because of protests earlier in the semester. The response to the protests were very militarised. I wondered if the vehicles the police were using would still be called an armoured vehicle, like the kind they use to transfer money between banks, or if it was actually a tank. Some of the officers personalized their tank with decals of wolves on the front. As though the driver and occupants of the tank were a wolfpack chasing their prey. The decals on the doors said, "Legends Endure". What kind of legends were these officers making intervening in protests for a more just South Africa? By the grace of the political climate, sheer luck, something… no RhodesMustFall or FeesMustFall protesters were killed by police during the student uprisings. The enduring legends brought to mind by White police officers standing next to their tanks are moments in South Africa history like Sharpeville, the Soweto Uprisings, the police brutality in townships during the 1980s, among others. Those legends should endure. However, the heroes of those legends are not the police, they are the African people who stood up against the denial of their dignity and humanity by the Apartheid state.

Figure 8: The Wolfpack Tank

There is a Black man in a blue uniform[82] who sat in front of me in the shade that day. He was the only Black person other than the security guards. Many of the Black-bodied people on campus were like him: low-skilled employees. The students of movements like #FeesMustFall leveraged their position as university stakeholders to try to improve the wages and lives of workers like him. As Shaeera Kalla articulated it: "Comrades we have neglected our mothers and fathers being abused at the hands of outsourced companies on our watch on our campus under our gaze" (Africa is a Country, 2015) [83]

> *The architecture, the flora, and the people of Stellenbosch could have been, for the most part, transplanted from Europe.*

Varsity hadn't started but my friends had begun to trickle back into Stellenbosch. A group of us decided to go out for afternoon drinks at Bohemia. It was sweltering out. The long

---
[82] Commonly worn by general labourers.
[83] Read more: https://brooklynrail.org/2016/03/field-notes/outsourcing-must-fall

end of the black deck was in the shade. We filled up a picnic table at the end, overflowing, sitting on the railing. Our crowd stuck out because of the eleven or so of us, only two were White. We met all during Open Stellenbosch or FeesMustFall the previous year, stomping over the rooiplein together, marching down Victoria street singing struggle songs and carrying signs calling for an end to racial exclusion at Stellenbosch, an end to rape culture or an end to financial exclusion from university. I was happy to be with them because supporting their cause made me feel like I was contributing to something worthwhile; that my life mattered toward something greater than myself. Being surrounded by people who were Black, Coloured and Indian was what I imagined my university career in South Africa to be like. When I arrived at UCT, two-thirds of my class was White and my professor was a White-American. It looked like I hadn't left McGill. The same weirdness I felt studying about Africa without any Africans teaching me that I had in undergrad came back to me. I questioned my choice to study at UCT. I attended the Youth Day Congress that Open Stellenbosch hosted a few weeks after I arrived in South Africa, where there was significant participation by people of colour. It felt like I was really listening for the first time.

But now we were having fun. We were a couple of rounds of drinks in. I think the table ahead of us –of White rugby-loving boys– were too. They were having a very loud and impassioned conversation. Loud enough that we were having trouble hearing each other as we plotted creative ways of having the land returned to children of the soil. Our waiter, a small, White Afrikaans-speaking, man very sternly told us he didn't like the conversation he was hearing. The other White woman who was there responded to him in Afrikaans angrily. Their spat ended quickly. A White-American woman waiter seemed to take over our table from him.

The rugby boys upped their volume. Someone began singing a struggle song. Then we were all singing, laughing, and smiling. Our waitress asked us to keep it down. She apologized but said someone complained. One of our crew jumped down from the rail to the sidewalk to smoke. He said, "What's the difference between singing a struggle song on a deck and the sidewalk next to it?" We all agreed to the arbitrariness of it all. He began another song. The rugby boys looked annoyed. We were happy: high on disrupting whiteness. Our waitress returned. She apologetically asked us to stop.

When the third song rang out, it was not the petite White waitress who asked us to stop, but the two large Black men who were bouncers. They walked towards us with a White man, who I assumed was the manager. He asked us to leave. He said we were disturbing guests. He suggested we not return to Bohemia in future. As we walked away, we heard the rugby boys talking.

Black, Coloured, and Indian students and White students are held to different noise standards at a bar next to campus.

Stellenbosch was a 45-minute drive outside of Cape Town. I left UCT and watched the landscape change. First, houses shrunk from comfortable walled-in houses and gated flat-blocks with lawns or gardens to duplex and triplex RDP[84] houses before the airport. Cape Town International Airport welcomes tourists from all over the world on the left of the N2 Highway, on the right are those living in shacks, mostly made of corrugated iron, almost stacked on top of each other, their inhabitants hustling for their basic needs. Using public transit, it takes over an hour to get from these neighbourhoods to the city centre. The Apartheid Group Areas Act created designated racial groups to particular neighbourhoods: putting White people closest to the city centre or areas of natural beauty, pushing out people who were Black, Coloured or Indian residing in those neighbourhoods to move White people in, in the case of Cape Town, out onto the Cape Flats. Layering so-called Coloured people between themselves and the 'pesky' urbanized natives. This was possible thanks to BJ Vorster, prime minister at the time, who consolidated the implementation of the notorious Group Areas Act (Johnson-Castle, 2014) (Britannica 2018).

---

[84] Reconstruction and Development Program, housing built for disenfranchised people who were Black, Coloured or Indian as restitution for Apartheid.

On the left of the N2, the commercial areas surrounding the airport and the airport itself stretch on. Bridges over the N2 allow people, and sometimes cows and goats, to pass over the N2 without dodging cars. There are only three of them in 20km, so from time to time people still dangerously cross the massively busy highway. There was a brief green area just before the exit to Stellenbosch. The other side remained informal housing throughout, since the beginning of the airport.

As we turned off the N2 onto the access road to Stellenbosch, I saw the first sign was for wine tasting. After some more RDP housing and a gated-community, mountains stood as a shield on the right; on the left rolling farms and vineyard hills. There was a break from the urban of Cape Town. It doesn't feel suburban. The area felt very rural; suddenly there were large farms instead of neighbourhoods.

As we keep moving, the mountains begin to inch in front of the horizon. The mountainous shield is now facing me. The farms are dotted with small concrete houses. Some of them painted coral. Some painted white. Some are dilapidated, with fallen roofs and broken windows. These were houses for farm workers, who around here, historically tended to be Coloured people. During Apartheid, many farmers used the 'dop' system. They paid a portion of their labourers' salaries with cheap wine, trapping them in a cycle of poverty (Larkin, 2015). This system has ramifications of alcohol dependence to the present day. Especially since there are farms that continue to illegally use the dop system (Larkin, 2015).

Barbed-wire fences split the farms. A train line running parallel to the road came into view as we passed the 'Zettler's gas station and farm stall'. A sign for Spier wine farm sat across from train tracks. The entrances of wine farms were walled with flags from the United States, the Netherlands, France and other countries from the global north.

We turned onto a road with more vines. Trees lined the road. Floral bushes grew through the metal fences around a brandy distillery. I saw a piece of the sidewalk painted yellow that said "Adam Tas". Adam Tas helped lead a rebellion by free burghers against the administration of the Dutch East India Trading company (SAHO, 2011). His name is now used as the name of a society devoted to "the preservation of Afrikaans instruction language at the University of Stellenbosch", also serving as "the alternative Afrikaans student society", whose motto is "Passion for Afrikaans" (AdamTas). Across from the brandy distillery there is a stone house with a thatched roof. The car turned into the sun, the summer heat hit my shoulders.

We turned onto Merriment Road (a main arterial, into Stellenbosch), where there is a sport-field on the right. On the left, commercial buildings. After a second set of robots, there was a sign for the University. It introduced a grey rectangular building: The Arts and Social Sciences Building[85] but was once the BJ Vorster[86] Building. Voster, in addition to the Group Areas Act, Vorster supported the teaching of secondary school subjects to Black learners in Afrikaans, which led to the Soweto Uprisings. The building named after him was built on land that was expropriated from the Coloured people who lived there so that Stellenbosch University (which only accepted Whites-only at the time), could expand (SU, 2013). Specifically, the forced removals of the neighbourhood *Die Vlakte*[87] where those classified as Coloured and Black people who were pushed to spatially disconnected and racially segregated suburbs on the town's margins: Kayamandi, Cloetesville and Idas Valley (Valley, 2014). The Lückhoff School - where children of *Die Vlakte* were educated - became the University's Fine Arts Building (Grundlingh). Today more than 60 percent of Stellenbosch students are White, the total population White people in South Africa is barely 9 percent (Stellenbosch Statistics). On the left, there are small White houses with green doors. These houses, which sit on opposite the BA Building, were slave lodges until the middle of the nineteenth century (WCPHS 2002: 45).

I was dropped off just inside the University underneath some leafy trees near the rooiplein. At other times, there are bake sales or residences and clubs selling tickets to events.

---

[85] Colloquially referred to by students as the BA building.

[86] BJ Vorster was the prime minister of South Africa from 1966 to 1978. The Terrorism Act and the Steve Biko crisis also occurred during his term (SAHO, 2016).

[87] *Trans*: "The Flats".

Perhaps it is also red because it contains the lifeblood of the University. There are raised grass-lawns on the right-hand side of where I am sitting that are bordered by trees and succulents. Some of the trees are palm trees.

> *This vignette illustrates argument that access to capital has the ability to compress space and time. The vast majority of people travelling between Stellenbosch and Cape Town cannot afford the use of a ridesharing application.*

I left my house in Walmer Estate, walking across the bridge to Woodstock. The urban giraffe-like cranes of the Foreshore interrupted the view of Table Bay and rolling hills behind the Northern Suburbs. From the freestanding houses of Walmer Estate everything seems much smaller in Woodstock where houses are attached blocks, with small concrete yards. Mountain Road flattens as it meets Main Road. I waited for a minibus-taxi headed to town. A taxi finally comes into view as its caller yells "Town! Town girl?" I nodded, and it pulled over.

There are about 13 seats. I checked for an empty one, manoeuvring to the back. The air inside was stiff and hot. The taxi blared some R&B remixes. I sat too far away to reach the windows politely, so I silently sat in the heat, sweating. The ride to town was not long. The driver asked if we minded stopping on Strand instead of the taxi rank. It was an unlicensed taxi. They tended to avoid official taxi ranks to avoid police checks. No one puts up a fuss. We arrived at Cape Town station; I shot across the street, past the Sea Point taxis into Cape Town Station. It was roughly 20 minutes since I left home.

The station was very open with many entrances and exits. Light streamed through its bright, high windows. There were many Black and Brown-bodied people, some perusing the small shops tucked along the wall opposite the trains. I peeked at my phone in the inside pocket of my backpack as I stood in the ticket line. I was running a little bit late. My palms became sweaty. I was anxious about missing the train because if I missed it, I'd have to wait almost an hour and a half, which would be less safe because it wouldn't be as busy. I notice an older White woman wearing a large backpack and a baseball hat. My gut tells me she is going to Stellenbosch as well; it's a popular tourist destination and many tourists in South Africa dress like this woman but not many tourists make it onto South African commuter trains. I finally reached the front of the line.

"A ticket to Stellenbosch please."

"First class?" Asks the lady behind the glass.

I nod, but I'm not going to sit in first class because it has less people and it makes it less safe. I slide R25[88] onto the wood beneath the gap at the bottom of the glass separating me and the ticket agent and she returned R4.50 and my ticket. I checked the platform of my train on the electric time board hanging from the ceiling, as I speed-walked toward glass doors branded with prasa's[89] logo. The doors aren't synced with the issued tickets, but one is open for passengers to pass. During the week, the tickets of those passing through the open stalls were checked by a prasa employee but since it was a Saturday afternoon there is no one there.

I checked the platform again as I passed onto the platform hallway. It was shadowy and darker than the bright station hallway. Water trickled down the walls, even though there was sun on the platforms. I had a minute to spare but there wasn't a train at the platform. I stepped back into a crowd that also seemed confused about the missing train. I watched the time board: 1:33pm, the time of departure for Stellenbosch. Then, as the time switched to 1:34pm and the time of departure stayed 1:33pm. I listened to the people standing near me speaking about the train to Strand, which was scheduled to leave a few minutes after Stellenbosch train. A train arrived at the platform down the hall that was going to Strand and the crowd rushed toward it. As the Stellenbosch die-hards stayed, a young Black woman with long black braids asks if I am going to Stellenbosch. I said yes. She told me last time she took the train she got off too early and had to get a rideshare for the last stretch. I told her I often take the train but it's confusing after Bellville because all the stops are so far apart from each other, but she could follow me. We stood a little closer together and watched what the others around us were doing, looking for guidance as to

---

[88] About $2USD at the time
[89] Passenger Rail Agency of South Africa

how we were going to get to Stellenbosch with no apparent train.

We wandered down the hall. She was braver than me and walked forward to ask someone else if the train is going to Stellenbosch. They said that it was. I was nervous but since this woman has mentioned she had a ridesharing app so I was confident that we could split one if something went wrong. It had been more than an hour since I left my house at this point.

We walked past the first-class train compartments; my train partner and I picked a compartment that was mostly full. Unlike the first-class compartment seats which were padded, these seats were hard plastic, set up along the wall of the train. There wasn't any privacy. They ran continuously on either side of the walls of the train. My train partner sat next to me but put her headphones in…. she didn't want to chat with me.

Figure 9: Local Performances on the Train from Cape Town to Stellenbosch

Everyone in the compartment were Black-bodied people, with the exception of me. A trio of people who are Black, two women and a man, in their 20s broad the train and squeezed in on my left side. The train jolted to a start. The sound of metal scrapping metal pulled us away from the station. My travel partner asked, "how long does the train usually take?"

"An hour and ten minutes, but that is if there aren't other delays along the way."

At the first stop of the train, it screeched and rocked. A group of Black children got on, boys and girls: the girls were wearing white shirt and skirts of the same print. The boys were wearing white on top and dark bottoms, keeping vaguely in line with the girls. Around their feet were severed tops of soda-cans tied on through wire. They began to sing and drum. It was jovial. One at a time the children danced solo. People began shouting and joining in their song. Next, two boys danced as a pair, in unison. The trio next to me were cheering the kids on in isiXhosa, smiling. A kid took out a hat for donations; they started on the other side of the door we sat next to but then came toward us. I took out R5 for them. My travelling partner also donated some coins and so did the trio next to us. The kids stayed with us until the next station when the train creaked and swayed as it stopped. They hopped off to get onto another train.

Many people got off at that point because it was an interchange station. As the train took off, people were now sitting on the floor. The windows were missing from one of the doors allowing a Coloured man to stick his head out the window and smoke a cigarette as the train ran. At the next stop, a Coloured man got on the train with an older boy-child[90] and two boxes of bananas. He began selling three or four small bananas for R5. They sold quickly. He would put the bananas in a plastic bag and his younger business partner would bring them to the buyer and collect the money, returned it to his elder as he went to get the next bag of bananas. They only had a few left. I decided to buy some. By the time the next stop had come, he had sold out completely. In one smooth movement, he put the two empty boxes together, slid them under the bench by the door and exited the train. Many people started to laugh. I asked the young man sitting next to me why people were laughing. He said

---

[90] Not quite a teenager, but not a young child either.

because of how smoothly the banana-salesman exited the train. We had now passed Koeberg Road, Maitland, and Woltemade.

    The man sitting next to me was showing pictures to his friends on his tablet. My eyes strayed toward them. He seemed to be a dancer. He chatted to his friends in isiXhosa but when he noticed I was looking, he showed me a picture he took of a dog wearing Nike branded dog shoes. I laughed at the picture and he told me he saw the dog at the Waterfront with a White lady. I said: "You know a hectic way to make White people angry: ask them how much they spend on their dog; follow up by asking how much they pay their domestic worker." A smile stayed on his face but looked slightly forced. He didn't talk to me much after that. The train lurched between Mutual, Thorton, Goodwood, and at Vasco, the trio next to me departed. Then the train just stopped. There were no announcements. The doors stayed open. My travelling partner asked if I knew where we were, and I said we were almost in Bellville. We waited. The doors closed... then opened again. I looked at my phone to see if there were rideshares nearby. A couple of men selling chips passed and we waited. Next, someone selling q-tips and external batteries and chargers and regular batteries passed. Even someone selling ant traps came through. You could have done all your shopping while you waited at this irregular stop. Finally, the sound of engines started. The train jolted forward, slower than usual but then sped up to a regular pace.

    I felt anticipation as we passed through Parow and Tygerberg. I worried we would have to change trains in Bellville. I was anxious as the train was already delayed so we would arrive in Stellenbosch later than I thought, even considering I knew the trains run a little behind. If we had to change trains, we would have to wait for one to arrive. Trains on weekends were infrequent. Bellville is known to not being a safe area, although I had taken the precaution of not bringing my laptop with me. My phone is replaceable. This made me a little less worried. When we pulled into Bellville. The train stopped. Some people got out. Most continued sitting. A few joined us. The train stopped for longer than usual... not as long as the previous random stop.

Next, we jolted from Bellville to Kuilsrivier, from Kuilsrivier to Blackheath, from Blackheath to Melton Rose, from Melton Rose to Eerste Rivier, from Eerste Rivier to Lynedoch. When we were at Lynedoch, I asked my travelling partner if it was where she had gotten off before. She looked around. She was pretty sure this was it. We were very close, I said. In a short period, we had gone from the densely populated urban Bellville, to the more suburban Kuilsrivier, Blackheath and Melton Rose, to the liminal RDP housing of Eerste Rivier. The distance between stops kept getting longer. After Eerste Rivier, the land was more open and the mountains came into sight. There were less than a quarter of the people we started with in Cape Town on the train. It was empty. There were visible grape vines, in neat lines, tied to and growing around wooden posts. We passed a stop labelled "Spier" for the winery across from it. In my experience, the train never stopped there. At Vlottenburg, I looked out the window and saw a few small free-standing houses. They were generally for the farm workers.

Between Vlottenburg and Stellenbosch, the train goes through a game farm. I peeked out the window to look for zebras and wildebeest. I was surprised when of all things, I saw a caribou, one of the animals so important to my Inuit ancestors. I was shaken but then I considered the farm probably breeds exotic animals, it didn't seem outside the realm of possibility. I stood up, signalling to my travelling partner that we were almost in Stellenbosch. I began to look in my pockets for where I put my ticket in case someone wanted to check it on my way out. As we arrived, me and the man standing opposite me had to pull on the door to open it. About three hours after I left my house, I arrive in Stellenbosch. My next journey was to get to where I stayed in Ida's Vallei[91]. Idasvallei is almost an hour's walk from the train station. I decided I would walk to the University and then take an Uber to my house. Idasvallei was the only place I could find a room for the short-term that didn't cost upwards of R6000-R8000, or even more. Prices for AirBnB and guesthouses were set for European tourists or wealthy locals. On a student budget, I couldn't afford either. I planned on going to an event, it was going start in two hours.

---

[91] Also known as Idasvallei or Idasvalley

Normally I wouldn't think it to be worth it to trek to Idasvallei but because of how tiring the train was, I wanted rest. The Uber between the University and Idasvallei cost more than my train ticket between Cape Town and Stellenbosch.

> *Here, the converse, when one does not have access to capital: the cost being less than a tenth of a ride from a ridesharing platform, but the time is about three times longer.*

I walked from my flat in Idasvallei to the University. My flatmate was a White-German girl out came to South Africa to volunteer. She lived in Mitchell's Plain. Her boyfriend still lived there. She spent the weekend 'at home' with him and his family. When I moved in she told me there was a White Afrikaans man who had also been interested in the room but when his mom drove him to see it, she vetoed him staying there because "nice White boys don't stay in Coloured areas".

It was hot. I was sweating. It felt sparse. 3 o'clock in the afternoon… almost no one else was walking. I turned the corner of my street; there was a dry, grassy field with some exercise-jungle-gym equipment. A fence divided the field from the double-lane busy road. There were only two breaks in the fence where one could cross to the 'Stellenbosch' side of the fence. I thought about the Uber-driver who picked me up the last week. After entering Idasvallei, my house was the first sharp right turn. A road ran parallel with the road on the other side of the park for a couple hundred meters, then it turns up to the road where I stay. The Uber-driver turned too early. When he realized his mistake, he kept driving for a short while, thinking there would be another opportunity to turn left. There was not. Helshoogte Road begins ascending the Helshoogte Mountain. He turned around because *there was only one entrance to Idasvallei*. The Apartheid creation of Idasvallei for expropriated residents of *die Vlakte*. Only having one entrance and exit was probably purposeful by the Apartheid regime as a means of control. Easier to monitor who was exiting and entering if there is only one place to do so. When he explained, I joked with him: "Yeah, can't have easy access to a Coloured neighbourhood, obviously". He laughed and said, "Yes, have to keep the thieves away from the Spar", sarcastically. He noted Cape Town is also often this way.

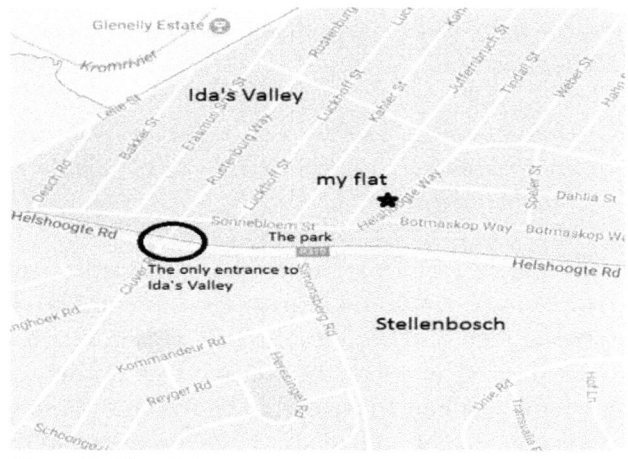

Figure 10: Idasvallei

From the robot, on the Stellenbosch side of the fence, I saw the stripmall, with a large grocery store, petrol station, pharmacy, a few restaurants. I walked through the stripmall's parking lot, dodging a car or two, on to the sidewalk of Culver Street. As I look down the street, I can see there are some groups of young people, also walking ahead of me. Their clothes were neat, not faded or thinning out due to wear and tear, though there are some stylistically placed holes in jeans. Most people are walking on their own or in small groups.

As I reached a large roundabout, there was a woman whose shopping cart tipped over. Her clothes had splotches of dirt and dust. I thought she might not have a home. She looked to be a Coloured person. No one stopped to help her, as I imagine they would if a student's bag ripped.

Infrastructure in Stellenbosch has not been remade since Apartheid.

I thought about what it means to touch Stellenbosch. Anthropology privileges the visual. Many interpretations of participant observation focus on visual and auditory observation and participation. There are two distinct anthropological observations that 'touch' opens up. One is touch as a form of intimacy that both creates and demonstrates a sense of obligation in people. Even between strangers, if someone was clearly distressed and yelling "Oh, no! Oh, someone help!" and that someone touched a person walking by on the sidewalk, the act of touching the passer-by make it more difficult for them to move on without even acknowledging the distressed stranger. Even if the touched passer-by does not end up helping the distressed person, the thought of them stays in the mind of the passer-by probably longer than if they had just heard someone yelling "help!"

Secondly, venturing into the realm of touch and tactility corroborates the spatial privilege of Stellenbosch as a municipality. At the core of the town, the University was incredibly smooth to the touch. The bricks on the rooiplein were expertly laid, incredibly evenly. There was barely a dip between the bricks and the grout. They don't jut out at strange angles, they aren't broken off. The bricks were symmetrical. Even the bricked stairs going down to the library didn't seem worse for their wear, though they seemed to be more at risk than their flat brethren for being cracked off or broken. Rarely was there broken glass on the rooiplein. When it appears, it tended to be cleaned up quite quickly by a person on the cleaning staff.

Figure 11: The Smooth Bricks Of The Rooiplein

The buildings surrounding the rooiplein were made from what looks like smooth concrete. If one ran one's hands along the building there was little risk of injury, perhaps one would feel the minor ripples in the concrete. The metal frames of the windows were sturdy, unbent. They held uncracked windows into place. As one exited the rooiplein on to Victoria Street, towards the cluster of student residences (in the opposite direction of Kayamandi and Cloetesville), the sidewalks of the roadside closest to the rooiplein were bricked in the same expert way as the rooiplein itself. Smoothly and evenly. Between the bricked sidewalk and the pavement of Victoria Street is a lane of soft grass almost as wide as the sidewalk itself which could easily accommodate four or five people walking shoulder to shoulder on it. Another barrier between the pavement and the bricked sidewalk is a drain that itself is announced to one's touch by a line of bricks before plunging down 30 or 40 centimetres and just under half a meter across. A friend told me they were called "storm water drainage". These were very common around the historically White streets in Stellenbosch. A hazard for parallel parking though.

Figure 12: Lush Green Trees, Smooth Pavement, Being Protected By Police

As one walked further up Victoria Street, past the creamy-white JH Neelinthing Gebou with its orange-y tiled roof, the tiles were even and undamaged. The roots of the large, towering trees that line the road are the only thing that uprooted the sidewalk. Crosswalks were made of bricks. As was a large plateauing speedbump. The bricks are fitted together like perfect puzzle pieces, laid in the same way as those in the rooiplein. If you felt your way along Bird Street in the direction of Cloetesville and Kayamandi, from the Eikestad mall, from the University: things become more jagged. The sidewalks begin to crack; not immediately, but gradually they erode as the walk continues. There weren't brick crosswalks or speedbumps except, at the driveway of a cluster of car dealerships. The bricks seem to divide the Toyotas and the BMWs from the sidewalk. At the intersection of Bird and Adam Tas, about a kilometre away from the University, you'd find broken glass laying with the rocks, as an obstacle to vulnerable feet. A little further toward Cloetesville and Kayamandi, passed Du Toit train station, on the left there's a taxi rank and faded pavement that leads into Kayamandi. The pavement on the R304 is noticeably black, it feels more compact, stronger. There's some paved roads in Kayamandi but most of the sidewalk crumbled leaving red dirt and rocks to walk on. The many houses are made of corrugated iron with jagged edges. Their windows have wooden frames. Sometimes the wood is bloated, from exposure to rain and temperature fluctuations. It looked risky to run your hand over it. It might splinter and pierce the skin.

It's not a coincidence that the areas of Stellenbosch near the University, near where the White people lived, were the areas where maintenance was done most consistently. Infrastructure that isn't jagged, buildings that are crisply painted, indicated the presence of maintenance. Maintenance has a clear cost associated with it. This is part of the Apartheid hangover: funds being consistently dedicated to areas where White people live. Apartheid set an explicit and implicit standard for how people who are White should live: at a standard above rest, above the people with melanin. Yet, it is doubtful that German tourists stop flocking to Stellenbosch if not for flowerbeds in downtown.

The municipality of Stellenbosch is also responsible for the lives of people in "Franschhoek and settlements such as Klapmuts, Koelenhof, Kylemore, Johannesdal, Pniel, Jamestown and Raithby" (Stellenbosch Municipality 2015); no mention of the predominantly Black settlement of Kayamandi which was on the way to Koelenhof from

Stellenbosch. Spatial inequality here had a double signification of income inequality and racial segregation. White people are not "supposed" to be in areas that are jagged. People who were Black and Brown are only supposed to be in pretty areas under specific circumstances. The circumstances under which people who were White and people who were Black or Brown touch, were very rigid.

Touch is another dimension we can use to understand the racial and income inequality in Stellenbosch.

On my way to the University gym at the Coetzenberg complex, it was like students were coming in colour-coded waves. It reminded me of a time when I was observing on the rooiplein and after an hour of observation I noticed most of the groups I saw were either of a single gender or a single race. It felt strange how little people seemed to be socialising with people who were different from themselves. During the first thirty minutes of that observation, I did not see a Black person on the rooiplein. I thought about when I was in Kigali or Bob's Bar on Long Street in Cape Town, I stuck out because I was White, but the students of colour in Stellenbosch stick out, not the White people.

After I left the gym, I saw people playing rugby. I asked a White girl with brown hair who was playing. She was sitting by herself. She told me Elsenburg[92] and Olympus[93]. She asked if I was looking for anyone special and I said no, I was actually doing research about language. She noted rugby was a good place to observe because it was better than soccer in terms of the variation of languages as it was a more integrated sport. Then she laughed and said rugby games were "not a pure language" because of nicknames players get and the initiations they do. They did benign things like count in Afrikaans, but there were more crude things like swearing by using sexual names for girls. She said there was not much between rugby players' ears. As an example of initiation, she told me that Elsenburg showed up to their last game with whips. This was the first tournament of the year. Rugby speak, she tells me, is mostly Afrikaans. She asked if I knew

---

[92] The Agricultural College
[93] The Private Student's Organisation (PSO)

what was going on and I said yes because I played in school. There were some women's teams, she said, but women don't really play; "it's not sexist but we don't have the patience to be tackled around on the ground".

We continued to chat. She was from Joburg. Lots of people come down here to study, I observed. She agreed: "here or Potch". Her dad wanted her to study through UNISA and stay at home, but she had convinced him to let her come here. Her family was Portuguese, which reminded me that the Afriforum representative at their debate against Open Stellenbosch had a Portuguese name. I asked her about the connection between the Portuguese and Afrikaners, and she said it was because both came from cultures of hard work with conservative values.

UCT was "very sensitive/political", she said, whereas Stellenbosch was conservative enough that she is comfortable, even though there is stigma attached to Afrikaans universities, it's actually what drew her to here. When it came to traditions around initiation, she told me that they were very toned down since people died in them in the past. Now, they are accepting because, "human rights and all that", but traditions are still sometimes seen. Like in Olympus when men lose at games during the first week they had to shave chunks of their eyebrows. Her friend Jack shaved his beard. I asked her what she liked about her PSO, she told me there was less hierarchy than at other residences or PSOs because all hands on the ship are needed to make the ship work. Other residences prims[94] or house committee members can make mentors[95] get them drinks.

Her friend found us on the field. They talked about Valentine's Day. The girls had chatted with someone they lived with who said she was not celebrating Valentine's day because she was a feminist to which they told her: "if feminism was successful, Valentine's Day would have been cancelled years ago".

> *My casual talk with this woman on the rugby pitch to me was demonstrative of the attitudes of conservative leaning students at the University.*

---

[94] The head of the residences or PSOs.
[95] Mentors are lower in the hierarchy than prims.

At the Boland Debating League, I chatted with my former debating student. She was a first year at Stellenbosch. She had long blonde hair and blue eyes, quite conventionally attractive. She grew up with an Afrikaans-speaking parent and an English one. She spoke English as a home-language but took Afrikaans in school and could more than get by in it. However, she told me that when she tried to speak Afrikaans with the Afrikaans-home-language women in her residence they often giggled and commented on her accent, then returned to speaking to each other without including her in the conversation. If someone who looks as though they could belong at Stellenbosch is rejected like this by not meeting the linguistic standards of her Afrikaner peers, I wondered how those who look out of place and don't meet the linguistic cut off get treated?

I was surprised to hear how my former student was excluded by her peers who looked like her because she did not sound enough like them.

Conclusion

This chapter has highlighted some less traditional anthropological ways that can be used to open up and understand space, place and people. These vignettes highlighted the continuity of apartheid spatialities in Stellenbosch, through sight (the flowerbeds in town centre) and touch (feeling our way from the University to Kayamandi). It also looked at how capital can collapse space and time through comparing the journey to Stellenbosch by car to a journey to Stellenbosch by train. The last argument made through these vignettes is that there are set norms in Stellenbosch that coerce different peoples behaviours: White men yelling about rugby are welcome to take up space at a bar but a table of Black, White, Coloured, and Indian people singing struggle songs are not welcome. Or that exclusion can happen even when people look alike if their language skills are not up to snuff.

Chapter 5

Silent, Concrete Walls: Black and White, and the Grey Areas of the Making and Re-Making and Maintaining of Interracial Friendships

Introduction

The ghosts of apartheid continue to haunt South African lives. For example, Panashe Chigumadzi reflects that though she had crushes on the White boys in her primary school later, in high school, a taboo appeared:

> [We] were witnessing many of our childhood friendships lose their colour-blind innocence, [we] understood the tacit rule that we didn't date each other. Sure, we were now free to go to school with each other and live in the same suburbs, but interracial love still represented a kind of final frontier yet to be fully explored (2018).[96]

The argument of this chapter is that Chigumadzi's experiences in high school hold true in the context of Stellenbosch: the structural ghosts of Apartheid haunt Stellenbosch University students' friendships and their ability to make friends across racial lines. As I spoke with my participants and observed their social groupings, and the social groupings of the University, I noticed a tendency towards homogeneity along the lines of race and often gender. This tendency towards the homogenous, I also saw in the physical structures of the University itself; academic and administrative buildings were built in the same style as the older buildings on campus, even if they were built decades after the fact. Their colour went unaffected by the dust and wear-and-tear that seasons bring as the buildings were kept in that way by some very busy grounds-keeping staff. Each year, I saw buildings being maintained a crisp white-cream colour, receiving new coats of paint.

---

[96] Online article

The demographics at Stellenbosch University make it impossible to write about this place without writing about whiteness and particularly South African whiteness. Stellenbosch University as a 'place' and the town of Stellenbosch as a 'space' which are heavily associated with Afrikanerdom informs who is made to feel welcome there. Both of these topics will be defined and briefly explored in the introduction to this chapter. I will also outline theory about what facilitates the makings of friendships and some challenges to becoming friends. The experiences of Wanjiku speak to how the whiteness of Stellenbosch has the ability to isolate Black students. Her views will be corroborated by Hugo, a Mozambican student who is also Black (possibly Coloured in the South African context).

My interviews with Anneke and Ané focus on the experience of White students and attempts to cross the racial boundaries. Randy, a young Coloured woman, was the person I met in Stellenbosch who had the most diverse friend group. Her experiences highlight how places become associated with particular ethnicities, and therefore become more or less comfortable for people who do not come from that shared background. Catherine's voice adds to how spaces become type-cast to particular cliques or types and Hugo's experiences also speak to the 'colourization' of space in Stellenbosch. My argument is that the dominance of whiteness and the whiteness of the place of Stellenbosch puts strain on the ability for interracial friendship to thrive. Implicitly, there is a sense of risk for people who are Black, Coloured or Indian that being friends with a White person carries with it a risk of being made to feel more abnormal or out of place than with someone who looks similar to them.

Whiteness and South African Whiteness

The scientific thought of the Enlightenment created a lasting racial taxonomy that continues to perpetuate notions of White supremacy into the present. In 1776, Blumenbach published *On the Natural Varieties of Mankind*, which posited five divisions of humanity that started with "Caucasians" and ended with Africans and Indigenous North Americans (Bouie, 2018). Succinctly expressed by Melissa Steyn:

"Whiteness and Blackness were co-constructed, so were Europe and its others" (2005: 123). Much of critical race theory has focused on the 'Others' as created by this Enlightenment ranking, however "concentrating on the racialization of the margins has functioned to keep attention fixed on 'other' as the problem needing explanation and needing to come in line with the centre" (Bouie, 2018: 120). This dynamic allows whiteness, which has centred itself for hundreds of years, to continue to construct itself unproblematically as the norm (Bouie, 2018: 120).

Pigmentation can be the starting point for analysing power, privilege, and opportunity, but Nyamnjoh cautions us to dig deeper for the nuances by which people of all races manipulate their appearances and cultural connections beyond those given to them by birth (2016: 59). Power and domination are central "to the belief in being white, and without it, 'white people' would cease to exist for want of reasons" (Coates, 2015: 42). At moments across histories, the physical specificities of the characteristics of whiteness have been flexible to accommodate those willing be part of the subjugation of the other through lynching, redlining, testing hair with pencils, the issuing of passes, the issuing of numbers instead of taking the time to understand difference[97], the building of walls and fences, among other tactics (Coates, 2015: 42).

In his own experience, as a Cameroonian, Nyamnjoh was taught that 'the ways of the White man' were synonymous with the ways of the civilized. He was put in school because his "parents had embraced the idea that it was possible to become civilized by copying the ways of those who presented or imposed themselves as receptacles and vehicles of civilisation (2013:109). Elsewhere, Nyamnjoh asks readers to consider separating "whiteness" from the people with pink pigmentation. The wishes of Cameroonian parents, for example, for their children to become White, not through bleaching, but by studying hard because "what such parents really want [is] for their children to aspire to attain the

---

[97] The Canadian government, frustrated by Inuit not being neatly assimilated into southern Canadian white-settler colonialism bureaucracy issued Inuit numbered discs which were to be worn at all times or sewn into clothing (Library and Archives Canada Blog 2016).

perceived luxury, effortless, enjoyment and boundless abundance of power and privilege which they have come to associate with White skin or body" (Nyamnjoh, 2016a: 1). Similarly, van Zyl-Hermann and Boersema note that though explicit European imperialism has ended in Africa, White settler-descended communities and expats retain notable wealth such that White skin continues to denote a position of privilege and power (2017: 655).

At its most basic, whiteness – in the sense that it is used in whiteness studies – is "a configuration of power, privilege, and identity consisting of White racialized ideologies and practices, with material and social ramifications" (van Zyl-Hermann and Boersema, 2017: 652). In Steyn's early work, she notes that much of the scholarship done on 'whiteness' has come from the centres of whiteness, in particular North America, to which she then posits: "If whiteness is all about power, an analysis of whiteness in any context has to start from examining the power base that whiteness wields in that particular context" (2007: 421). Steyn is currently a leading academics on South African whiteness, a whiteness she names as "diasporic" because of its encompassing of "two diametrically opposed identity positionalities: the 'centre' of mainstream racial identity construction, whiteness, and its relationally marginalized counterpart, diaspora" (2005: 120).

Unlike whiteness in traditional "centres" of whiteness, the South African historical and political configuration has meant that "Whites have never experienced their whiteness and the advantage it afforded them as invisible… what *was* taken for granted, however, was the 'naturalness' of being thus privileged" (Steyn, 2005: 122). Steyn notes that "White-South Africans held on to many of the colonial assumptions that helped underwrite the social construction of whiteness with particular tenacity" (2005: 122), and posits that perhaps the fact that White people were never a majority in South Africa, as the reason why these assumptions have been so ardently embraced.

Since the end of Apartheid "Whites need to find new narratives to explain who they are, what they are doing in Africa, and what their relationship is to the indigenous people and to the continent" (Steyn 2005: 122). Of particular noteworthiness on South African whiteness is the great deal of choice they have in their ability to claim symbolic ethnicity either in "Africanness" or "Europeanness"; "this is hybridity very much on their own terms: White-South Africans can invoke, or deny, the tensions of living at the intersections at will" (Steyn 2005: 126-127). Thus, the White students at Stellenbosch University with whom I was interacting, whether they were consciously aware of it or not, are taking part in that negotiation.

Drawing on Said's (1978) *Orientalism*, as the West used stereotypes from the East to create themselves as superior, so too did Afrikaners with the Brown and Black-bodied people around them. In the 19th century, Afrikaner/Dutch-settler identity for so long was predicated on a foil using the 'Other'[98]: there was a double foil, on the one hand from the English and, on the other the pure and White Afrikaner contrasted with the impure, 'savage', people who were Black and Coloured[99] who surrounded them, and with whom they often shared very intimate connections. The Afrikaner's foil is distinct from orientalism in that the use of orientalism by those in the West, because the foil is not against an abstract, far away culture. Yet, people who raised Afrikaner children, cooked and cleaned for their families, worked side-by-side on farms and in gardens, remained at arm's length because of their 'difference' that was meant to preserve the 'superiority' of the Afrikaner race. Given the greater integration between English and Afrikaners due to the economic rise of Afrikaners (Charney, 1984: 269-270), further integration between Afrikaners and people who were Black, Coloured or Indian could be seen as another threat on the Afrikaners being a distinct people in South Africa.

Nyamnjoh and Page proposed that the 'Other'– in their study with young, Black Cameroonians – can contest or subvert essentialised ideas of whiteness (2002: 608). The framework in which their argument is set, argues for considering not just that the Occident has the ability to gaze at the Orient but also that the Orient is actively gazing back. Indeed, that the "Black Cameroonian self is maintained through the production of the White other" (Nyamnjoh & Page, 2002:609). In the context of their study, the White body

---

[98] See Chapter 2.
[99] And later Indian people.

was seen as simultaneously repulsive and as representative of abundant material comfort and power; White people were perceived as "both vehicles for, and obstacles to, the realizations of dreams of the West and Western 'ways of live'" (Nyamnjoh & Page, 2002:609: 612). The participant's perception of White people is that they treat each other fairly but unfairly between themselves and Black people. They were characterized also as:

> Cruel, exploitative, selfish, arrogant, jealous, ignorant, racist, hypocritical, violent, unemotional, physically weak, cunning, deaf to rhythm, unable to eat African food, not very attractive, cold, shabby, unnatural, *unreliable in friendship*, far behind in terms of body hygiene […] (Nyamnjoh & Page 2002: 615, emphasis added).

Furthermore, the informants pushed back against the pigmentation of White people and emphasized that "White people" were in reality, pink (Nyamnjoh & Page, 2002:617)[100]. However, "despite the often negative personal experiences, the Whiteman is still seen very much as a solution to misery and impoverishment" (Nyamnjoh & Page, 2002:627). Thus, there was a recognition of the economic power and the social power associated with the so-called White people but that socio-economic power does not align with good personal qualities. Like Nyamnjoh and Page's study, I hope to shed some light on how 'the Other' understands and experiences whiteness.

'Place' in Theory

The town and University of Stellenbosch are associated with historical pageantry within the Afrikaner elite communities. To briefly discuss "a sense of place", a concept which posits that places are significant because they are the focus of personal feelings. People infuse places with meaning and feelings. Meanings of a given place can become so strong that they can manifest as a central part of identity to the people experiencing them (Rose, 1995: 88). However, the experience of a person's sense of place are largely shaped by

---

[100] As does Salman Rushdie in *Midnight Children*.

the social, cultural, and economic circumstances of those people (Rose, 1995: 89). People identify with places where they feel that they belong to that place; they experience a feeling of comfort, as if they are 'home' (even if it is not literally their home, their hometown, region, etc,) (Rose, 1995: 89).

It is important to note that space itself is never neutral. Fiona Ross notes that,

> Coming to know a space [is] not the product of solely visual relation with a landscape but an embodied one… [there can be] emotional and intersubjective experience over time, to an interrupted sense of bodily placement in relation to features in a landscape, and to a puzzle about the relation of the senses to the modes and products of categorisation and classification (2010: 58).

Racial classifications during Apartheid speaks directly to the political and inexact nature of categorization. When the government actually had to categorize people in the Population Registration Act, they realized that biological standards were unlikely to work, so instead they used appearance and social acceptance. When it came to whiteness, the Act stated that a person could be classified as White if they were "obviously…[or] generally accepted as White" (Thompsell, 2017)[101]. It was possible to appeal one's racial status between Black and Coloured or between Coloured and White through appearance and social acceptance.

Edward Soja notes that during the 19th and 20th century, "time and history have occupied a privileged position in the practical and theoretical consciousness of Western Marxism and critical social science" (1989:1). Thus, he argues that it is "the 'making of geography' more than the 'making of history' that provides the most revealing tactical and theoretical world" (1989: 1). Given the racially exclusive spatial planning in the history of South Africa, I find it easy to accept Soja's claim that space is never neutral and rather is set up ideologically (Ross, 2010: 59). In the context of friendship, space is particularly important because:

---

[101] Online article

Sociality relies on movement— we visit friends, hug those close to us, etc. Our bodies are expansive, and motility is productive of our social worlds [...]. Yet, movement is constrained by ideas about properness, about the appropriate distribution of persons in space. Colonialism and apartheid produced racially and ethnically segregated spatialities and a distinction between places of 'work' and 'home', places of familiarity and those to avoid. We should not forget these are legally enforced, sometimes violently (Ross, 2010: 60).

There is an importance to the knowledge that the majority of students at Stellenbosch are White and that the institution used legally enforced rules of racial exclusion to obtain land. The BA Building stands as those ideas of entitlement and properness were intact when the parents of the current generation of Stellenbosch students attended the University. The end of Apartheid has meant that the formal legal barriers have fallen but the attitudes produced by colonialism and Apartheid have not been transformed, yet.

A tool of transformation that aims to push against Apartheid practices of spatiality has been the renaming of places: streets, buildings, entire cities. At Stellenbosch University there is only one building named after a Coloured person and none named people who are Black or Indian.[102] Michael Jackson argued that "A place name is... the trace of a story, the story about how a name came to be given" (1998: 175). The student protests at Stellenbosch used renaming buildings as one of their acts of defiance. Open Stellenbosch gave the name 'Winnie Mandela House' to a building previously known as Administration A Building. FeesMustFall Stellenbosch renamed the RW Wilcox Building to Lilian Ngoyi Building. The story in Stellenbosch then remains one where the prominent characters are White, except for the by the demands of protesting student whose names were not accepted by the University[103].

---

[102] Huis Russel Botman is a senior residence named after the Rector and Vice-Chancellor of Stellenbosch University who unexpectedly died in 2014, half way through his second term (Dirk 2014).

[103] Though for a time some departments did call 'Wilcox' Lilian Ngoyi instead

Space is also shaped by those who occupy it and different kinds of people occupy space differently: "men and women, young and old do not occupy space in the same— their movements are moulded by (implicit) social rules of age and gender" (Ross, 2010: 60-61). This analysis can also be applied to ethnicity, class, race and other social characteristics. Ross points out that in colonial society there is a firmly embedded notion of 'knowing one's place', that particular people belong in specific places. These notions are what create "the rules of hierarchy through which power is expressed and maintained" (Ross, 2010: 61), which postcolonial societies must struggle to dismantle.

This chapter centres the experiences of Wanijuk, Shane, Hugo and Randy, who shared with me about how space in Stellenbosch has felt during the University experience, as people who are Black or Coloured; and predominantly Anneke and Ané with some comments from other informants who spoke about their experiences of the space as White students.

Characteristics of Friendship

Graham Allan characterizes friendship as egalitarian, supportive, and non-instrumental (non-exploitative). He points out that "friendship should not be seen as a universal relationship but a culturally variable one. […] Sometimes, as in discussions of "true" friendship, it refers to a highly significant form of relational solidarity; at other times it has a much wider reference, being almost any tie of voluntary sociability" (Allan, 2003: 513). This chapter is interested in both ends of the friendship spectrum cited here by Allan, but particularly seeks to examine the seeming lack of deep friendships across racial lines.

There are three broad characteristics of friendship that Allan describes. The first: friendship is a non-hierarchical tie "in that friendship does not involve differential power or authority" (Allan, 2003: 513). Thus, while a pupil might have a positive relationship with a teacher, their relationship is not one of friendship, if it ventured into the realm of friendship that would be considered inappropriate because of the power the teacher is able to laud over the pupil. The second is that friendship is personal rather than being based on social roles or arbitrary proximity, like neighbours being neighbours by virtue of living near one another or work colleagues being colleagues by virtue of being hired by the same company. Though friendships may (and often do) start from these proximities, they go beyond these contingencies to a closer relationality. If a colleague quits a workplace their relational ties will fall out with people who did not take their relationship a step further to voluntarily spending time together (Allan, 2003: 513).

"Friendships are personal in that their content is not prescribed by others", as at a workplace the boss or supervisor decides who works together on projects, the rooms people occupy at what times, and more (Allan, 2003: 514). Friends decide together how they will spend their time together. Finally, "friendship is normally seen as non-instrumental— that is, it is not viewed as a means to some other end", though that "is not to suggest that friends never turn on another for help or never advantage from their friendship" (Allan, 2003: 514). Rather, what makes friendship non-instrumental is the utility people gain is not the basis of the tie (Allan, 2003: 514). When people are seen as only being part of a friendship for gain, that friendship is thought of as hollow, or as Allan puts it the reciprocity between friends "signifies that the friends are not using one another in inappropriate ways or in a manner that would undermine their solidarity" (Allan, 2003: 514).

The idea of friendship itself is a contested one that is culturally situated. The students from Western Europe, in a study by Patrick Williams, found that they had a different understanding of the word 'friendship' than their American peers. The students reported to him that in their countries, friendships are taken more seriously than in America and that many Americans claim people for friends that Germans or Swedes would not." (Williams, 2001: 28). The American definition of "friend" seems to include what are, for participants, acquaintances. (Williams, 2001: 30) In this chapter, I will be using the word acquaintance to describe people within the social sphere of informants with whom their connection is impersonal, like a classmate or someone who lives in the same residence as them. I will reserve the word friendship for relationships that meet the three characteristics as outlined by Allan. Many of the interactions across racial lines that I was told about seem to those in the category of 'acquaintance' as they were based more on social roles or arbitrary proximity rather than the personal nature that friendship has. For example, Wanijuk interacted with White women when she lived in residence, but those interactions never became personal to a point of creating a friendship.

Challenges of Making Friends

The challenge of making friendships across racial lines is that for most people social circles are their comfort zones. As Tanya Menon described in an interview with American National Public Radio (NPR): "It's easy, we're talking to people who are similar to us. There's no threat in that, they're not going to reject us". Menon's research work is about networks between people, like how we choose who to surround ourselves with. Menon asserts that "one of the most basic ideas in psychology, [is] that people form cliques" that "any little tiny scrap of commonality" is what people have a tendency to gravitate toward, even something as simple as being "the same height, we just feel comfortable standing there, talking to each other" (NPR, 2018). Menon witnesses a moment of openness at the beginning of each year at the business school where she teaches:

> Day one, they're so open. At that moment in their lives, they are connecting with everybody, they're having lunch with all different kinds of people, they're sitting with new people but literally in a matter of weeks it crystalizes they all find their friends, they find their people who are usually looking just like them and they sit and cluster together… and that wonderful moment of openness ends. All of those other connections wither away (NPR, 2018).

Menon makes the connection to the anthropological concept of "liminality", which she defines as "these moments in our lives where we're just open, we're living in a grey area, we're between worlds… we're out of the boundaries that normally constrain us… it's only a few weeks later where they stop this" (NPR, 2018).

Liminality has become a popular concept in anthropology and sociology. For example, in Patrick Williams' work among exchange students from Western Europe, he describes liminality as a "phase during which individuals who have entered into a new social environment actively pursue a means of combating negative feelings and emotions. The liminal phase is seen as a process in which the participant is active and conscious of his or her cultural situation" (Williams, 2001: 21). I would posit that the difference between Stellenbosch and the rest of South Africa could feel so extreme that perhaps Black students always or often feel as though they are in a liminal phase that creates feelings of alienation; as if they are exchange students in their own country because of how strong Afrikaner norms are. In most cases in Williams' study, the exchange students became comfortable with their US setting "once they had met other international students and established relationships with them" (Williams 2001: 26). Liminal feelings, he found, were most poignant for students before they were able to establish relationships of some kind in America but as "students developed relationships in their new environments, they passed out of the liminal phase, though cultural boundaries continued to exist" (Williams, 2001: 26).

The strong norms of whiteness and Afrikanerdom that are entrenched in Stellenbosch were alienating to my informants of colour. Applying Menon's assertion that social circles are many people's comfort zones here, I believe that many people who were Black, Coloured or Indian were cautious about widening their social circles and unnecessarily spending energy on being in liminality (feeling alienated) as so much of their time in places like residence and class were spent in zones of liminality where they were not able to be comfortable. The friendships of students of colour were precious to their ability to have moments of comfort in a place that otherwise was quite alienating. This would explain why Anneke felt that maintaining friendships across racial lines took more effort because perhaps to build trust and comfort between a person of colour and a White person, required work by the White individual to prove to the person of colour that they could be comfortable around one another.

Friendship relations across racial lines are challenged by contextual perceptions that make it difficult for them to be experienced or seen as being egalitarian, supportive and non-instrumental. For example, in the Cameroonian context studied by Nyamnjoh and Page, many participants felt considerable scepticism about interracial marriages and relationships as they were seen as very materially asymmetrical, thus being seen as an instrumental kind of relationship or presenting too great a challenge to the equality necessary for love (2002: 623). Many of their participants felt that couples in interracial marriages were rarely happy (Nyamnjoh & Page, 2002). This is the perception from these participants rather than actually people in interracial relationships. However, these observations by the participants of Nyamnjoh and Page point to the scepticism toward white people and interracial relationships which might prevent people from making an effort across racial lines or might make it difficult to maintain a relationship if racial lines are crossed. If people were constantly questioning or being judgemental about a relationship between two people, the social pressure might affect the ability of that relationship to flourish or exist at all.

The taboos about racial mixing in South Africa are not just romantic. Similar to the description by Balibar, they are maintained by the dominant classes and to an extent the state. For example, the racial segregation continues to be facilitated by policies like the charging of extensive tuition fees to allow the maintenance of former Model-C schools as "public" schools (Balibar 1991, 24). Once while I was coaching debate, I watched as a White student of mine, who went to an Afrikaans-medium school, asked a Black student how she got her hair to grow so fast. Since a previous session, Black student had her hair put in protective braids with extensions. This meant the White student had no experience or understanding of very basic information related to Black women's hair. This is similar to the shocking revelation shared in Chapter 3 that a Black student could be wealthy enough to bring his own mini-fridge to residence demonstrating the conflation by those White students that to be Black in South Africa is to be "poor". Their presumption is likely coming from a similarly institutionally legitimated place that normalizes being schooled only with people who are the same race and class as each other. This kind of institutional legitimation of continued segregation "functions as a unidirectional block on expression and social advancement" argues Balibar (Balibar 1991, 25). He observes in a European context that:

> No theoretical discourse on dignity of all cultures will really compensate for the fact that, for being a 'Black' in Britain or a *Beur* in France, the assimilation demanded of them before they can become integrated into society which they already live and which will always be suspect of being superficial, imperfect or simulated is presented as progress as an emancipation, a conceding of rights (Balibar 1991, 25).

In South Africa, all school curriculums teach about apartheid ("theoretical discourse on the dignity of all cultures") and yet we see in the hair example and fridge example the level of "otherness" and ignorance demonstrated by White students who have attended (by and large) former Model-C schools (and/or private schools). I imagine it must create an internal hurricane of feelings (shocking, demoralizing, heart-breaking, etc) within Black, Coloured, and Indian students who are South African, and know that the vast majority of South Africans have lived experiences like theirs but now being in an institutional culture with such an intense expectation of "assimilation demanded of them before they can become integrated". Almost all of this students are South African, almost all of them are African, but this environment of intense whiteness, in a living museum of Afrikanerdom positions students of colour of "always be suspect of being superficial, imperfect or simulated is presented as progress as an emancipation" (Balibar 1991, 25).

When the exchange students in Williams' study arrived in America, they felt boundaries in most aspects of their daily lives: "participants reported encountering various things that made them feel uncomfortable, disoriented, or frustrated" (Williams, 2006: 26). These moments were described by Williams' as stumbling blocks: "discrepancies in the meaning attributed to signs and objects" (2006: 21). During the liminal phase of settling into their new environment, Williams' argues that:

> Stumbling blocks are symbolic representations of host-cultural values or behaviours that contradict the values or behaviours found in the sojourner's native culture. Stumbling blocks represent situations in which individuals encounter new behaviours or actions and interpret them within the context of their existing understanding of the host culture (Williams, 2001: 26).

In this instance, the stumbling blocks for my informants were the Afrikaner norms, as with Shane who went as far as to describe his feeling as "culture shock". Williams posited that "stumbling blocks can reinforce ethnocentrism and sharpen criticisms of the host culture, thus reinforcing boundaries" (Williams, 2001: 26), though I would not completely support that characterization. I would say that the alienation felt by Black, Coloured and Indian students could be why they do not seek out friends from the dominant culture.

Then how do we move past the stumbling blocks and alienation? John Rawls created a thought experiment called "the veil of ignorance". He asks people to create a society from behind a veil of ignorance: we do not know who we are, our race, social class, disability status, status of our mental or physical health, intelligence (Rawls, 1999: 11). Not knowing who we are, he asks, what rules and structures would we create in our society? In this iteration here, I extend Rawls' test from society structures to interpersonal behaviour, to the question of how we would treat a newly arrived neighbour. Perhaps apart from those with extreme social anxiety, we expect a certain sense of sociality: at minimum a kind of acknowledgement, a wave or nod, small pleasantries; on the other end of the spectrum, the more extroverted among us might be pleasantly surprised by a bigger gesture like a fruit basket might also be nice. All these social interactions come with a certain level of risk: if one attempted to visit a new neighbour and be brushed off or rejected it would feel like a blow, possibly as though the neighbour is superior. If we focus on the person moving in, a circumstance where neighbours do not make an effort, given this risk of rejection: would you risk it?

This dilemma is a first mover problem. This is similar to situations of romance where two people may well have romantic feelings for each other but because of a plethora of possible reasons, like uncertainty, shyness, intimidation, a relationship or date may never manifest because neither is willing to make the first move. In situations with elevated factors of social risk, people are less likely to make an effort to socialise with or befriend people who they believe pose a higher risk of being rejected. Through my observations and interviews I will explore what it is about the social context of Stellenbosch that makes it challenging for people to make the first move.

To just make the first move toward making friends with someone, one would first need to meet them. Based on the feedback from my participants, there were conspicuously few spaces in Stellenbosch that are comfortable for both people who were Black, Coloured or Indian and people who were White to be comfortable in. In their study of teenage parties in Denmark, Demant and Ostergaard note that the space that parties constitute are important to the teenagers taking part, that "the zoning of the party is crucial for creating what can be termed not 'my space', but 'our space'. It is a collectively created space, distinct from other spaces created with parental or adult supervision […]" (2007: 533). They argue that in the party space, which they and their peers create, teenagers are free to relate to each other according to their own rules and organisation, rather than how authorities tell them to.

The lack of spaces in Stellenbosch that are co-constituted by people of multiple backgrounds means that spaces are lacking where people feel comfortable to relate to each other in ways other than those they have been taught through societal sociality. Furthermore, Oxley's study of men's friendship in the context of bars found that, "typically men met in the bars in the town and created a highly egalitarian form of tie in which status and class differences were rendered irrelevant". The space of the bar was a defining aspect of those interactions, as the "invisibility of status would be difficult to achieve if the relationships were defined more broadly and activated in other settings, such as the home, in which lifestyle differentials are more evident" (in Allan, 2003: 513-514). Bars and other spaces with alcohol are not the only place where friendships across different identities can take place.

In their research on African-Americans in interracial congregations, Emerson and Yancey note that African-Americans who spent extensive amounts of time with White people, including at church, did not significantly affect their attitudes. This demonstrates that "African-Americans are not losing their racialized perspectives on racial/social issues in these multiracial settings" (Emerson & Yancey, 2008: 312). Significantly, from each of these studies is that these different spaces are able to reach across differences that often divide people. It is intuitive that if many social spaces continue to be socially segregated (and not legally so), then that is a barrier to being able to interact outside of the structures that institutions dictate that people should interact.

A section of this chapter examines the physical space and social spaces at the University such as bars and sports. Svašek argues that "'Belonging' or 'feeling at home' […] should not be defined as a static form of rootedness in one physical locality but can best be conceptualised as a cognitive and emotional process in which people identify with particular experiences and feel familiarity with their lifestyles" (2008: 215). The dominance of Afrikaner imagery and symbols at the University make it easy for students from that background to feel rooted in that space. Based on the experiences of my participants, it seemed as though the commonality between White English students and White Afrikaner students mean that though English students were not necessarily raised steeped in the symbols and imagery of Afrikanerdom, they become accustomed to it in a way that allows themselves to become rooted in Stellenbosch. Students of colour I spoke with were mostly not able to feel that same sense of belonging or rootedness at the University. For example, in the documentary *Luister*[104], members of the Open Stellenbosch Collective speak about feeling as though

---

[104]Trans. "Listen". Accessible at https://www.youtube.com/watch?v=sF3rTBQTQk4 . Accessed 20 January 2016.

they are excluded or as though they don't belong at the University (Contraband Cape Town, 2015).

The noticeable rarity, almost to the point of absence, of interracial friendships in Stellenbosch implies that there is not much interracial physical contact. Anneke specifically noted that "it's like so abnormal for me to see even like two people of different races like going on a date or sitting having coffee… it's like a weird thing to see in Stellenbosch." This absence of physical contact indicates that people do not feel obligated to the "other" across racial lines. Touch is important as touch causes obligations between people. Even those who are not tactile are often the most comfortable with being touched by members of their immediate family, who are often seen as those we are the most obliged to. People we feel obliged to, tend to meet the characteristics of friendship as set out by Allan, particularly that of being supportive. For example, DeVault observes that women often described the work they did in feeding their families as "love" and "caring", though it was labour intensive: cleaning, provisioning, knowing what people liked, and the cooking itself (1991: 13). This is not to be overly simplistic in arguing that interracial romantic relationships and interracial babies will solve systemic problems of racism. As Danielle Bowler eloquently, states:

> Having mixed raced children will not end racism and result in a racial utopia, as questions and experiences of race cannot be bred away, but often appear with greater force when mixed bodies appear (2016)[105].

Rather, it is to say, that physicality is a mechanism by which people tend to demonstrate who they feel most obliged to. In her study of transnational Italians, Baldassar notes the numerous ways in which people attempt to replicate physical co-presence in their transnational relationships. For example, transnational objects, like photos and letters, were considered important by her informants due to their "tangibility- they can be touched and held and thus take the physical *place* of the longed-for person or location" (Baldassar, 2008: 267). They represent, or more specifically,

---

[105] Online Newspaper Article

"stand for" the absence of being" (Baldassar, 2008: 267). Her informant, Signora Eva, cradled and kissed a picture of her child, unable to physically do so because of the distance of her transnational daughter (Baldassar, 2008: 267). Baldassar found that physical co-presence was more highly valued than virtual co-presence, which could access through information technologies such as webcams as there was an implicit "need to touch each other, to embrace" (Baldassar, 2008: 260). Thus, I am positing the converse: that the implicit lack of touch between White students and students of colour implies the absence of those bonds. The implication of this is incredibly sad: that people are not learning to care about one another across racial lines.

Menon's research says even though it is difficult to force ourselves out of our social comfort zones, we all have the ability to do it (NPR, 2018). The issue I observed occurring at Stellenbosch University thus, is not unique but is perhaps exacerbated by the environment and history of South Africa and of the University as was explored in Chapter 2. Even in the encyclopaedia article on 'friendship', Allan notes that "because it can actually be quite difficult to develop egalitarian relationships across wide social and economic gulfs, in reality, friendships usually develop between people who share similar social locations" (2003: 513).

Furthermore, given the segregation and ghettoization of peoples across the globe, one might posit that what I observed in Stellenbosch is not that exceptional but given the close proximity of students to one another in their classrooms, church services and residences, the question this chapter posits is: why does the gulf of difference loom so large even among people who appear to have so much in common? After all, these students all attend the same university, many take the same subjects and live in the same residences and apartment buildings; why are these relationships not becoming personal across racial lines? Using the concept of liminality, belonging, and place, this chapter has examined the effects of Stellenbosch on friendship.

The structure of Apartheid itself demanded that White people isolate themselves from the rest of the peoples of South Africa. The people who were Black, Coloured or

Indian that they did interact with, sometimes in intimate situations like acting as a caregiver to children, were in socially and economically subordinate positions to White people. In a country that remains incredibly segregated and thereby haunted by consequences of Apartheid policies, I believe that to achieve true transformation at Stellenbosch would involve changing some of the current characteristics of the University, particularly demographics. During a conversation with Christoff we spoke about his growing up in Bloemfontein. He was born into a family he described as very Afrikaans and Grey College, a former Model-C school, where he was instructed in Afrikaans. "I've lived in South Africa my whole life surrounded by White people. It makes zero sense. Predominantly Afrikaans White people."[106] Christoff speaks to a phenomenon that unfortunately seemed to continue to be fairly common.

Whiteness Isn't Only Skin Deep… Sometimes, It Has Little To Do With The Skin.

Wanijuk completed her undergrad and honours at Stellenbosch in December 2016. She is an international student from Kenya who found her way to Stellenbosch through her father who completed a graduate degree there. She told me that she "had a lot of loneliness and feelings like I don't belong here [in Stellenbosch]", that she "found it so hard to really be with people [in Stellenbosch]"[107]. Wanijuk experienced the stumbling blocks found by Williams to be moments where individuals encounter new behaviours or actions in their host culture that contradict the values or behaviours found in their own culture that made her feel alienated from her classmates (2001: 26). For example, once when taking part in an inter-residence singing competition, as part of the costume the girls were supposed to put paint in their hair, Wanijuk tried to explain to them that because her hair was different than their hair she could not put paint in her hair. These girls, who were White, told Wanijuk that she was being "difficult" and a "diva" for refusing to take part in the hair-paint portion of the costume. She felt that in Kenya,

---

[106] Interviewed 2 November 2016
[107] Interviewed 16 December 2016

where she was likely to have been surrounded by Black people, no one would have ever suggested putting paint in her hair. Wanijuk's alternative was to wear a head wrap, which allowed for her to have colour on her head without putting paint in her hair: "That [experience] was a point where I was like, you guys don't even know, you don't even know how my hair works and you stay with me every day."[108] As pointed out by Svašek, belonging can be conceptualized as "a cognitive and emotional process in which people identify with particular experiences and feel familiarity with their lifestyles" (2001: 215). While the White women in Wanijuk's residence were happy to put paint in their hair, which perhaps was familiar to them from previous experiences of costuming in theatre, this experience emotionally alienated Wanijuk from these women thereby making her feel like she did not belong.

While she felt that whiteness in Stellenbosch contributed to her feelings of loneliness, it was not the only reason she singled out, another being a general lack of awareness:

> I found South Africans very ignorant, both Black and White. Like with… the same way Africans go to America and… they're asking the same questions Americans would ask. Do you have lions as pets? Not that extreme but that kind of vibe. I can see they think that the rest of Africa is nothing to think about, it's a jungle. So, in that sense the whiteness it's not only with the White people, it's also with the Black South Africans, I felt it a lot. Lack of awareness.

Here Wanijuk reminds us of Nyamnjoh's argument that whiteness is not just a skin tone but also a set of relations and connections that people; that whiteness and blackness, "far from being a birthmark, can be acquired and lost with circumstances, by Whites and Black alike, regardless of how they define and identify themselves or are defined and identified by others" (2016: 59). In this circumstance, of an African foreign national studying at a predominantly and historically-White university, Wanijuk, as Nyamnjoh and Page's participants in Cameroon, identified the adjective "ignorant" with Whiteness. The ignorance displayed by

---

[108] Interviewed 16 December 2016

South Africans, White and Black alike, significantly contributed to the emotional alienation felt by Wanijuk: "I didn't belong with the White people, I didn't belong with the Black South Africans, so, where was I? I was like ???"

She did, however, find some solace among other Black, African nationals at Stellenbosch:

> I don't know if it was the fact that we were both foreigners, but I connected a lot with other African nationals aboard. I don't know if it's because we shared the same thing, or because like I knew something about them, there was a place to connect. They'd ask me "where are you from?" and I'd say Nairobi and they say "Oh! The capital." Just like those little things, I wouldn't know everything but at least I would know some things… so I think that whiteness wasn't just necessarily from the White people.

The inability for Black South Africans that Wanijuk met to identify capitals or show understanding of the rest of the continent meant that she found it difficult to identify with them. As Menon notes, we have a tendency to gravitate towards those with whom we have even a "tiny scrap of commonality" because we want our friendships to feel safe (NPR, 2018). This feeling of alienation, a feeling that one is strange or out of place, was further emphasized to Wanijuk by being Kenyan, rather than South African: "I was super made aware of my foreignness, my Blackness was made aware of but even when I was interacting with White people I was made aware of, like when they found out that I was from Kenya, their tone changed."

The kinds of friendships that seemed to be encouraged to cultivate in Stellenbosch residences, where Wanijuk lived for three years, were not the kind that Wanijuk valued: "I like depth in friendships, I don't care about how many friends I have. It doesn't matter to me." In residence, she felt as though the social events were not "genuine" and rather "forced":

> The thing is, I wanted a place to stay; I didn't want sisters. If I wanted sisters, if I wanted friends I'd go look for them and make sisters from them. Don't force me to be sisters with people. If there is no chemistry, like stop. Also, the same people

who are sisters, they didn't want to accommodate me so like what kind of friendship is that?

This experience of Wanijuk was her White peers having difficulty seeing themselves in her, who they experience as the 'other'. In *Midnight's Children*, Salman Rushdie's Amina Sinai speaks of losing her "city eyes" as she enters a Delhi slum:

> When you have city eyes you cannot see the invisible people, the men with elephantiasis of the balls and the beggars in boxcars don't impinge on you, and the concrete sections of drainpipes don't look like dormitories (2006: 105).

In South Africa, Apartheid taught White-South Africans to put on snow-goggles and only see other White people as being fully people, seeing the others they shared the country with only reluctantly as people. They were taught that those with Brown and Black-bodies were lesser than them. The argument for Apartheid was that the 'Other' was evolutionarily behind White presenting people, thus they must develop at their speed (SAHO, 2017).

At many robots[109] there are people asking for money. The vast majority of these people are Black (though from time to time they are a White person). This also happens in other parts of the world, even occasionally where I grew up in a somewhat remote Canadian city[110]. In Senegal and several West African countries (mostly all-Black societies), begging at roadsides is very common, and givers consider it their duty to share. Similarly, as I was told by a friend who is Xhosa— from Eastern Cape, well-off and surrounded by other Black people— that when people would come to ask for money, it would be in the form of asking for work, her mother would give the beggar a task like sweeping out the kitchen but would over pay them for their work.

Given the levels of segregation and inequality in South Africa, Wanijuk's experience is demonstrative that young

---

[109] A South Africanism for traffic lights

[110] In my hometown street-involved people are almost entirely White, though in other parts of Canada there are a disproportionate number of street-involved Indigenous people.

White-South Africans, 'born-frees', are having trouble shaking the 'city eyes' that Rushdie describes. I believe that being trained not to see or acknowledge Black pain is in and of itself a form of dehumanization, as what it functionally does is train humans not to recognize the humanity of other humans. Though not all White students at Stellenbosch will have grown up in circumstances that are implicitly foregrounded by this dynamic, it only takes a few negative and uncomfortable interactions between White and Black students to have the Black student feel unwelcome. Given that students of colour are demographically overwhelmed by White students, they are already likely to feel alienated; feel conscious of being in an ambiguous cultural situation (Williams 2001: 21). A direct negative interaction with White students could be a tipping point.

In the introduction of this chapter, I spoke of what could be considered the ideal social expectations for a newly arrived neighbour if we were behind Rawls' veil of ignorance, noting that the risk of rejection is often what makes people shy to make the first move. Here, I want to tie the perception that White students are ignorant about everyday aspects of Black lives (such as hair), to the idea of rejection. If Black students are feeling vulnerable and alienated in Stellenbosch, if White students are seen by them as not making an effort to be their friend and friendship with them seems to be at risk of feeling more moments of alienation, then it seems like a reasonable calculation for Black students to be particularly averse to making the first moves toward friendships.

Wanijuk said it was only in her honours, her fourth year of study, that she felt like she had friends at the University:

> I have friends…. this year my study group was just White females, so everyone I studied with was White and the only reason I was actually able to get along with them was 'cause they… aren't ignorant. It was a nice experience. For the first time a White person invited me to their home… after all the years I've been here. That's the first time someone has ever invited me to their place.

Hugo, who grew up in Mozambique, noted to me that "I know that there is an invisible wall between the Whites, the

Blacks, the Coloureds… It is not something aggressive, but it is like just that silent wall."[111]

Wanijuk's and Hugo's observations were consistent with what were pointed out to me by White informants, like Anneke[112]: "people just don't tend to associate that much with people of other races…" Anneke is a very bilingual Afrikaans-speaking student I met through the Stellenbosch University Debating Union. Her father is Dutch, but he speaks Afrikaans fluently and her mother's dad is German, but she was also raised Afrikaans. Before Anneke's family moved overseas, she attended an Afrikaans primary school but was schooled in English abroad and continued her education in English after she returned to live in Johannesburg in the eighth grade. Johannesburg is widely thought of as being less racially divided than Cape Town (Hosken, 2016). Anneke's comments point to the fact that elsewhere in South Africa she was able to make friends with people who were Black, Coloured or Indian but something about Stellenbosch seemed to make it more difficult:

> I don't really have a single very good friend [at Stellenbosch] that is not White. That's interesting to me because I came from a school where it wasn't strange for me to be like "hey mom, I'm going to sleep at my friend's house" and that friend happened not to be White. That was never a thing I even thought about. I had like lots of friends that weren't White growing up. Then I came to Stellenbosch and I don't have any. Not because I don't want to but because the dynamic is very interesting because it's still really divided.[113]

How Anneke phrased her last comment alludes to separation having been the norm during Apartheid and in the period shortly after but was not her experience in Johannesburg where she grew up. This comment of hers was corroborated by my experience in the field[114] and the experience of another participant, Randy who said: "When people see interracial couples their eyebrows still lift… its

---

[111] Interviewed 10 November 2017
[112] Interviewed 16 September 2016
[113] Interviewed 16 September 2016
[114] See Chapter 3.

2017"[115]. Randy's emphasis on time here implies a way of emphasizing that interracial couples should not be something worth raising one's eyebrows about. Similar to Canadian Prime Minister Justin Trudeau's defense of his cabinet ministers being half women, half men which was "Because it's 2015" (Ditchburn, 2015).

Anneke went on to describe how different her upbringing felt from her time at Stellenbosch:

> I've grown up in very... almost like colour-blind, you know [race] didn't really matter... but then I came here and it's like so abnormal for me to see even like two people of different races going on a date or sitting having coffee... it's a weird thing to see in Stellenbosch. People just tend to group themselves in terms of their race.

Anneke's observation of the absence of interracial social interaction is demonstrative of my argument that people at Stellenbosch, in large part, were not making friends across the racial divide. Social science studies of romantic relationships in teenagers have found that "peer group as the prime socializing force for adolescent romance their importance for the transmission of cultural knowledge about romantic love", though experiences differ by culture and ethnic associations as well as of different crowds (Milbrath & et al, 2009: 316). While I am not specifically interested in romantic relationships, my sense is that something similar may be happening among students at Stellenbosch, most of whom are in their late adolescence and early young adulthood. If many, even most, peer groups are noticeably homogeneous then it signals to each other that it is normal not to have friends from other racial groups.

This nervousness of making the first move is almost similar to a collective action problem, where although each individual in any given group may share common interests with every other member, namely finding interesting and fulfilling friendships, individuals may also have conflicting interests (here a fear of rejection). In collective action problems, when taking part is seen as costly, then people avoid having to take part (Dowding, 2013). Thus, while many

---

[115] 15 Interviewed February 2017

might have observed the problem, most do not act on it because it seems costly to do so. However, it could also be more than an issue of first moves. Towards the end of our conservation, Anneke posited that:

> I have personally found you have to make a lot more effort if you want to make a friend of a different race, like it doesn't come as naturally, like you kind of organically become friends with people but at Stellenbosch I find you don't organically become friends with people of different races. And I don't know if that's because I wasn't in rez or like haven't had anything to relate to maybe? But definitely in the class experience it's like they definitely identify themselves as [a group].

Alternatively, Anneke notes that "Not that I've ever seen people be overtly racist, I've definitely seen lots of tacitly racist things", which corroborates my conjecture that interracial friendship can seem emotionally costly to people who were Black, Coloured or Indian. If they have been witness to or been hurt by tacit racism by their White peers, then that would possibly deter them from wanting to develop relationships beyond those of happenstance like taking a class together or living in the same residence. Without a want to move those relationships from one of proximity to becoming a personal one.

While speaking to Ané, I mentioned Anneke's experience of her friend group lacking in diversity since moving from Gauteng to Stellenbosch. Ané, a White, Afrikaans woman who grew up in Randburg, Gauteng, agreed: "Where I am from it's pretty White but there were a lot of Black people. Like I knew Black people,"[116] thereby implying that she does not currently know Black people or perhaps not to the same extent or not nearly as many. Ané's observation confirmed that Stellenbosch is noticeably White even when compared to other parts of South Africa. In her residence, Ané noted that people of different ethnicities did not mix with one another: "Coloured girls in res, they would kind of flock together. Like I made friends with them individually… kind of."

---

[116] Interviewed February 22nd, 2017

"Was it hard to break in with them?" I asked.

"Yeah, but there was more of a divide between Black people and Coloured people. The gap between being friends with Black girls was harder than it was with Coloured girls. Coloured girls, they got along together better, I guess… […] the Coloured girls spoke mostly Afrikaans. Most of the friends that I made were English girls, and then… they wouldn't necessarily always get along with the Coloured girls because they don't have that connection. But I would, I would speak Afrikaans with them it and it was a lot of fun."

Ané's description here of why it was easier for her to make friends with the girls in her residence who were Coloured than it was for the girls who were Black in her residence to make friends with them was because both Ané and the girls who were Coloured shared a commonality: Afrikaans. This is just as noted by Menon, that people cling to commonalities when they socially interact.

Ané went on to describe what she saw as the root to the lack of diversity at Stellenbosch:

> I thought about it and just the population here is SO White like its… my boyfriend, […] from Pretoria, he came here and is literally so flabbergasted like "it's so White I can't believe it", and I forget. I forget it's so White… it's definitely something that is a prominent feature of the day to day. Like when I think about Black people I think, just because they're really a minority here. And they're not a minority in the country, they're a minority here because this is a really privileged space. And I feel like, they might feel like they need to stick together.

Ané illustrates her observation with an anecdote about her one close Black friend, that friend as having a primary group of friends (of which Ané is not a member) who are Black, which she understands. Ané's observation is congruent with the argument of this chapter: the deep connections at Stellenbosch to whiteness made people who were Black, Coloured or Indian feel alienated which pushed them to seek commonality where they could find it.

Ané met some Black women she "really got along with" during extracurricular activities but their friendships never moved beyond their extracurricular activities. "It almost never goes to that next level" she said, alluding to the element of friendships needing to be a relationship that becomes personal rather than proximal through an institution like work. As Anneke noted, as a White person, more effort had to be made if one wanted to make a friend of a different race, unlike making friends with White people, which she used the words 'natural' and 'organic' to describe. There is no such thing as "natural" and "organic" interactions as all human culture and society are built on our social constructions and agency.

Kara noted a lack of cosmopolitanism in Stellenbosch. She is a White, Afrikaans-speaking woman who was raised in Cape Town and attended a former model-C[117] Afrikaans high school. She imagined that university would mean a lot of very different interesting people and people who would be open to new ideas. After arriving and settling in at Stellenbosch, she was surprised at how little diversity there was at the University and felt that people were apathetic about its lack of diversity.[118]

Randy, a Coloured woman who was in her third year of a drama bachelors when we spoke, talked about her best friend, "a White male, Afrikaans […] from Springbok, homosexual […], he's got a lot of struggles together"[119]. This description by Randy was foregrounded by a description of the importance of respect which implied to me that characteristic need for equality as pointed out by Allan's analysis of friendship. She went on to speak about the kinds of shared moments of physical intimacy with her friend: "We always hug each other, and we dance crazy and we kiss each other on the lips". Which Randy stipulated was not sexual but that many others assumed was: "we are inseparable, people would think we actually in a relationship". Comparing Randy's experience to the observations my other participants made about feeling separated or isolated from people from other racial groups, is a moment of my fieldwork that pushed me to consider how that touch acts both as a manifestation of care and devotion but can also be one of the steps that brings care and devotion with it.

---

[117] A "model-c" school is "a state school in South Africa that used to be for White children only and is now mixed" (MacMillan).
[118] Interviewed September 28th, 2016
[119] Interviewed February 15th, 2017

Randy noted that sometimes she felt people were staring at her and her White best-friend when they were together and visibly touching. Once she was so upset by it that she and her friend went home. She told him that it had upset her to have all those people looking at them. People tend to stare at things that seem out of the ordinary. For example, a redheaded friend travelling in Japan was often stared at and taken pictures of because Japanese people almost uniformly have brown or black hair so seeing someone with red hair is a rarity. Thus, in the context of Stellenbosch, based on the reaction of those around them of staring: a Coloured woman and White man dancing together, hugging, etc. was out of the ordinary.

During Apartheid, the Prohibitions of Mixed Marriages Act was one of the first pieces of legislation passed by the National Party in 1949. It "prohibited the marriage or a sexual relationship between White people and people of other race groups" and "also nullified interracial marriages of South Africans that occurred outside of the country" (SAHO, 2012). The fear of miscegenation was related to the Apartheid regime's fear of *gelykstelling* or "equalisation" of the other races in South Africa to White people (Falkof, 2016). Implicitly, this fear shares a common assumption with Allan's analysis of the basic tenets needed for friendship that there must be equality between people for them to be friends (Allan 2003: 513). After escaping the stares of people Randy realised:

> No, let them look. Let people look. This is clearly upsetting towards them, eye-opening or something. Let them look, you're my best friend. I don't really care what the outside world thinks of it. In fact, if people want to look they must look. I'm here for that, I'm not here for them. I'm here to have a good time.

This attitude of Randy's demonstrates a very high level of courage because it is a refusal to bow to social pressure created by her staring peers. Implicitly, her White-male-Afrikaans best friend must at least to some extent share this attitude if he does not retreat from the stares. If he did, that likely would be something noteworthy enough for Randy to mention. Thus, if the dominant social order is one where interracial friendships or relationships are unusual or are made to seem out of place, then based on the success of Randy's interracial friendship it implies that both parties must be courageous enough to cope with going against social norms.

On the other hand, Jason's experience speaks to the cultural closeness of the English and Afrikaners. Jason was from an English farming family in the Eastern Cape and was in his final year of his Bachelor of Commerce in economics. Even though he was from an English background, since where he grew up was fairly Afrikaans, people at Stellenbosch often did not realize that he was English[120]. He had a cultural competency with Afrikaans culture that was likely less available to his Black peers due to his White privilege. When residents of Orania defend the fact that technically people of colour could move to their town they emphasize the "cultural" difference of the town to attempt to separate it from the explicit racial character the town has. For example, in a 2019 interview Carel Boshoff IV (the President of the Orania movement and the grandson-son of the first Apartheid Prime Minister Verwoed) said: "There's no rule that says that you can't. It's an Afrikaner town. Afrikaans is the language. Your neighbors and your friends would be Afrikaners. That's it." (Smith and Pitts). What is being left unsaid is to what extent those Afrikaner neighbours would want to be friends with Black, Coloured, or Indian people, especially those who might deviate from Afrikaner norms. Though Jason might be more camouflaged than other of his English classmates, this does speak to the greater integration between English and Afrikaners (Charney 1984: 269-270). Marc, a completely Anglophone and White PhD student in the Music Faculty, felt that his positionality and linguistic abilities (rudimentary Afrikaans) did not disadvantage him in Stellenbosch, the town and the University.[121]

Social Spaces in Stellenbosch

This section examines the types of social spaces in Stellenbosch. As mentioned in the introduction to this chapter, if social spaces are not co-constituted or zoned in

---

[120] Interviewed 1 March 2017
[121] Interviewed 13 October 2016

ways that signal that they are different to dictated social spaces, such as classrooms, that might cause a barrier between students. As Ané and Hugo mentioned, sports is one place where people have an opportunity to meet. Another, as I spoke about extensively with Randy, are bars.

There seemed to be a consensus that different bars and clubs had set social standards, many associated with particular ethnicities. Catherine described the feeling as having to "to like conform to a place to be able to go there".[122] I asked Catherine to speak more to the kind of culture she saw as being associated with clubs in Stellenbosch, and she responded that a kind of confirmation bias existed where: "people go together in different places, so you will find more of the same people with the same people, and more of the same people will go there". Catherine made specific reference to a kind of dress code that was socially expected at these places: "It's almost like if I were to go to Catwalk or NuBar in like my sneakers and my jeans and a hoodie people would look at me funny like I was not meant to be there. I tend to stay away from those places." The top three search results on Google about Catwalk are two blog entries accusing it of being racist as well as a YouTube video accusing it of racial profiling.[123]

Strict dress codes and racist practices are connected. RAB May has focused on what he called "velvet rope racism", the practice of excluding racial or ethnic groups from participating in nightclub social life (2018, 45). May argued that there is an implicit rationale held by the owners of nightclubs that practice velvet rope racism: "the mere presence of undesirable racial or ethnic groups in nightclubs

---

[122] Interviewed 7 October 2016

[123] Hendricks, Jay. "I don't get into Catwalk because I'm Coloured" Published 22 February 2012. Accessed 15 May 2018.
http://www.bonfiire.com/stellenbosch/2012/02/i-dont-get-into-catwalk-because-im-Coloured/

Username: Tintin. "Catwalk, it's time for another talk". Published 25 April 2016. Accessed 15 May 2018.
http://www.bonfiire.com/stellenbosch/2016/04/catwalk-its-time-for-another-talk/

B. Phil. "Stellenbosch club accused of racial profiling". Uploaded 18 March 2012. Accessed 15 May 2018.
https://www.youtube.com/watch?v=2W9oPbPuanM

negatively affects the social desirability of those nightclubs for the targeted clientele" and that this could happen because of "their patrons' negative racial attitudes, the owner's assessment of profitability, or simply the owner's racist attitudes" (2018: 45). These practices prevent people from different racial and ethnic backgrounds from being able to interact with each other in space outside of classrooms. This hindrance from being able to access places where people can transition from acquaintances— having met out of proximity— towards friends— a more personalized association.

Hugo pointed out that "the club scene still has a lot of Afrikaans, so there is a lot of Afrikaans people. People of colour rarely go there, myself included".[124] It is significant Hugo perceived clubs as being a very Afrikaans space which people who were Black, Coloured or Indian rarely go as he sees them as spaces which would be very far out of his comfort zone. Randy had a different experience of clubs and bars. She noted different bars attract different ethnic groups: "when I go with my White friends we go to Mystics, Bohemia, or Happy Oak." Bohemia and Happy Oak were predominantly sit-down bars, Bohemia sometimes had live music and had a foosball table. Neither had a dance-floor. Mystics, short for Mystic Boer, had a specified dance-floor upstairs but also had areas to sit down on the ground floor.

"When I go with my Coloured friends," Randy continued, "it's normally Cubana, Entourage, Stones, although we also go to Mystics because the music!" Cubana and Entourage were both known for being places for dancing. Cubana also had hubbly[125] and tables to sit at. Both Cubana and Entourage in the Stellenbosch imaginary, as I understood it, were places that people who were Black, Coloured or Indian went. Randy focused on people's taste in music:

> "The music is different. Depending on who I'm going out with I'll go [to different places]. Some of my White friends are like 'you know what? Let's go to Cubana, let's go to Entourage, why we don't we go there?'… some of [my other White friends] you can see it's not really their scene and I respect that."

---

[124] 10 Interviewed November 2017
[125] Also known as hookah or shisha

Here Randy pointed to some of her White friends either not feeling uncomfortable in spaces that were most people were Black, Coloured or Indian, that those friends were willing to cross out of their comfort zone and be in a place with people who did not look like them. Others, either disliked the music in Cubana or Entourage so much that they would not be willing to go there, even with friends who did enjoy the music in those places.

The ability to make friends is contingent first on being able to meet. As was pointed to by Ross, ideas of 'properness' and where people 'belong' constrain people from entering places (2010: 60). Like, like the young, White-Afrikaans man who was going to move in with my roommate, but his mom told him he could not live in Idasvallei because "nice White boys do not live in Coloured areas". Or velvet rope racism as explored by May which obsesses with "the "appropriate distribution of persons in space" (Ross, 2010: 60). The importance of people crossing thresholds is to challenge the vestiges of "Colonialism and apartheid produced racially and ethnically segregated spatialities [...] places of familiarity and those to avoid" (Ross, 2010: 60). Colonialism taught people to stay in their respective zones, the places the most familiar to them. Before and during Apartheid this meant creating "a distinction between places of 'work' and 'home'", people who were Black, Coloured or Indian were allowed to be in the homes of White people but as workers not as guests (Ross, 2010: 60). Similarly, only White police officers, in townships for their work, were allowed in areas meant for people who were Black, Coloured or Indian.

These divisions were apparent during my fieldwork in many ways. Even in the bars and clubs where White people are the most comfortable there will be a few Black or Coloured there: some as patrons and some as the bouncers, bartenders, dishwashers, domestic workers. The remnants of ideas of improperness and the subtle social norms of de facto segregation as Chigumadzi came to understand as a teenager, that "we [White and Black people] were now free to go to school with each other and live in the same suburbs, but interracial love still represented a kind of final frontier yet to be fully explored" (2018); make crossing the divide from either side incredibly difficult. It is difficult as beyond the normal fear of rejection that grips people as they seek out new friends because there is an added layer of going against the grain of social norms.

Hugo spoke about sports as a way of building trust across racial lines. Hugo played on a basketball team organized by his residence with people of different races participating: "You have to work together so you get that energy form them, like I need you, you need me then you just build on that and it becomes a friendship"[126]. Sports teams are co-constituted spaces. Team members are all present voluntarily and work together towards a common goal (try, or wicket). The recreational nature of the team Hugo played on could also be key as Siphe, had quite a different experience. Siphe played netball at the inter-varsity level for Stellenbosch. Her experience on the team stood out in her mind as having made her feel Black:

> When I got there, I was the only Black girl there and I wondered why Black girls were not there when they love netball so much. Then I realised that it's not the most welcoming space for people of colour or English people because we get coached in Afrikaans"[127].

These different experiences with sports show that the similar activities can be alienating or comfortable based on how those spaces are built, thus linking back to Demant and Ostergaard concept of 'zoning'. In their study, teenagers co-creating a space that is "a collectively created space, distinct from other spaces created with parental or adult supervision […]" allows them to socialize feeling independently and create new bonds with their peers and friends (2007: 533). Thus, the same group of teenagers in the physically same space but having it been put together by adults who were supervising would not have those same bonds. In the case of sports at Stellenbosch, when it is a co-constituted space, as in Hugo's intramural team, it seems as though people from different backgrounds can be comfortable, given Hugo's experience of having a diverse group of teammates. Whereas Siphe's experience of playing on a varsity team, where the

---

[126] Interviewed 10 November 2017
[127] Interviewed 2 March 2017

space is curated by the coaches who have a degree of power beyond that which members on the team have, Siphe was the only Black woman on her team and she felt very alienated.

Conclusion

This chapter has argued that the overwhelming whiteness at Stellenbosch remains a barrier for people who are Black, Coloured or Indian and White people to be able to easily enter into friendships with one another. The first section of the chapter examined the concept of whiteness in the South African context: its linkages to power and privilege (beyond physical whiteness) as well as that White people in South Africa have always been a minority. Their minority status makes whiteness in South Africa less naturalized than in other settler-colonial contexts where White settlers have become the majority. Next, theories of place were noted and tied to the Stellenbosch context. Namely that people infuse places with meaning in such a way that the physical place becomes tied to their identity. Whiteness, which is already linked to power, is associated with Stellenbosch because if a place has been coded historically as an influential place of whiteness, people who are not part of that same form of whiteness are made to be outsiders from the outset.

The final theoretical section defined characteristics of friendship. It considered some nuances of why making friends can be difficult. I explained that many people seek to stay within their comfort zone, especially in liminal settings. In this context, students are conscious of cultural differences which can cause stumbling blocks. I thought through how people would want to be treated, imagining we sat behind a veil of ignorance, raising the question of how we would treat a newly arrived neighbour. This brought up the risk of rejection or awkwardness involved in social interactions. Social interactions require someone to make the first move; that person has to be willing to take on a degree of vulnerability. A necessary step to even being able to make the first move is the act of meeting. If there are no co-constituted spaces where everyone is equally comfortable then it is unlikely people will be able or capable to make the first move. Finally, I noted that a lack of physical touch between people from different racial groups implies that White students and Black, Coloured, and Indian students lack those bonds. Thus, it seems that people are not learning to care about one another across racial lines.

Drawing on the experiences of my participants, I have established that Stellenbosch is very White in relation to the rest of South Africa and the African continent and that these demographics cause Black students to feel out of place at the University. Furthermore, the need for friendships to be personal rather than just proximal— like a member of a group project for a class— there is a lack of spaces where it is easy for interracial friendships to blossom. My experience and the experiences of my participants indicate spaces in Stellenbosch were coded either implicitly through a confirmation bias effect of similar people going to the same place, or through more active means like velvet rope racism. However, spaces that are co-constituted and zoned by peers, such as intramural sports, are hopeful and allow for a personalisation of relationships to a greater degree than places like residences, as was the experience of Wanijuk.

Chapter 6

"You Can't Just Leave Us Here"– Caught Between Bloemfontein and Perth

Introduction

Chapter 5 focused on the difficulties and barriers that people who were Black and Coloured Stellenbosch felt about their sense of belonging there. This chapter focuses on the identity crisis of Afrikaners in South Africa (van Zyl-Hermann, 2014), where Stellenbosch acts as a central battleground, particularly the process of reinvention and sense-making of the identities rooted in being White and Afrikaans. The debates around the language policy particularly between Open Stellenbosch and Afriforum gave me the opportunity to have conversations with my participants about access to and how transformation at Stellenbosch also speaks to transformations happening in Afrikaner identity. Steyn's research noted a sense of alienation in the Afrikaner community from the rest of South Africa, that (at the time of her research) the community was experiencing a strong need to "preserve something of value, rehabilitate some element of Afrikaner idealism […], not see everything the Afrikaner stood for dismantled" (Steyn, 2004: 154). Steyn argues:

> The pursuit of "true" Afrikanerness has been central to Afrikaner ethnicism and sought to hegemonize this version of whiteness in competition to other discursive possibilities. Afrikaner ideologues placed a great deal of emphasis on the organic link between culture and nationhood, suggestion that the volk was "a natural, pure, and integrated entity" (Dubow 1992. 12). [This...] has involved Afrikaners in ongoing, self-conscious, and contested discursive activity for more than a century- the quest for the holy grail of "originary unity and racial purity" (Steyn, 2004: 148).

I witnessed the ongoing contest that Steyn describes among my informants and at Stellenbosch. On the one extreme sits a protest witnessed on the rooiplein in October

2017. It was small, there were maybe 15 to 20 people present. A Kaapse Klopse band walked toward the Jan Marais statue. Those that were not playing instruments carried signs that said: "Afrikaans is 'n taal van dekoloniasasie"[128], that Afrikaans was the victim of "kultural terrorisme"[129], and other slogans of a similar nature. The band was outnumbered by the group of White people marching behind them. The band stopped playing music, the protester gave speeches, but only White people spoke. Including the woman who asserted that it was the divine mission of Afrikaners to be in South Africa.[130]

---

[128] Trans. "Afrikaans is a language for decolonization"
[129] Trans. cultural terrorism
[130] Protest occurred 21 October 2017.

Figure 13: Language Protest on the Rooiplein

I was with a friend who was a fluent Afrikaans speaker who translated. She spoke to the protesters for me in Afrikaans and helped me get acquainted with them. Only one protester was a student at Stellenbosch. At the end of the protest the White members of the group put money into a hat for the Klopse band which implied the Coloureds at the protest were being paid to be there. I wanted to interview the Stellenbosch student that was involved, so I asked Kristina to introduce me to the protesters and was able to get her phone number. Unfortunately, that interview never took place as shortly afterwards I initially sent her a WhatsApp message, she seemed to stop receiving my messages.[131] Though I was unable to have a more thorough conversation with the supporters of this protest, their blatant references to the Apartheid national anthem and having called the Black people of South Africa "uncivilized", implied to me that some Afrikaners do not see much of the past as bad or wrong.

Conversely, I understood people making good faith efforts to confront their historical baggage. When I asked if Christoff identified as "White, Afrikaans", he smiled coyly. He told me that there is dispute within the community as younger people prefer not to call themselves Afrikaners but

---

[131] They were only getting one tick on WhatsApp which means a message has been delivered but not received.

he would rather say "I know I'm Afrikaans-speaking and White but I'm not an Afrikaner". He believed they did this because the word 'Afrikaner' "carries the weight of other things", particularly Afrikaner nationalism and Apartheid. Young White, Afrikaans-speaking peoples in his mind looked to "wash [...] their hands with innocence" by approaching the issue of identity by caveating the idea of "Afrikaner" with "I'm not completely comfortable identifying as... It's almost as if identifying as an Afrikaner means suddenly Verwoerd is wandering closer to you", he said[132]

More and more Afrikaners are leaving South Africa. Pinning down the number of White-South Africans leaving is difficult as the government does not keep emigration records. The numbers are disputed but range from 520,000 to 850,000 from 1989-2006, with the rate of emigration rising (Griffiths & Prozesky, 2010: 28) (Singh, 2017). Though it is not only White-South Africans leaving South Africa they make up a significant proportion of the emigrants. Historically, the nickname for English-White-South Africans among Afrikaners was 'soutie' or 'soutie-piel'[133]. Afrikaners saw English settlers as having one foot in South Africa and one foot in England (and thus their genitals hanging in the saltwater) (Redkozubova, 2013: 222-223). Perhaps English-South Africans are thought of as being more willing to leave South Africa (many still holding dual citizenship with the United Kingdom), more than 500,000 South Africans live in Britain alone (though not all of these are White, and some could be Afrikaners) (The Economist, 2008). There is an increasing willingness to leave also from Afrikaners, particularly among young, White-South Africans who are leaving at such a high rate that their population profile is regarded as abnormal (Steyn & Foster, 2008: 26). My fieldwork ties this willingness to the ability to speak fluent English. The burden of post-Apartheid identity crisis makes Afrikaners want to flee South Africa, in hopes of escaping it.

In Stellenbosch, there is a notable focus on the international. Wine farms fly flags from Britain, Germany, and the United States, and sometimes other countries like France, the Netherlands and China, as a gesture to make

---

[132] Interviewed 2 November 2016.
[133] *Trans*. Salty, salty penis.

international tourists welcome. Additionally, internationalization is of concern for the University as Professor Hester Klopper's, a vice-rector, portfolio is of "internationalisation" which is described as a "main priority" (Stellenbosch University). Part of my argument is that the sense of dislocation of Afrikaans is important. It can be connected to the attitudes towards the adoption of English, a language which Afrikaner nationalists historically characterised as a nemesis of the *volk*.[134] There was a strong sense during my fieldwork, that English was understood as a 'global' language 'needed for business' or 'economic opportunities'. The focus on the global rather than the local is a strategy to draw attention from the local. This spoke to the existential struggle for a sense of belonging that Afrikaners are grappling with more broadly in South Africa. It was odd to me that young people who grew up speaking Afrikaans do not imagine working in an Afrikaans environment even though Afrikaners run a substantial amount of economic ventures in South Africa and the legal system in a number of provinces still operates in Afrikaans.

In her study with young Afrikaner men in Stellenbosch, RA Leitch observed informants struggling with what a democratic South Africa meant for their economic security. Johann, one of her informants,

> believed that the previous generation [of Afrikaners], who are mostly retired, were not required to change. No longer economically active, they were able to carry on and live the way they did before 1994. Johann perceived his generation of men as being forced to 'adapt or die,' as change for them is inevitable. […] This conscious strategy of 'adapt or die', was used to bridge the discrepancy the men felt between their past expectations and their perceptions of present economic circumstances. Their expectations of institutional stability can be seen as deriving from the rhetoric of the apartheid government, whose power and authority gave entitlement to the Afrikaners in various institutions. Yet, in view of the new political milieu of affirmative action and BEE these men are shifting from an institutional expectation to a more entrepreneurial notion of employment. In doing so, 'adapt or

---

[134] *Trans*. People.

die' was used to bridge the experienced dissonance. (Leitch, 2005: 43).

My informants are approximately a generation younger than Leitch's and have not yet faced finding a permanent job, but it seems as though younger Afrikaners are seeing English as an indispensable tool during their generation's turn to 'adapt or die'.

Open Stellenbosch framed the use of English at Stellenbosch as part of "its responsibility to redress historical injustices, promote equity and build social cohesion" and chose it as the language to spearhead their campaigns for accessibility at the University (2015). However, for many White-South Africans who if they were only proficient in Afrikaans would stay in South Africa for employment, the exposure to English makes the ability to get employment abroad increase significantly. Those who are most financially well-off and well educated have the means and resume to be able to settle abroad with relative ease. What makes Afrikaners different than other South African citizens with itchy-feet is twofold: first, that Afrikaner nationalism's curation of Afrikaner identity tied Afrikaners to South Africa as their multi-generational African roots made them distinct from the Dutch who stayed in Europe. Afrikaners are often portrayed as having "nowhere else to go" (Swarns, 2000).[135]

Secondly, that there is an intergenerational obligation given the mass amount of privilege and opportunities Afrikaners gained from Apartheid. I acknowledge that White English-speaking South Africans carry a similar historical burden but the combination of the burden and betrayal to historical ideals of Afrikanerdom is what makes the situation with Afrikaners emigrating distinct. This was brought to my attention by Christoff and will be explored more in-depth in this chapter. As was mentioned in Chapter Two, English- and Afrikaans-White-South Africans have become more mixed under Apartheid and into the present. As settlers who have benefited from Apartheid and colonialism, this chapter explores the relationship between belonging and historical obligation.

---

[135] Online newspaper article.

In considering the local, as has been established, the locality of Stellenbosch is "Seen historically as the home of Afrikaner intelligentsia, [it] can be seen as a special place where Afrikaner thoughts and ways of life come together" (Leitch, 2005: 3). By using attitudes towards the English language as my entrée, during my fieldwork I noticed a gap between the beliefs of the White, Afrikaans-speaking university students with whom I was speaking and those being espoused by Afriforum, a group that claims to defend the interest of those very same people. I came to understand that there are barriers to being able to have public discussions about Afrikaner identity when there is much to discuss (See van Zyl-Hermann, 2014). This chapter outlines a theory detailing South African whiteness with specific reference to the idea of the 'Afrikaner' in post-Apartheid South Africa. It gives an overview of social attitudes surrounding emigration and the link of emigration with historical obligation of White-South Africans. Christoff's experiences will be used to illustrate a young Afrikaner confronting questions of emigration and historical obligation.

Mediums of Instruction

Afrikaans is the only language other than English of South Africa's 11 official languages that is used as a medium of instruction in secondary schools and universities. Stellenbosch University was the first university in South Africa to use Afrikaans as a medium of instruction, which was a factor that caused Afrikaans to become more standard and academic (Deumert 2004: 1-2). Thus, in some ways, the ability for Afrikaners to be taught in Afrikaans at university is one of the last vestiges of Apartheid privilege.[136] Officially, Stellenbosch University commits itself to multilingualism "by using the province's three official languages, namely Afrikaans, English, and isiXhosa (Stellenbosch University, 2016: 2). The policy describes the "contextual considerations" for using each language. Afrikaans is cited as having "developed an academic repertoire over decades, to

---

[136] See the special issue of the journal of *Arts and Humanities in Higher Education*, "State of Urgency" eds. Peter Vale & John Higgins; and the writings of Tinyiko Maluleke.

which SU has contributed significantly. Applying and enhancing the academic potential of Afrikaans is a means of empowering a large and diverse community in South Africa" (Stellenbosch University, 2016: 2); contrasted with English characterization of English:

> Speakers of the various South African languages use English to communicate with each other, and English has significant academic, *business and international value*. Therefore, SU uses English routinely, but not exclusively, in its academic administrative, professional and social contexts (Stellenbosch University 2016: 2; emphasis added).

The University itself emphasizes the internationality and commerce potentials of English but does not mention English has much in common with their characterization of Afrikaans. Open Stellenbosch argues that switching to English as a medium of instruction is vital to being able to achieve transformation at Stellenbosch University, English is a means of empowering a large and diverse community in South Africa (Open Stellenbosch, 2015).

Finally, the Stellenbosch language policy characterizes isiXhosa as:

> Used by one of the largest language communities in South Africa. By means of specific initiatives, SU is contributing to the advancement of isiXhosa as a developing academic language in addition to expanding isiXhosa as an internal language of communication (Stellenbosch University 2016: 3).

Thus, despite this, isiXhosa does not seem to warrant usage in the general contexts that English does, like the academic, the administrative, professional or social.

Practically, concerning learning and teaching, there are three different possible approaches to language in the classroom. The first is one referred to as parallel-medium, having separate lectures in Afrikaans and English (Stellenbosch University, 2016: 4). The second and third make up the characteristics that are colloquially referred to as "t-option"[137]. These are classes where both Afrikaans and

---

[137] Translation option

English are used in the same class group or lectures are only in one language. The classes where Afrikaans and English are used in the same group, the University's language policy commits that:

> During each lecture, all information is conveyed at least in English and summaries or emphasis on content are also given in Afrikaans. Questions in Afrikaans and English, at the least, answered in the language of the question (Stellenbosch University, 2016: 5).

As well as committing to offering other "facilitated learning opportunities" like "office hours, or routinely schedule tutorials and practicals"; and in first year classes making simultaneous interpreting available during each lecture, a service which must be requested to the faculty in later years of study (Stellenbosch University, 2016: 5).

In classes only offered in one language (either English or Afrikaans), the University's language policy makes simultaneous interpreting available in English or in Afrikaans (as needed), as well as making "facilitated learning opportunities" like "office hours, or routinely schedule tutorials and practical's" available to students in the appropriate language for them (Stellenbosch University 2016: 5). The one exception is if students unanimously agree (by means of a secret ballot) to have a module presented in Afrikaans only or English only (Stellenbosch University, 2016: 6).

The confrontations surrounding the Language Policy have brought many questions of identity to the forefront because this policy is the mechanism Afriforum have used to keep Afrikaans in classrooms. Publicly, people have tied Afrikaans offerings at Stellenbosch to accessibility of university to Coloured people. For example, Giliomee writes that:

> Coloured Afrikaans-speakers are the community with the lowest participation rate in tertiary education. A switch by Stellenbosch to predominantly English-medium instruction will be a lethal blow to this community's hope to shake off centuries of neglect under slavery, segregation and apartheid (2015).

There are complex politics around the use of Afrikaans/Kaapse and English by Coloured people particularly in the Western Cape, but it is notable that there are differences between the 'standard'[138] Afrikaans used in the University and the Afrikaans spoken in Cape Coloured communities. For example, the experience Shane, a Coloured and Afrikaans-first language speaker, who initially registered for his studies in Afrikaans but switched to English because:

> Afrikaans here is different from the one I did in school and it has to be in full Afrikaans sentences. I did my first essay in Afrikaans when I spoke to my tutor about postgrad. She said it's better to start with English now as the transition will be difficult in my postgrad years. I also started challenging myself and did my work in English and even my lectures I take in English now.[139]

There are certainly Coloured-Afrikaans speakers who benefit from the language policy but there are others alienated by it, like Shane. Ross notes that Cape Flats-Afrikaans is "considered of low status compared to the slower forms of *suiwer-Afrikaans*, ostensibly closer to Dutch" which demonstrates how proximity to Europe continues to create value (2010: 139). The boundaries created by dialects and language are surmountable. For example, Ross notes the impressive way that her informant code-switched within Afrikaans and learned English quickly during the time of her fieldwork. However, the experiences of my informants speak to the external factors that cause even those that have a common language to feel separated from one another.

It is worth observing some of the discourse surrounding the policy. There are, however, gaps between the ambition of the policy and the reality as experienced by students. Pierre de Vos notes that:

> Some Black students at Stellenbosch argue that this policy, in effect, discriminates against them because the interpretation service provided is often of a poor quality. Even when the

---

[138] Also known as "*Suiwer*" Afrikaans.
[139] Interviewed 2 February 2017.

interpretation is adequate something is invariably lost when you have to rely on a translator whispering into your ear (2015).

De Vos was writing when more Afrikaans was used in Stellenbosch classrooms, but what is particularly important is that students still felt as though they had missed something in class, even when the translation was adequate. The evidence of this thesis aligns with the De Vos' observation of the "Afrikaans-first" attitude that Stellenbosch has held historically: "the "Afrikaans-first" that Stellenbosch University publicly supported until recently created "an atmosphere in which Black students are deliberately or inadvertently 'Othered' and made to feel unwelcome because they cannot speak the language of those who belong to the dominant culture at the University" (2015). However, the rest of this chapter will be dedicated to examining the effects of greater use of English on the dominant culture at the University.

Being White/African/Afrikaner: History and Obligation

The end of Apartheid caused a massive shift in the discourses surrounding whiteness in South Africa. Historically, Afrikaners were characterized by the English as less White, but the empowerment Afrikaners received from the Apartheid regime led to them having greater power over the discourse of South African whiteness. Steyn notes that Afrikaner discourses of whiteness use the British as a point of contrast:

> There certainly has always been an element of defiance in Afrikaner whiteness against the more secure, powerful, whiteness of the English who had the culture of Empire backing them. As a resistant whiteness, the constellation of the victim has been highly salient in the discourses of Afrikaner whiteness. They saw themselves as besieged, having to fight for the "right" to their own brand of White supremacy (Steyn, 2004: 148).

Steyn argues for viewing White-South Africans as having a diasporic kind of whiteness. Though, unlike other diasporas that are often drawn together by suffering, Steyn argues that "Eurocentric expectations of privilege relative to 'others', which comes to be experienced as the norm, forms the common, uniting structure of feelings" (2005: 126). The liberation of South Africa from Apartheid means that "White-South Africans cannot assume the same privileges, with such ease [as they have historically], when state power is overly committed to breaking down racial privilege" (2007: 422). Elsewhere, Steyn notes that "White-South Africans draw toward White people elsewhere: "home" is where other Whites are" thereby explaining their moves to places like Australia and Canada: places where they have necessary reason to settle other than a continued proximity to whiteness (2005: 126). As transnational media is dominated by Western interests, there is a disproportionate amount of coverage of the victimhood of White people living in Africa as being "under threat and in need of Western sympathy, if not protection" (van Zyl-Hermann & Boersema, 2017: 656).

Emigrating is seen as a solution for some. Griffiths and Prozesky argue that the failure of White-South Africans "to come to terms with the historical forces that shaped their identity and to recognise the legacy of a past that cannot be erased by emigrating" (2010: 29). Afrikaners cannot escape the fact that the Apartheid regime was put in place in their name (Steyn, 2004: 150). Louw characterizes part of Apartheid as "a state-sponsored attempt to actively halt the Anglicization of South Africa" where "the Afrikaans language received significant political patronage from the Nation-Party-run state" through institutions like schools, the media and the state bureaucracy itself (Steyn, 2004: 45). Christoff wanted to face the historical forces that shaped his identity head on. He noted the close link he saw between Afrikaners learning English and moving abroad.

Based on her research, Steyn points out a number of tropes of "White Talk" by White-South Africans. The two examples she drew on which I encountered most often were privileging the global over the local and refusing the past (Steyn, 2005: 128-129). As Hall argues, "identities are constructed within, not outside, discourse, we need to understand them as produced in specific historical and institutional sites within specific discursive formations and practices, by specific enunciative strategies", thus part of this chapter is using historical context to further illustrate the tie some feel (or don't feel) to the place of Stellenbosch and the use of English in this historically Afrikaans place (1996: 4).

Louw notes the shifting context and power relations during the 1960s, 1970s, and 1980s, when Afrikaners gained access to capital and became more integrated with the English: "Anglos/Anglicization was no longer considered the key threat to Afrikaner identity. Decolonization pressures and threat of Black majority rule set the new contextual framework within which Afrikaners constructed their identities" (2004: 51). On the other hand, among White-South Africans who stay there is still the consideration that they "may claim belonging and African identity, but nevertheless remain part of structures of racialized power and privilege that mean they carry little of the burden African identity may otherwise entail" (van Zyl-Hermann & Boersema 2017: 658). White people claiming belonging on the continent increasingly seems to be representing themselves in a rhetoric of victimhood or besiegement (van Zyl-Hermann & Boersema, 2017: 658).

During the language debates at Stellenbosch, however, there became a sort of confluence between these two identities as calls for more access to English were made by Open Stellenbosch, "a movement of predominantly Black students and staff at the University who refuse to accept the current pace of transformation" (Open Stellenbosch, 2015). Afriforum began making the preservation of the Stellenbosch language policy an issue and fought to retain Afrikaans as a medium of instruction (News24Wire, 2016). When I spoke with students at the University, many of them had diverse and nuanced opinions which were very different from those expressed by Open Stellenbosch or Afriforum. Many of the young, White-South Africans I spoke with were grappling with their place in the New South Africa.

Post-Apartheid, Afrikanerness was experiencing 'dislocation' (as noted by Steyn (2004) and Louw (2004)):

> [dislocation] can be understood as occurring when social changes result in the previously unseen or denied being made forcibly visible, when the representations and constructions that shaped identities are recognized, and the boundaries of the

approved have moved to such an extent that new horizons for the social imaginary have to be forged (Steyn. 2004: 150).

The Afrikaner identity has historically been reliant on Afrikaner nationalism which based itself on "religious, racial, and cultural purity, superiority, calling, and the struggle for autonomy against oppression—which included the struggle for an independent language" (Verwey & Quayle, 2012: 553). Thus, the end of the Old South Africa, for many Afrikaners is accompanied by feelings of loss which compounded with the TRC, which attached elements of shame and guilt— of disgrace—to the social positioning of the Afrikaner (Steyn, 2004: 150) (Leitch, 2005: 2). Du Toit witnessed this sense of loss when he was on a road trip in the Free State: "it was so strange the way they thought about apartheid, about the government in the past, still like reflecting on it. They had this positive view of it and some of the stuff, and I'm like what? Wow!" [140] In some circles, these sentiments have been questioned through interacting with the Fallist movements[141]. However, many reactions to the Fallist movement from White-South Africans were negative, as was reflected in popular media which "condemned the Fallist protests as disruptive and infringing on peace and tranquillity the mythic rainbow nation offers" (Mpofu, 2017: 364).

In the Canadian settler-colonial context, Paula Reagan's work argues that "non-Natives [in Canada] must struggle to confront their own colonial mentality, moral indifference, and historical ignorance as part of a massive truth telling about Canada's past and present relationship with the original inhabitants of this land" (Alfred, 2010: x). As part of their settlement of a class-action lawsuit against the Canadian state, survivors of residential schools paid for a Truth and Reconciliation Commission to document the history and impacts of the program residential schools as overseen by the government of Canada (Truth and Reconciliation Commission of Canada). Reagan argues that racist attitudes

---

[140] Interviewed 18 August 2017

[141] The term *Fallist* refers to movements like #RhodesMustFall and #FeesMustFall which sought to disrupt the post-Apartheid status quo (Mpofu 2017: 353).

are still alive in Canada today, rooted in settler historical myths and colonial mind-sets (Reagan, 2010: 6).

She advocates that Canadians need to ask themselves difficult questions to confront how policies like the Indian Residential School policy were able to continue (2010: 6). Less than three years after the release of the Canadian TRC report, Chelsea Vowel[142] declared that "reconciliation is dead" in the wake of the acquittal a White farmer who killed a young Indigenous man[143] (Gleason, 2018).

Twenty years after the end of the South African TRC, similar scepticism is coming to light (Borowski, 2014). Obviously, TRC at the end of Apartheid is a very different context as it was part of the agreement reached in negotiations at the end of Apartheid to reach a peaceful transfer of power to democracy (Lansing & King, 1998: 759). Mangcu notes that Mandela had to make many compromises with the Apartheid regime to prevent violence and resistance from White settlers, government officials and citizens alike (2003: 106). Recently, many young South Africans have expressed criticism of Mandela's presidency (SAHO, 2018) (Boshomane, 2016). All this to say, that the apologies and efforts to make amends between settlers and indigenous peoples in contexts of settler-colonialism have left those being apologized to feeling as though justice has not been served.

'Should I Stay, or Should I go?': Emigration and Remaining

In the early 1990s, there were social norms that painted White-South Africans planning to emigrate as "too cowardly or too racist to make the effort to live in the new South Africa" but Griffiths and Prozesky note that norm has waned to a point where by the 2010s emigration had become less something to be ashamed of and more of a practical move (2010: 28). The main reason often given for the large exodus of White-South Africans as crime (van Rooyen, 2000: ix). Other reasons include: "Weak political leadership, uncertain

---

[142] A Metis public intellectual.
[143] See Joe Friesen: "Gerald Stanley acquitted in the shooting death of Colten Boushie"

long-term economic stability, poor government, and municipal operation com[e] together into a pervasive, pessimistic belief that "things are getting worse" all contribute to a general sense of unease" (Griffiths & Prozesky, 2010: 29). Enclaves of White-South Africans can now be found in most large cities of the English-speaking part of the developed world (van Rooyen 2000: xii). This is significant as given the historical relationship of Afrikaners to English mass exoduses to Anglophone countries demonstrates a contextual willingness to use English to get to where they want. My focus is on that most of the people leaving are "affluent and educated", as many of the White-South Africans at Stellenbosch fit this description (Griffiths & Prozesky, 2010: 28).

The choice to stay in South Africa does not necessarily indicate a willingness to be part of society. Ballard notes the tactic of some South African-White people of so-called 'semigration', a combination of emigration and segregation that is used to retreat to self-contained comfort zones (Ballard in Blaser & Van der Westhuizen, 2012: 386). To illustrate, "the largest Afrikaans newspaper Rapport use the notion *inwaarste migrasie* [144] to denote an inward turn and withdrawal from public life among Afrikaners"; so, while physically present are returning to an exclusivist ethnicity rather than joining the others in pursuit of a rainbow nation (Blaser & van der Westhuizen, 2012: 386). Less drastically, semigration can also be considered gated communities and enclosed neighbourhoods (Ballard, 2004: 52). These less drastic measures allow those who cannot emigrate (those who do not have the significant resources or the particular life circumstances (like higher education or language)) to continue to live exclusivist, separate lives almost as if Apartheid has not ended (Ballard, 2004: 60).

Another strategy of Afrikaner identity re-invention involves "'the globalization of the Afrikaner' through an embrace of neoliberalism, in particular its dictum of 'depoliticizing social and economic powers'" like the trade union Solidarity which, though it avoids explicitly referencing neoliberalism, advocates for a "competitive 'growth-oriented' free market with low company taxes" thereby corresponding

---

[144] *Trans:* inward migration.

with key tenets of neoliberalism (Blaser & Van der Westhuizen, 2012: 386-387) (van Zyl-Hermann & Boersema, 2017).

Those White-South Africans who choose to stay in South Africa have choices between encouraging the 'Others' who surround them assimilate—which "attempts to control desegregation by reforming otherness" (Ballard, 2004: 64)—, to semigrate—thereby acknowledging the impossibility of assimilation and a failure of the market to defend Western modern cities from the 'Other'—, or to integrate (Ballard, 2004: 64). Integration means an openness to accepting unassimilated otherness, thus engaging with it without trying to reform it to resemble the familiar (Ballard, 2004: 64).

Discussion and Hierarchy among White-Afrikaans People

Leitch noted the prevalence of institutional identification among her young male participants because the institutions of Apartheid meant they "were allocated a social identity that was strongly connected to power and privilege in terms of education, job security, and material assets" (2005: 31). She argued institutional identification was being an extension of the generational hierarchy: respect and deference to authority during childhood expected of Afrikaner children: "In almost every conversation with the men about their familial upbringing mention was made about the childhood expectation that one never 'back chat' one's parents. Deon, for example, noted that it was a gross violation of generational respect to speak up against any adult" (2005: 25). She observed that these same norms were present in relation to the men's attitude to the church as well as the education system "which was characterized by a strict adherence to prescribed codes regarding behaviour towards teachers and principals" (2005:25). My research observed a similar phenomenon when I explored why there had not been more public debate about Afrikaner identity. This institutional identification can be witnessed in a statement by Hein Gonzales, a spokesperson for Afriforum-Jeung:

> It is necessary for personnel, students and alumni that are pro-Afrikaans, to start using the institutional decision-making

structures of the US to ensure the place of Afrikaans on the campus in the long term. It can only be done if personnel, students and alumni participate actively in the process followed to compose *these structures* (Batt 2016, emphasis added).

This call to action shows how some people believe Afrikaans needs to be defended against the imminent threat of English becoming the primary medium of instruction at Stellenbosch (Batt, 2016). However, there would still be Afrikaans offerings even if English became the 'primary' language of instruction. Some circles of the Afrikaner/Afrikaans community believe the loss of higher functions of a language[145] leads to a loss of prestige of a language and thus, with it, a lowering of its usage in everyday life, as written about by the Afrikaner scholar JC Steyn (1980). Afrifourm, whose headquarters are in Pretoria, flew Hein Gonzales to Stellenbosch to debate against Open Stellenbosch (USDV, 2015). Instead of the Cape evangelizing the interior to protect Afrikaans from the influence of outside groups, it is now the interior evangelizing the importance of protection from outside groups to those at the Cape.

For example, my ex-boyfriend was a peripheral member of a group called the Volksverraaiers[146] as was Megan. Megan told me the group was founded after the prim of a residence spoke out:

> appealing to the Afrikaner-nation to think twice about the way they were trying to preserve their culture through the language issue and trying to get them to think with an open mind. Then he was called traitors to the Afrikaans culture then we made a group on campus to show that not all Afrikaans people were the Afriforum types.

There is criticism that the media tried "to make it seem like all Afrikaners have always thought the same" (Citizen, 2016). Organisations picked up on by the media are Afriforum and Solidarity who pushed a specific narrative of Afrikaner identity rooted deeply in Afrikanerdom. Furthermore, these organisations imply that those who

---

[145] That is, in a university setting.
[146] *Trans* "traitor of the volk", a word with deep meaning to Afrikaners

supported and held the views of their organisations are the 'true' Afrikaners (Hatton, 2015). Though Afriforum does represent many Afrikaner, reporting 200,000 members paying R30 per month to maintain their membership (Fairbanks 2017). Some of the informants expressed some sympathy with the cause of Afriforum, most did not align with the rhetoric they used.

Young, White, Afrikaans home language speakers have been shaped by discourse. Post-Apartheid, there was a massive tonal shift in Afrikaner media platforms from the ideology of Afrikaner nationalism to the 'ideology-free ideology' of consumerism. Simultaneously, there was an attempt to redefine the Afrikaans language and culture as a saleable commodity, rather than a marker of 'race' or ethnicity. Afrikaans media also engaged in new Afrikaans identity politics (Wasserman 2010: 22). The new identity politics of formerly Afrikaner centric platforms like *Die Burger*[147] have given focused attention to language issues that are particularly directed at the White-Afrikaans speakers who tend to have a greater fear of the 'extinction' of the Afrikaans language more than brown and Black-Afrikaans speakers. Though Black and brown Afrikaans-speakers outnumber White-speakers, White-speakers still hold a significantly greater amount of economic power.

Language and Identity at Stellenbosch

At the University, I found a wide spectrum of beliefs and understandings about the roles of Afrikaans and English and to what extent each should be used in the classroom. Some passionately supported use of Afrikaans but all spoke to the needs of accessibility: that Afrikaans should not be used at the cost of students who do not understand the language. Many saw multilingualism as an asset. For example, Freddie, a White, Afrikaans-speaking law student spoke about his bilingualism as an asset, he described his classes where lecture slides were read in English and Afrikaans as getting "taught in two languages for the same price" [148]. For him the protests

---

[147] A conservative Afrikaner newspaper.
[148] Interviewed 2 March 2017

surrounding language brought a sense of awareness about himself:

> […] then things started changing with the protest regarding language. It was weird in that it was a first time I was confronted by, I would say, my privilege in that sense. And it was quite something to get over, and to get used to. But it wasn't much of an issue for me, although I think there a lot of people who it is still a massive issue to them. Especially to Afrikaans speakers who were taught in Afrikaans from primary and high schools, so for them to suddenly think in English academically is quite a shift to make. [149]

Freddie grew up in Mpumalanga initially in Komatipoort and then in Nelspruit.[150] Though he spoke Portuguese and Afrikaans as a child he lost touch with his Portuguese heritage but began to speak English and some Swati in addition to his Afrikaans. As a bilingual person, Freddie may not have noticed the benefits that accrued from it without conversations and perspectives from people who were not bilingual, both from the side of those who can only learn in English and from that of those Afrikaans speakers for whom learning in English is a challenge. He had some friends from Afrikaans-speaking home and schools who really struggled with the new language policy:

> Yes, I pity them that they have to make this shift of language, it is also a life shift. And I think it is quite cruel in a sense and I think that the University can help them land a bit softer. Because I had some friends who called me and cried that they can't get over this shift after three years and now the system has changed. [151]

Another informant, Jason commented that multilingualism was a privilege to have that was bestowed on him by parents whose choices meant that he picked up isiXhosa and Afrikaans at a young age. He spoke to the kinds

---

[149] Interviewed 2 March 2017
[150] Which was renamed Mbombela in 2009, though it was protested by the Lowveld Chamber of Business and Tourism (see Mbuli 2014)
[151] Interviewed 2 March 2017

of insights he received from being trilingual in English, Afrikaans and isiXhosa, emphasizing that speaking people's languages was significant to communicating and understanding people's viewpoints because:

> they can express in their own language but you also by understanding you understand more than just the language you understand the culture as well where they're coming from. I can understand the Afrikaans culture and their sentiments, and I can understand the Xhosa culture and their sentiments and then the English as well. When you put that together you can see how South Africa in the past has had vast divides between those three. Then you're like "wow, okay I can be all three". And from the past they've had such big differences but, yet it shouldn't be that way. You bridge that gap and you look past all of that and you get past things so easily in life because you understand and speak and understand the culture. That makes a big difference.[152]

However, in addition to opening doors and creating greater understanding, the knowledge of a particular language can be a signalling mechanism for more exclusivist tendencies. Freddie noted how some people still use the ability to command Afrikaans as a signalling mechanism for trust: "big business Afrikaans people in Afrikaans it would work well since it has a massive psychological difference if you work with someone and they are part of your ethnic identity"[153].

This kind of exclusivism was what I expected to find among the White students at Stellenbosch. During my time in Open Stellenbosch before I started my fieldwork, I was enthralled in a binary, Black and White narrative of Stellenbosch University. White people who were not explicitly for us, I believed, were pro-Afrikaans, anti-Black, and clearly did not understand mechanisms for substantive equality. Part of my process during my fieldwork was using the hermeneutic circle of Hans-Georg Gadamer to help counteract my biases. Gadamer argues, in the context of one's interaction with text, that one be explicit about one's

---

[152] Interviewed 1 March 2017
[153] Interviewed 2 March 2017

prejudice: "The important thing is to be aware of one's own bias, so that the text can present itself in all its otherness and thus assert its own truth against one's own fore-meanings" (Gadamer 1960: 282).

I was surprised and pleased to meet Justin who challenged my preconceived notions of what Afrikaans-speaking White people believed about the presence of Afrikaans at Stellenbosch University. Justin grew up in Pretoria in an Afrikaans-speaking home and was a Bachelor of Science in Human Life but ultimately wanted to study medicine and become a doctor. Justin identified as Afrikaner but seemed baffled by the University's choice to continue to offer Afrikaans as a medium of instruction. Justin was educated in English for his entire life, but English was not spoken in his home, only Afrikaans.

> A lot of people turn to feel like Afrikaans is under attack at the moment, because personally I believe it shouldn't be at the University. I don't understand why because the world is in English, so I don't know why you would teach in a language that is only spoken by eight percent of the population in the country. So, it's a bit counter. I understand why the University is Afrikaans because it started in Afrikaans and the country was very Afrikaans. I just believe that time has passed now. You want to be world class and you can't be world class in Afrikaans. You can try, but you are not going to be able to work in Afrikaans. You can't go overseas; you won't be international.[154]

The link Justin provided for the importance of English lying outside of South Africa demonstrates this fixation on the international. When I noted that there are still quite a few companies in South Africa that operated in Afrikaans, Justin retorted that those companies were:

> Only in South Africa though, and the world is a global market now. It's not just working in South Africa, but if you want to stay in the country then it is cool. But if you want to expand then you can't... well you can, but it's going to be difficult.[155]

---

[154] Interviewed 1 March 2017
[155] Interviewed 1 March 2017

His phrasing implies that English is an important step to being able to work outside the country and alludes to international connections being particularly important for, presumably, the growth of a business or person's professional network. The fixation on internationality notions at a desire to join superiority within Balibar's framework of race without races which privileges connections to the international community (1991, 25).

Similar concerns were raised by Philna, a second year philosophy, politics, and economics student who took all of her classes in English. For her, the practical benefits of English outweighed loyalty to the Afrikaans language:

> Although, I am proud to be an Afrikaner, relatively I like being an Afrikaner. But I feel that English is more important to be able to speak it well professionally. And in an academic sense that's how the world operates. Being able to write in Afrikaans is not going to help you that much.[156]

Philna's post-graduate ambitions were to become a psychologist. She said could imagine herself practicing in both English and Afrikaans, but it was important to speak English "professionally". Similarly, Justin's ambition to become a doctor made him feel he would need to be comfortable knowing a few languages but his academic work would be in English. He emphasized Afrikaans is "definitely going to carry on as a living language" but did not see its life as tied to academia:

> It will definitely live on because the Afrikaans population in South Africa is very strong. Just because people are not using it academically does not mean people are not going to speak it. I mean it is a language and it is going to be carried down. It will definitely take a bit of a back foot, but if you speak Afrikaans at home, you are not going to stop speaking it. I mean, I can't imagine speaking English to my parents, it would just feel weird.[157]

---

[156] Interviewed 21 February 2017
[157] Interviewed 21 February 2017

Many informants, like Justin, spoke with great fondness about Afrikaans. Justin's aversion to speaking English with his parents and his understanding of English as an academic language connotes Afrikaans having a particular level of intimacy that is shared between family and people that one is close to. An analogy would be if one always hugged their family members and suddenly started shaking their hands instead. Others spoke with similar fondness about other languages. Like Jason, for whom isiXhosa signalled a particular sense of home: "We'll in our household speak Xhosa to each other because there are somethings you just can't say in English like that. You can just express yourself better in that way. And it's so cool. I miss it when I'm here." [158] Or Siphe, a Zulu woman I spoke with who found comfort in speaking isiZulu: "I honestly become so happy when I speak to someone in Zulu who is from Johannesburg because we understand each other and it's refreshing in a space where we always speak English." [159]

Different languages also allow access to different kinds of privileges. Melissa, a Zulu engineering student, spoke to why it was problematic for instruction at universities to only be available in Afrikaans or English as it excludes people who are unable to speak those languages. At meetings in her residence, people who were more comfortable in Afrikaans would speak and have someone translate into English. She did not believe the same thing would happen for students speaking languages other than Afrikaans:

> I definitely have a lot of cousins […] who don't speak English as well, anywhere near as well as I do, like at any level, they just don't really speak it and like I feel like the same courtesy would not have been extended to them if they had come here… I don't even think they would have been able to come here because of that.[160]

Thus, even though Melissa's cousins would likely be able to communicate with many people in South Africa due to

---

[158] Interviewed 1 March 2017
[159] Interviewed 21 October 2017
[160] Interviewed 3 November 2016

their fluency in isiZulu because they do not speak English they are functionally barred from the University space.

My initial interview with Christoff was the first time someone had explicitly drawn the links between learning English in university and emigrating, though he wasn't the only one to do so. Freddie also spoke frankly about the fact that most South Africans stay in South Africa. He specifically noted the moral obligation he felt to stay that he cautiously extended to others:

> The reality is that not all of us are going to end up oversees, and we shouldn't I think. The work to be done is here. I don't want to speak in moral terms, but I really feel morally obliged to stay here. We have to try to get people's lives on track, our best prosecutors for example, they leave to go overseas. They are good at what they do, because they have seen some bad shit. That's the same with our doctors, my mom moved to Canada and she is a doctor, and that's the thing, we have lost them. We lost people who can command three languages, never mind the languages, just people who can do stuff are leaving and that is massively frustrating.[161]

Christoff was the first person I met who identifies as Afrikaner and I thought could be characterized as 'progressive'[162]. He grew up about a kilometre from where his father grew up, in Bloemfontein. He described Bloemfontein as a lower-middle class community. Attending Stellenbosch was very intention choice on his part because he looked forward to the "ethos of being at an Afrikaans university"[163] as well as the people he would get to meet here. Additionally, "knowing other people coming from similar background to mine, was a comforting feeling"[164].

While Christoff understood the impulse of his peers who identify as "White, Afrikaans-speaking", he called it cowardly as one is not instantly acquitted of what happened "because

---

[161] Interviewed 2 November 2016
[162] The vocabulary around political beliefs is in a constant state of flux but at the time of writing in 2018, 'progressive' signifies someone on the left side of the political spectrum
[163] Interviewed 2 November 2016
[164] Interviewed 2 November 2016

you decide to call yourself something else"[165]. He placed an importance on the need to acknowledge how the system of Apartheid would have recognised him, an Afrikaner. During our conversation Christoff pointedly corrected me when I said, "Afrikaans people" while implicitly referring to White, Afrikaans-speaking people: "you mustn't say 'Afrikaans people' as there are many other people who speak Afrikaans, even if the history of South Africa has been built on the narrative of Afrikaners". [166]

Christoff believed that those running away from their own history often do so literally:

> Sort of people who tend to say, "I'm White and Afrikaans, not an Afrikaner", I take disproportionate offence at people saying that, those are the people who will move to Perth, they will leave. Then what have you made of our people? Now we are plunderers" we came and we took and we left. [167]

He said that Bloemfontein, where he grew, was "the people that have remained behind are the people who don't have the means to leave, not that they don't want to go to Perth but that they can't go to Perth" [168] as emigration requires a great deal of means that people in Bloemfontein generally do not have. He pointed to the White, Afrikaans speaker elites living in places like the Western Cape and Johannesburg, as those most likely to leave:

> [they are] quick to say country gone to shit, we're just going to take our things and leave because Zuma doing that and that, you just find your poltergeist and you just aim your anger at time. 'Don't have a choice, have to go now'[169]

As pointed out in Chapter One by Christoff, there is an unlikely alliance between Afrikaners looking to Anglicize as an important step on the journey of leaving South Africa and predominantly Black, Coloured and Indian students who do

---

[165] Interviewed 2 November 2016
[166] Interviewed 2 November 2016
[167] Interviewed 2 November 2016
[168] Interviewed 2 November 2016
[169] Interviewed 2 November 2016

not want to have to learn Afrikaans to finish their degrees. As Christoff says:

> English becomes easy compromise because they [White people] want to be international and go to Perth and they [people who are Black, Indian, or Coloured and do not speak Afrikaans] want to understand what's going on in class, so now they have a common way forward. But they come from completely different: One is patently disloyal and the other is marginalized, end up benefitting from the marginalized's needs. It's quite sickening for me. [170]

Marc, the white-Anglophone PhD student, made comments that build on Christoff's indictment of English:

> When I travel I do my best, like two years ago when I was in Spain is did my best, I tried to speak Spanish but it was a godsend when someone could speak English. That's a problem and I think that especially for people like me who went to schools where Afrikaans was a compulsory language as much as there is a requisite on the institution side to open up there is also a responsibility on our side to acknowledge that we are not the ONLY people in this country, this country cannot just be English. You were speaking about how Zulu is a compulsory language in KZN. Why is Xhosa not a compulsory language here? [...] what happened is that English people have gotten off and said "well, you must all speak English" and while I agree there needs be a common language that we can all speak even if some of us are not as good as the others there also needs to be responsibility on those who hold that power to say, "I will do my best to adapt".[171]

Returning to Ballard's options of how White-South Africans can choose to interact with people who were Black, Coloured or Indian in South Africa: forcing people to attend university in English or *suiwer*-Afrikaans can be seen as a tactic of assimilation ("attempts to control desegregation by reforming otherness" (Ballard, 2004: 64)). If language is one of the means by which otherness is demonstrated, then to communicate a common language is needed. By using the

---

[170] Interviewed 2 November 2016
[171] Interviewed 25 October 2016

international prevalence of English as a justification for its use as a lingua franca in South Africa, it is easy to overlook the historical baggage of racial privilege that language carries with it. A willingness to learn an African language would be symbolic of openness to accepting unassimilated otherness, thus engaging with it without trying to reform it to resemble the familiar (Ballard, 2004: 64).

How Afrikaner identity gets positioned and understood is influential in relation to questions of how those people who understand themselves as 'Afrikaners' choose to relate to South Africa. In the view of Freddie:

> I think some of the older generation, like those who were born or grew up in apartheid, like you late 1980s and early 1990s, being called an Afrikaner is being subjected to staying in South Africa in a closed community. Being closed, like being apart, and I think there were really yearning to be world citizens, they didn't want to identify with just this one identity. So many of them fled the country, they really literally fled, like my cousin went to Australia, another to Canada. [172]

Christoff was adamant that the act of fleeing, as Freddie described it, was an incredibly dishonourable thing to do. Speaking about those who leave, he said:

> You don't think about that there are still going to be people that are left behind and stay here. You came, you brought your friends... took a lot of shit from the Black people, and now you left and left your friends to deal with the aftermath. [...] I take huge offense at people who come to study here to get an international qualification and emigrate. You can't just leave us. [173]

At the time when we spoke, Christoff said the issue of Afrikaners selectively using English to their own advantage hadn't come up in internal Afrikaner dialogues. There was a notable divide in the White, Afrikaans/Afrikaner South African community. My own observations agree with Christoff's. To illustrate, friends of mine and participants in

---

[172] Interviewed 2 March 2017
[173] Interviewed 2 November 2016

my study at times corrected me when I called them 'Afrikaner' rather that they identify as White, Afrikaans. However, organisations like Afriforum and Solidariteit explicitly provide programs and support for "Afrikaners", particularly those having trouble gaining access to institutions. Why then are the more educated elite withdrawing from the idea of "Afrikaner" and, if Christoff's observations are correct, from South Africa?

Don't Rock the Boat

I believe it is good wisdom in any context to say that the loudest voices are not the most representative. In looking at the situation in Stellenbosch, to consider the loudest voices in the language debate is to forget the anthropological nuance of the situation. This section explores how hierarchy in the Afrikaner community prevents public dialogue about Afrikaner identity. One afternoon in February 2017, Anneke—the White law student and member of the debating union from Johannesburg who grew up in an Afrikaans-speaking household—and I were walking down Ryneveld Street. Though it was a hot summer, it had rained that day, so the trees had greened up a bit.

On our way to get some take-out, I mentioned to Anneke my surprise at the views my informants expressed. I explained that many informants, if not explicitly, tacitly agreed with the calls from Open Stellenbosch to have more English offerings at the University. I wondered aloud to her: where were these voices in 2015? Why did none of them come to meetings of Open Stellenbosch? Anneke told me that "They probably didn't want to rock the boat." I asked her to explain what she meant, and she explained that in Afrikaner culture there was a taboo against speaking out against authority: "Even if you disagree," she said "you keep that quietly to yourself. That way you don't cause a disruption." This could be an explanation as to why, as Christoff noted, there hadn't been a dialogue about emigration and historical obligation in the Afrikaner public discourse.

Du Toit, a White, Afrikaans-speaking, was a poet who studied drama at the University. When we first met he had recently turned 21 and was nearing the end of his undergraduate studies. He witnessed the commitment to hierarchy as pointed out by Anneke when reading a poem of his to some Afrikaans-speaking Christian, White kids in their teens when reading a poem that contained explicit language and spoke against homophobia. He asked the kids: "Why wasn't any of you reacting? All of you were looking away. It was the first time I saw people being so uncomfortable in their environment [...]".

He empathized with them and reflected that when he was once their age and in their situation. Du Toit grew up gay in Springbok, a small, rural town in the Northern Cape that he described as conservative, Christian and very Afrikaans. He went on to engage the students:

> Aren't you all like against homophobia and racism? And aren't you all questioning your Christianity or your religion at least? And all of them were like, yeah [...] but we are just like afraid to say it. Okay, you are afraid to say it, react to it then. Then you can start to open yourself up to it because now you are complaining in all these small circles to your mom, and to your boyfriends, friends and whoever but nobody is hearing you because it is the small stuff. I feel it is so important for people that if you have an issue, complain about it.[174]

Resistance to the conservativeness of Afrikaner culture has happened through music. Jack Parow played a concert in February 2017 and in the lead up to his concert I asked informants about him and his music. I was curious as to how he was received in the Afrikaans community. Living in Canada, I knew of Die Antwoord and became acquainted with Jack Parow while I lived in South Africa. Freddie spoke with great passion about how the genre of rock and punk rock created spaces for Afrikaners who did not agree with the mainstream current of their culture. He told me that in the late 1980s, near the end of Apartheid, the Voëlvry movement was started by students at Stellenbosch who were men:

> who felt that they can't handle the system anymore and wanted to make some really good music that would take on the political

---

[174] Interviewed 18 August 2017

system. They incorporated punk elements and started attacking the system, like Johannes Kerkorrel. [...] Afrikaans society was very suppressed culturally. Because it was like, rock music is from Satan, whatever (laughs). [175]

Voëlvry[176] musicians were those who played with the Gereformeerde Blues Band (GBB)[177]. They redefined "elements of Afrikaner ethnicity in the eighties without fully rejecting it" thus "Voëlvry did rock the boat, but more gently than has often been assumed" (Gundlingh, 2004: 510). The explicit aim of Johannes Kerkorrel[178] was to help Afrikaners "find a new meaning in the country and a new place for us in the country" (Grundlingh, 2004: 496). Some Afrikaans universities banned GBB from performing on campus. The ban of GBB from Stellenbosch was a shock as it was supposed to be the heartland of 'liberal Afrikaners'", however, at the time PW Botha (the second last Apartheid prime minister) was the chancellor of the University (as had BJ Vorster before him) (Brink, 2005: 2).

After the end of Apartheid, the next band that, in Freddie's narration, really spoke against the Afrikaner establishment was Fokoffpolisiekar[179]:

> They challenged the Afrikaners themselves [...] regarding how we think about norms and values, Christianity, and free choice as to what your belief and your own values in life are. The political scene has already changed and they challenged the social scene. Although we went through political change in most of our communities we were still conservative about morals and how we think about life in general. They challenged that and succeeded, and rock-music moved up in Afrikaans. [180]

---

[175] Interviewed 2 March 2017

[176] "Voëlvry" can be interpreted to mean 'free as a bird' or 'outlawed', likely this double meaning was intension given the band's satirical name and lyrics which satirized the Apartheid state, Afrikaans political leaders, the South African Defence Force, and White middle-class values (Grundlingh 2004: 485)

[177] *Trans.* "Reformed", a deliberate play on the name of Dutch Reformed Churches.

[178] The lead in Gereformeerde Blues Band.

[179] *Trans.* Fuck off police car

[180] Interviewed 2 March 2017

Freddie spoke about Jack Parow as being part of this continuity of younger White, Afrikaans-speaking artists who challenge how Afrikaners see themselves:

> Jack Parrow was just a rap scene following [Fokoffpolisiekar]. He just took it further. I remember around 2007/8 most parents were like who is this gam/komon guy rapping with his swearing and shit? But the youth were like 'this is good stuff', so he spoke to people because he emphasised the working-to-middle-class Afrikaans speakers' lifestyles which is often seen (from a snobbish perspective) as very backward. Like urban gam/komon, those are terms you wouldn't really understand, but they just mean you are lower class. And he really challenged that perspective, and said aweh, but we can really make good music. Even if I come from the northern suburbs of Cape Town, I am not worth less, so he challenged how Afrikaners saw each other from class perspective. I really like that, and he mixes languages a lot because English speakers, especially White English speakers identify with him for some reason. I don't know why? I think it's because our communities are intertwined at some level, I mean in the suburbs, White Afrikaans and White English people still integrate a lot. I think that is still an apartheid legacy of White versus the rest. [181]

Jack Parow's willingness to mix English and Afrikaans goes against the quest for purity that architected the *suiwer-Afrikaans* dialect in the late 19th and early 20th century. Thus, given the hierarchy within Afrikaner culture, organisations like Afriforum may not speak for all those they claim to represent, as my research has demonstrated the reluctance for young Afrikaners to publicly disagree with those seen as authority figures. However, the places where one can see resistance to their narrative are not necessarily in newspapers or explicit public debates but rather in creative places like the music. While there are certainly other channels of resistance through film and media, literature, etc, my participants articulate their attachments to alternative Afrikaner-ness primarily through music.[182]

---

[181] Interviewed 2 March 2017
[182] For more on music and Afrikanerdom see the work of A Erasmus and R Truscott in the bibliography

I want to pause on this hierarchical constraint aspect of Afrikaner culture as it can relate to the hierarchies of culture discourse as observed by Balibar in the introduction. In grappling with the "Scarf Affair" Balibar observed:

> There is a certain the cultures supposed implicitly superior are those which appreciate and promote 'individual' enterprise, social and political individualism, against those which inhibit these things. These are said to be cultures whose 'spirit of community' is constituted by individualism (1991, 25).

Between the two White ethnicities in South Africa, English South Africans are seen as those which promote individualism the most. Afrikaners, as we've seen in this section, have norms within their community which provide more constraints on behaviour or have more formalized social threats for stepping out of line. In history, Afrikaners have been characterized as "less civilized" White people than English South Africans. Sometimes to justify the British takeover or consolidation of power in South Africa in the nineteenth century, or implicitly as the White people who "didn't do" Apartheid. I am curious about to what extent the Afrikaner commitment to the *volk* rather than to the individual contributed to the downgrading of the whiteness of Afrikaners.

To an extent, anthropology has struggled to effectively defend and communicate forms of agency that are less immediately legible to the framework of individualism. For example, in Saba Mahmood's work *Politics Of Piety: The Islamic Revival And The Feminist Subject*, she observes the liberal bias by and large built into anthropological work which always seems to see that "human agency primarily consists of acts that challenge social norms and not those that uphold them" (2005, 5). The subjects of Mahmood's study were women in Egypt, a predominantly Muslim country but with no legal mandates regarding head coverings for women, who were choosing to veil and partake in more conservative forms of Islam than were the norm within the country. She observed women making long commutes to mosques far from their homes to be part of congregations they felt aligned with their values. Leveraging their common Muslim faith, one of her interlocutors used her religious piety to get her husband to stop drinking and watching horror movies in their home (2005). Is it not agency to win arguments with one's husband? Though not the focus of her study, Mahmood's participants were members of faith communities. Those communities would be seen as "constraining" within the framework developed by Balibar. Many Western developed societies are experiencing crises of loneliness to a point that some, like Japan, are creating a government department to address social isolation. This is a major failing of cultures of individualism. I would bet that the women of Mahmood's study are not in the crisis of loneliness due to their strong social ties within their faith communities. Yet, we do not hear of anthropological critique of the 'culture' which has positioned itself as superior, as defined by Balibar. By failing to do ethnographic work about the 'culture' we lack the data to create such a critique.

Learning and Flexibility

This chapter has so far focused on the discussions being had by young Afrikaners, especially concerning emigration. It has been observed and argued that there are some who do not seem to want to learn to be part of the new South Africa. In the section that follows, I reflect on the change that is possible within people based on the experiences of my informants. Given the unexpectedly long time I had to do fieldwork due to a combination of bureaucratic and personal upheavals, I had the rare opportunity at this relatively beginner level of fieldwork to see my informants learn and change.

Catherine was one of the first people I interviewed.[183] She is White, was nineteen and a first year Bachelor of Humanities student when I initially interviewed her. The home where she grew up was an English-Afrikaans bilingual in Paarl, a farming town thirty kilometres down the road from Stellenbosch. Catherine commuted to university each day. In the first interview we did, Catherine seemed hesitant to speak about race. She implied that there were groupings based on language (English and Afrikaans) and interests ("the emos", "the jocks") but seemed rarely explicitly referenced race. She

[183] Interviewed 7 October 2016.

expressed that focusing on the legacy of Apartheid stops South Africans from being able to move forward, "I can't necessarily speak openly about the fact that I'm a White person or basically anything because I'm scared to be called a racist, and I'm not. […] just because I'm White doesn't mean I'm a bitch […]".[184] Catherine and I socialised through the USDV at Stellenbosch and about six months afterwards, she mentioned that she'd changed her mind about many of the things we had spoken about in our initial interview. This interaction really helped me consider the limitations of "the interview" as interviews are a snapshot frozen in time used to bolster the argument of the academic who recorded them.

Catherine, in her second formal interview, told me she started sitting in on a sociology class that some of her friends were taking in the 2017 academic year.[185] The professor teaching this class spoke about concepts she had never been exposed to before, such as gender being a social construct. She also enrolled in a course about experimental cultural production in South Africa offered by the English department. The course, as she described it, focused on some of the people who have been the most marginalized, such as lesbians of colour.

> So, it is things like that where the more you learn the more you start to build your own identity […] it opens your eyes to how much struggle there is out there, and it makes you aware of the privileges you have had and I would never be able to know what it is like, but it helps to empathize with them. That's all one can do, I mean obviously give back the land, like what the fuck (laughs). It is small things like that which constantly build up to changing oneself.[186]

Catherine specifically focused on trying to be empathetic as a mechanism for learning by trying to help her friends when they were struggling.

During my first interview with Catherine, she mentioned a poem that was performed in her English class by another undergraduate student named Du Toit, the same one who

---

[184] Interviewed 7 October 2016.
[185] Interviewed 18 August 2017.
[186] Interviewed 18 August 2017.

has become an informant of this work. The poem was about him pushing back against the connotations people drew from the fact that he was a White man, like the links between Afrikaans and patriarchy. At the time Catherine really related to it: "I think something like that really stood out for me and it was almost like WOW, I can relate to that."[187] Interested in this poem and the person who wrote it, I asked to be introduced to Du Toit through a friend in Stellenbosch. When I mentioned this performance, Du Toit remembered the positive reactions of Catherine's class. Du Toit was a member of the InZync Poetry Collective. A more senior member signed him up for the Open Book Poetry slam at the Fugard theatre in Cape Town. During his performance, the audience became agitated. A line of the poem was "so don't blame me for crimes I didn't commit", a line which pushes back on the intergenerational baggage Du Toit felt was put on him through the judgement of others… a line to which the crowd reacted by booing and swearing. Du Toit told me he was almost booed off stage. After his performance, the only people who congratulated him looked like very stereotypical Afrikaner ("boerjie" as Du Toit described them) men. Du Toit learned a lot from the experience and joked about returning to the Fugard poetry slam the following year to do a poem criticizing his poem from the previous year. At a poetry slam in Wellington shortly after the Fugard performance, Du Toit performed a poem about how disappointing DF Malan was to a more predominantly Afrikaner audience. In this instance, "this huge Afrikaner family like sitting in front, the father with his big beer [belly] and the small children, with the son looking up to his father and they were like frowning at me. And there was a bunch of these Coloured tannies[188] and they were like OOOH YAS, say it as it is".[189]

Du Toit and I did another interview about 10 months after our initial one. I had sent him the transcript of his first interview to read and reflect on. He described the experience as "quite scary" and that it "shocked" him because his beliefs and understandings had changed so much since then: "I have

---

[187] Interviewed 7 October 2016.
[188] Colloquial Afrikaans word for "Aunties".
[189] Interviewed 28 October 2016

been challenging my own thoughts the whole time"; particularly by getting closer with a Allison, a woman of colour in the InZync Poetry Collective. In addition to his performances with the Collective, Du Toit started to perform at the Stellenbosch drama department:

> It made them look in a whole different light at stuff, because they like okay cool; this is a person just like us with kind of the same background and you think if you study drama, all of us study drama. But I could become a voice in a certain extent, because we could start communicating about stuff. And then a lot of people came to me and said you made us change our minds so much.[190]

Du Toit told me that our first interview was "a huge turning point for me as an artist as well. That was the moment when I decided that, you had to speak, not like hiding behind anything". The work of Du Toit to constantly challenge himself and those around him through his poetry performances is one of the many ways conversations about historical responsibility are being had in Stellenbosch. We must make space for people to think through the complicated questions that have been put in front of them by being born in South Africa. As Du Toit pointed out "it is so human, it is so f***ing human to speak in contradictions mostly because your mind is going to change constantly".[191]

Du Toit and Catherine both had their horizons expanded and their minds changed through their interactions with others. As anthropologists, then, we must consider how we can do research in a manner that makes ethnography an ongoing conversation, rather than a quest for absolute answers, certitudes, and certainties. For me, it is intuitive to understand that the longer the fieldwork, the longer the contact between participants and anthropologist, the greater likelihood there is of a fuller picture being presented. If I had only interviewed Du Toit once and not had the opportunity to spend time with him, see him perform and then revisit our earlier conservation, I would not have learned about the extent to which he grew and changed as a person in less than

---

[190] Interviewed 18 August 2017
[191] Interviewed 18 August 2017

a year. Most master's fieldwork lasts 8 or 10 weeks, but because of my own challenges for health and support I was unable to complete my master's in a conventional way. I can now see what a wonderful gift my challenges have given me: a picture beyond the snapshot that short-stay anthropology offers.

I think there is value in shorter projects but what Catherine and Du Toit bring to our attention is the limitations of short contact projects. Similar to how I would hope people reading and ethnography from 1970 would not consider its conclusions as absolute given the amount of time that has passed since publication, I believe that at the same time scepticism should be considered when reading even recent ethnographies. What Catherine and Du Toit expressed to me during our first interviews was true when they spoke it, but the process of experience, listening and engagement with their surrounding made their truths change with time.

Thus, the value of ethnographies of all shapes and sizes should be weighed based on attributes like the nature of the relationships between the anthropologist and their participants with particular attention paid to the length of the time spent with them or the length of the correspondence with them. Interviews done between participants and ethnographers can reveal truths about the moment they take place in.[192] Even if that truth for that particular participant changes with time, the thought they share is quite likely to be one or similar to one that someone of a similar positionality in an analogous situation could share. These ethnographic moments can still speak to truths of the world, but they have to be understood for their limitations.

Conclusion

The future of Afrikaans and Afrikaners is dependent on the important discussions being had by young White Afrikaans-speakers who are interrogating their past and looking forward to their future. This chapter has explored the connections between Afrikaans and English at the present moment, particularly the strategic use of English as an important point on the map toward emigration for young

---

[192] On the condition that both are engaging truthfully.

Afrikaners. The first argument built on the work of RA Leitch with young Afrikaner men in Stellenbosch. Leitch noted that the learning of English by Afrikaners can be seen as a continuation of the 'adapt or die' strategy noted by her participants. In the introduction and medium of instruction sections, I noted the emphasis on internationalization: that in South Africa organisations and institutions like universities and wine farms are using English to connect themselves to the international sphere.

Next, I analysed the language used by the University to describe the three languages referenced in their language policy. It emphasized the internationality and commerce potentials of English. When describing Afrikaans, it emphasized that Afrikaans "is a means of empowering a large and diverse community in South Africa" (Stellenbosch University 2016: 2). It does not give English or isiXhosa the same credit; indeed, isiXhosa does not seem to warrant the usage that English does at the University, like the academic, the administrative, professional or social. Furthermore, the other 8 languages in South Africa were not considered by the policy. I also discussed the erasure of the nuances of the Afrikaans language by not acknowledging the existence of Cape Flats Afrikaans, the group of people the policy implicitly hopes to empower.

Thirdly, I discussed some of the subtleties of South African whiteness; that the levels of privileges accrued at the expense of Black, Coloured and Indian South Africans have been so extreme that, unlike other forms of settler-colonialism, it is very visible. Additionally, the privileges of whiteness in South Africa are no longer guaranteed. Thus, young Afrikaners were coming to grips with the baggage associated with the older conceptions of what it means to be Afrikaner and shaping how the idea of Afrikaner is viewed. While emigrating is seen as a solution to many, my informants were pushing back against it. Conceptions of Afrikanerdom are being challenged in South Africa, particularly through their musical choices of groups like Jack Parow and Fokoffpolisiekar. As described by Freddie:

> [...] many of us we grew up in communities that were unshackled. Even coming to university and having parties with lots of alcohol, screwing around, having fun and being young

was not an issue with us being Afrikaners. You can be Afrikaner and still do those things, you know. I don't really mind identifying as such, for me when I think Afrikaner in our history I also see the proud and interesting history. Having fun is part of that history, saying my people created Fokoffpolisiekar as a reaction to society as a whole is something to be proud of. [193]

These musicians are challenging Afrikaner norms that I outlined in the fourth section about discussion and hierarchy among white-Afrikaans people. It emphasized the strong institutional and generational deference that many white-Afrikaans people are taught as children which explains, in part, why there is such a disparity between the views of my participants and the views propagated in the popular media.

This chapter attempted to shed light on the complicated relationship between Afrikaners, Afrikaans and its place in the University. As explained by Du Toit:

> I love the language and I want to speak it for the rest of my life. I know that is what I want, but that is not what the best is for most people around me. I have also learned a lot to separate my subjective opinion and feelings for myself. Because I usually decide with my emotions, everything. There is a lot of guilt that comes apart with being Afrikaans and talking it. Even in front of you, like now as I'm reflecting on it. Sometimes it even smothers me because it is the most natural way I can speak. It almost this way of closing off people because I have different ways of speaking Afrikaans. [194]

The ethnographic section explored particulars of how different linguistic capabilities give students access to different experiences at the University. Fluently bilingual students are advantaged by the University's policies by receiving significant reinforcement in their classes when the material is explained twice in the best case and in the worst case to not being disadvantaged by the preferences of their professors. The prioritization of English and Afrikaans in the University is demonstrative of White-South Africans and the institutions they built continuing to operate in a similar vein

---

[193] Interviewed 2 March 2017
[194] Interviewed 18 August 2017

using tactics assimilation to try to force the Other to adapt to whiteness.

Next, I drew on the experiences of my participants to explain why there are not more public discussions and debates explicitly about Afrikaner identity. My participants highlighted the creative ways Afrikaans musicians are taking up this dialogue to push back against some of the more conservative aspects of Afrikanerdom, though not necessarily the historical baggage outlined in the earlier portion of this chapter.

Chapter 7

Ndiyazama Noko[195]

> Not everything that is faced can be changed but nothing can be changed until it is faced. – James Baldwin

Conclusion

The question that began my research in 2016 was "What does it mean for there to be increased offerings of English at Stellenbosch University, a historically Afrikaans place?" In the media in 2015 and 2016, English had been put forward as a compromise to help facilitate the integration and access to education to Black, Coloured and Indian students at South African universities. These calls were made in tandem for calls to "decolonize" South African universities. I understood these calls, I listened to my Black, Coloured, and Indian friends explain the alienation they felt from their universities. They were tired of feeling that they had to assimilate to the pre-existing (White) culture of their universities. The findings of this work reflect the continued separateness of the colours of the rainbow in the rainbow nation.

Even when I was involved in activism supporting Open Stellenbosch and FeesMustFall, I did feel there was a slight irony in calling for decolonization in a language of colonization. As my work for my thesis progressed, I saw how language was one of the metrics that can be used to understand the effort being made between people. I was incredibly surprised when I moved to South Africa at how few White-South Africans seemed to speak languages like isiXhosa or Sesotho. I called this chapter "Ndiyazama noko", an isiXhosa phrase which means "I am trying nevertheless" because I think it is an important phase that points towards the most hopeful possibility noted by Ballard, of integration– an openness to accepting unassimilated otherness, thus engaging with it without trying to reform it to resemble the familiar (2004: 64).

---

[195] I'm trying nevertheless

This book explored the webs and fractals of social connections at Stellenbosch University. They are intertwined between and split along and (in some instances) overcome lines of language and race. I contributed to an understanding of what the barriers to integration and transformation exist at Stellenbosch University. The domineering nature of Afrikaner symbolism at the University implied the space is zoned for white-Afrikaans-speaking people. The campus is haunted by the spectres from the histories of oppression and privileges of Apartheid. This haunting shaped the social landscape, particularly how students related to each other and their country of citizenship, or temporary residence for their studies.

There have been some interesting demographic changes at Stellenbosch between the time of my fieldwork and this compilation of it into a book.

Year	Black	Coloured	Indian	White	Withheld
2015	17.8	17.4	2.6	62.2	-
2016	18.2	17.6	2.8	61.3	-
2017	19	18.1	3	59.9	
2018	20.1	18.1	3.1	58.1	0.43
2019	21	18.1	3.2	56.5	0.77
2020	21.8	18	3.2	55.5	1.17
2021	22.5	18	3.4	54.4	1.37
2022	23.3	17.7	3.4	51.6	3.6
2023	24.6	17	3.5	49.8	4.6

Table 1: Demographic Change at Stellenbosch University from 2015-2023. Sourced from Stellenbosch Statistics Overview.

I do not know why the option to withhold race was introduced in 2018 but it does mean there is a margin of error as to what extent the number of White students at Stellenbosch is actually continuing on a downward trend or maintaining stability at just over 50 percent. After such an emphasis on the need for Afrikaans at the university to support Coloured students it is telling that the number of Coloured students, though relatively stable, has actually decreased.

Older statistical information is formatted in a bit less transparent way. Note students from Africa outside of South Africa but do not disaggregate students who were Black, Coloured, or Indian from each other.

Demographic Change at Stellenbosch University 2000-2012				
Year	Students from Elsewhere in Africa	Black, Coloured, and Indian Students	White Students	Total number of students
2000	461	5,658	14,763	20, 421
2005	991	6,281	15, 801	22, 082
2010	1,913	9,113	18, 581	27, 694
2011	1,963	9,278	18, 915	28,193
2012	2,031	9,221	18, 602	27, 823

Table 2: Demographic Change at Stellenbosch University 2000-2012. Sourced from Facts and Statistics, Stellenbosch University.

When the column for Black, Coloured, and Indian students and the column for White students are added together it is equal to the total number of students at the University during this period. This means that the students from elsewhere in Africa, who are statistically most likely to be Black, are being counted within the category of Black, Coloured and Indian. One can easily see how significantly the number of students from elsewhere in Africa increased between 2000 and 2012 from 461 to 2,031. Between 2011 and 2012, the total number of Black, Coloured, and Indian Students slightly decreased and the population of students from elsewhere in Africa continued on its upward trajectory. What does it mean for the transformation of Stellenbosch that a considerable portion of the students of colour are not South African? My ex-partner had noticed that many of the Black students he met were from Gauteng, about 1,400 km away from Stellenbosch. Whereas, to his knowledge, there was not a single student who had grown up in Kayamandi (the Black township in Stellenbosch) who attended the University. His theory was that the University was purposefully recruiting students of Colour from far away because they needed to improve their demographic profile as it related to transformation, but the University did not want to have people from Kayamandi to feel entitled to the public space at the University. This argument can easily be extended to our consideration of students from elsewhere in Africa: they advance changes to the demographic transformation of the University without changing the relationship between the University and Black, Coloured, and Indian South Africans.

As I began this work in Chapter One I hoped to underscore how closely Stellenbosch resembled apartheid-Stellenbosch at the time when I was writing– a time when the born-free generation was coming of age. To me this meant the university continued to reflect a time of explicit Afrikaner dominance, as Justice Khampepe's final report for the Commission Of Inquiry Into Allegations Of Racism At Stellenbosch University agrees. I considered what were the best strategies to not stand in one place to watch the language debate masquerades, along the lines of the advice of Chinua Achebe. In addition to participant observation, the cornerstone of anthropological research, I explained the Gadamerian hermeneutic circle I used to hold myself accountable to prejudices I might be harbouring, and the identity framework by Stuart Hall that would be used. It's argued that by including types of literature, like creative nonfiction of Chapter Three, should also be used as anthropological evidence as to do so is to take an expansive understanding of knowledge, which anthropologists profess to have. The common ethical challenges like consent and the ability to anonymize participants is discussed; but I also remind readers of the perception that texts create "permanency". I am connected on social media to some of my participants, and I know they have had experiences since this research was conducted that have profoundly changed them. Reading this work does not mean the reader now *knows* them, though it might feel that way, but rather that the reader knows what they were thinking when I interviewed them.

Chapter Two examined the relationships between settler colonialism, anthropology, and whiteness in Africa. I grew up in a settler-colonial, with Inuit family whose relationship to our land has been reconfigured through the project of Canadian colonialism. Similarly, in some senses to South Africa, we have experienced assaults on our culture and way of life resulting in significant trauma and social disruption even though Inuit remain the majority on our land. In my more contemporary academic work I explore Inuit history to try to parse how and why our relationship to settler colonialism is different from First Nations and Metis, the Indigenous people in "southern" Canada. This lived experience and the parallels it gave me insights which inspired me to make an extended consideration about to what extent "settler colonialism" as laid out by Patrick Wolfe and others, is relevant to the South African context. While the Western Cape has the strongest direct parallels to typical cases of settler colonialism, the reconfiguration of land relations and the access to land touched every corner of the country. In addition to historical analysis of regulations related to land, I analyse how anthropologists do work with White people in Africa in terms of the conclusions they draw about identity and place making as well as the ethical considerations of studying horizontally. There is a morbid fascination with communities like Orania where Apartheid culture continues. The relationship building done as a necessary facet of participant observation has the possibility of flattening or obscuring the structural privileges of interlocutors.

The more time I spent in Stellenbosch, the more I was reminded of subjects from the South Africa history course I had taken in my undergrad. Chapter Three gave historical background as to how Stellenbosch was settled and came to be home to the University. It highlighted that language became a rallying-cry around which Dutch-settlers organized themselves when the British restricted its teaching in schools. I hoped this would help readers understand the significance of Afrikaners becoming willing to be strategically Anglicized while at the same time fighting to keep their language at the University. Furthermore, it contributed to the understanding of the parts of history that Afriforum and similar organisations strategically draw on to characterize the victimization of Afrikaans. Additionally, I compared the debates around language in South Africa to debates about language in the broader African context because we must never forget that many African countries had these debates about language before South Africa decolonized.

Chapter Four underlined some of the features of physical landscape like well-kept infrastructure and flowers in historically White areas to consider what it means that the converse– the lack of investment in Black and Coloured areas– also continued. Features of the social landscape were also considered like the double standard people who do not look like they should fit in or do not sound like they should fit in are held to. It more broadly also spoke on how access to capital has material impacts on how people are able to spend their time. The first three chapters of this thesis contributed to formalizing knowledge that sometimes people take for granted or assume. Others push back against it, claiming this knowledge as untrue. These chapters created context for the arguments I made in Chapter Five and Six.

The Five Chapter demonstrated the sense of Otherness felt by many Black, Coloured, and Indian students. Wanijuk and Hugo, who are both black from other African countries, noted how overwhelmingly White the University is. For Wanijuk and Siphe (who is from Johannesburg), they both spoke about experiences that made them feel Black at Stellenbosch; white participants like Anneke and Ané also noticed the staggering number of White people. Importantly, Ané spoke to how the number of White people at the University became normalized to her, even though South Africa is 90% Black, Coloured and Indian. This demonstrates the power of whiteness to centre itself as normal at the University. As English and Afrikaner-South Africans have been becoming more intertwined with each generation, it seemed that English-South Africans do not feel as alienated by Stellenbosch as their Black, Coloured and Indian classmates. Jason —speaking Afrikaans, isiXhosa, and English— felt as though his language skills were able to bridge the common divides at the University. Students from all racial groups focused on the benefits of the internationality that English offers them. A common coping strategy for pain is finding something else to focus on. I believe one of the reasons why informants mostly focused on English's ability to bring people together is because they, on some level, are aware that it would be better if people did make the effort to learn a language other than English or Afrikaans, towards a form of collaborative cohesion. This chapter contributed to understanding the challenges that efforts of transformation face as projects of institutional transformation are dependent on the relationships between individuals.

Chapter Six focused on the relationship between Afrikanerdom, English and emigration. Though African countries have had their own debates about mother-tongue education (see Chapter Three), Afrikaans' unfair head start from the Apartheid regime adds a dimension to the South African debate. Stellenbosch University was a place built for Afrikaners to feel comfortable because it was taught in Afrikaans, however, more and more Afrikaans-speakers are learning or improving their English at Stellenbosch. Open Stellenbosch called for greater English offerings at the University as a means of access for Black, Coloured and Indian students. Though these offerings have the ability to bring people together by giving them a common language with which to speak, English's competing international appeal seemed to have won out over creating greater social connections with South Africans who come from different backgrounds, as was demonstrated in Chapter Five.

It is not only Afrikaners who are leaving South Africa. Afrikaners are not even the only South Africans with historical baggage who are leaving: English-White South Africans also carry privileges accrued during Apartheid on their flights to London. However, Afrikanerdom has publicly tied Afrikaners to South Africa, for example, through its claims that Afrikaners have nowhere else to go. This has created a feeling of irony when noting the large Afrikaner diasporas in places like Perth and Toronto (van Rooyen 2000: xii). Christoff's response to the dislocation of Afrikanerdom post-Apartheid has been to tackle it head on, through his involvement in *Volksverraaier*. The resistance to publicly rocking the boat in Afrikaner culture leaves these questions somewhat unanswered in the public sphere. Many young White-Afrikaans speakers are discussing them and coming to answers of their own, having had new possibilities of expression opened up through music like Fokoffpolisiekar. This chapter helps to demonstrate both why there has been a lack of public discussion about the issues raised in it as well as some views held by Afrikaners about their place in South Africa. Perhaps if figures like Reverend Naudé were more prominently celebrated it would create new routes for Afrikaners to negotiate their roots. My former debate student who graduated from high school in Cape Town in 2017 had never heard of Reverend Naudé. In prominent South African history texts, Naudé is mentioned in passing (Thompson 2001) (Davenport and Saunders 2000).

The questions raised about how to cross racial divides and create true friendships is an incredibly important one. In conversations with a dear friend of mine who studied psychology, we spoke about the fact that in the school system, very little is done to teach children about what it means to be kind. Teachers intervene when children are bullying each other but there are no lessons about how to care about each other. My ethnography details what the barriers to interracial friendships were at Stellenbosch University in 2016-2017. While some South Africans, particularly White South Africans, do not want to learn to live together and would rather move to Perth, there are those committed to trying nevertheless. I do not have the answers, but I am confident South Africans do.

References

Abrams M.H. (1953). *The Mirror and the Lamp: Romantic Theory and the Critical Tradition.* Oxford University Press: London.

Achebe, C. (1997). 'English and the African Writer', *Transition.* 75/76. pp. 342-349.

Achebe, C. (1988). 'The Igbo World and its Art', *Hopes and Impediments.* pp.62-67.

Adichie, C. N. (2003). *Purple Hibiscus: A Novel.* Chapel Hill, NC: Algonquin Books of Chapel Hill.

AdamTas. 'AdamTas: Passie Vir Afrikaans,' *Student Societies-Stellenbosch University.* ND. Accessed on 1st July, 2017 at https://www.sun.ac.za/english/students/student-societies/cultural-hobby-societies/adam-tas .

Adhikari, Mohamed. "A total extinction confidently hoped for: the destruction of Cape San society under Dutch colonial rule, 1700 –1795". *Journal of Genocide Research.* (2010), 12(1–2) March– June, 19 –44.

Africa is a Country. (2015). 'Our 11-Minute Film Capturing the Energies of #FeesMustFall', *Africa is a Country.* Accessed on 29th May, 2018 at https://africasacountry.com/2015/10/watch-our-11-minute-film-capturing-the-energies-of-feesmustfall-in-south-africa.

Afriforum. "AfriForum on its way to the UN to shine international spotlight on discrimination and hate speech targeting minorities in South Africa". *Afriforum.* Published 20 November 2023. Accessed 7 August 2024. https://afriforum.co.za/en/afriforum-on-its-way-to-the-un-to-shine-international-spotlight-on-discrimination-and-hate-speech-targeting-minorities-in-south-africa/

Alexander, N. (1989). *Language Policy and National Unity in South Africa/Azania.* BUCHU Books: Cape Town.

Alexie, S. (2000). *The Toughest Indian in the World.* Atlantic Monthly Press: NYC.

Ballard, R. (2004). 'Assimilation, Emigration, Semigration, and Integration: 'White' peoples' strategies for finding comfort zones in post-apartheid South Africa', in Distiller, N. and Steyn, M. (eds.) *Under Construction: 'Race' and identity in South Africa today.* Heinemann: Johannesburg.

Balibar, Etienne. "Racism Revisited: Sources, Relevance, and Aporias of a Modern Contempt". *PMLA*. 123 (5). Special Topic: Comparative Racialization. Oct 2008. 1630-1639.

Balibar, Etienne and Immanuel Wallerstein. *Race, Nation, Class: Ambiguous Identities.* New York: Verso Books, 1991.

Baloyi, Thabo. "Another urination scandal rocks Stellenbosch University". *The South Africa.* 23 October 2022. Accessed 12 June 2024. https://www.thesouthafrican.com/news/breaking-urination-scandal-stellenbosch-university-23-october/

Bandura, A. 1989. Human agency in social cognitive theory. *American psychologist*, 44(9), p.1175

Bernard, H. (2010). *Qualitative Data Analysis: Systematic Approaches.* Sage: Thousand Oaks, California.

Biehl, J., 2007. "Introduction: Rethinking Subjectivity". in Biehl, Jo, Good, B. & Kleinman, A.(Eds.) *Subjectivity: Ethnographic Investigations.* Polity Press: London, UK.

Biko, S. & Stubbs, A.(ed). (1978). *I Write What I Like: A Selection of His Writings.* Heinemann: Oxford.

Biddle, Nicholas, Francis Markham "Census 2016: what's changed for Indigenous Australians?" The Conversation. Published 27 June 2017. Accessed 2019-06-29. http://theconversation.com/census-2016-whats-changed-for-indigenous-australians-79836

Birnbaum, S. (2015). 'In South Africa, it's called the Black Ta', *The World* by *Public Radio International*, 24 November. Accessed on 21 August 2018 at https://www.pri.org/stories/2015-11-24/south-africa-its-called-Black-tax .

Blaser, TM & Van der Westhuizen, C. (2012). 'Introduction: The Paradox of Post-Apartheid 'Afrikaner' Identity: Deployments of Ethnicity and Neo-Liberalism' *African Studies* (71)3, December 2012.

Borowski, M. (2014). 'Truth and Reconciliation's Checkered Legacy', *Deutsche Welle*, 24 April. Accessed on 12 July 2018 at https://www.dw.com/en/truth-and-reconciliations-checkered-legacy/a-17589671.

Boshomane, P. (2016). '20 Years After the TRC Hearings South Africa's Pain Persists', *Sunday Times*, 10 April. Accessed on 12 July 2018 at https://www.timeslive.co.za/sunday-times/opinion-and-analysis/2016-04-10-20-years-after-the-trc-hearings-south-africas-pain-persists/.

Bouie, J. (2018). 'The Enlightenment's Dark Side: How the Enlightenment Created Modern Race Thinking and Why We Should Confront It', *Slate*, 5 June. Accessed on 9 June 2018 at https://slate.com/news-and-politics/2018/06/taking-the-enlightenment-seriously-requires-talking-about-race.html.

Bowler, D. (2015). 'Opinion: Mixed Race Children Will Not Solve Racism', *Eye Witness News,* 1 December. Accessed on 28 May 2018.

Boynton, G. (2016). 'How the Birthplace of Apartheid Became Wine Wonderland', *Newsweek*, 14 February. Accessed on 1 March 2018 at http://www.newsweek.com/how-birthplace-apartheid-became-wine-wonderland-426473.

Brink, C. (2005). 'Opening of the Workshop on Trans-disciplinarity presented by the Sustainability Institute', *Trans-disciplinarity and the Vision of Stellenbosch University*, 11 April. Accessed on 30 July 2018 at http://cetrans.com.br/assets/artigoscongresso/Chris_Brink.pdf.

Britannica (2018). "John Vorster–Prime Minister of South Africa" *The Editors of Encyclopaedia Britannica.* 6 September. Accessed 30 June 2016. https://www.britannica.com/biography/John-Vorster

Britannica, The Editors of Encyclopaedia. "National Party". *Encyclopedia Britannica*, 17 May. 2024, https://www.britannica.com/topic/National-Party-political-party-South-Africa. Accessed 1 October 2024.

Brock-Utne, Birgit; Holmarsdottir, Halla B. (2004) "Language Policies and Practices in Tanzania and South Africa: Problems and Challenges" *International Journal of Educational Development*, (24)1, Jan. Pp67-83. ISSN-0738-0593.

Brown, A. (2017). 'Give Back the Land', *The Documentary*. [Podcast]. BBC World Service. https://www.bbc.co.uk/programmes/p0571tjx .

Brulliard, Nicolas. "World Cup: Is South Africa's white town racist?" *Global Post*. 21 June 2010. Accessed 6 August 2024.

Bunyi, Grace W. (2008) "The Place of African Indigenous Knowledge and Languages in Education for Development: The Case of Kenya" in *New Directions in African Education: Challenges and Possibilities*. Ed. S. Nombuso Dlamini. University of Calgary Press: Calgary, Canada.

Business Tech. "South Africa's white population is still shrinking" *Business Tech*. Published 23 Jul 2018. Accessed 8 June 2021. https://businesstech.co.za/news/government/260219/south-africas-white-population-is-still-shrinking/

Cavanagh, Edward and Lorenzo Veracini. 2017. *The Routledge Handbook of the History of Settler Colonialism*. Routledge: New York, New York.

Cavanagh, Edward. "The History of Dispossession at Orania and the Politics of Land Restitution in South Africa". *Journal of Southern African Studies*, Vol. 39, No. 2 (June 2013), pp. 391-407

Censer, Jack R. 1995. "Series Editor's Preface" in *Segregation and Apartheid in Twentieth-Century South Africa*. Routledge: London.

Certeau, Michel de (1984) "Walking the City" in *The Practice of Everyday Life*. Trans. S. F. Rendall. University of California Press: Berkeley, CA.

Charney, C. (1984). 'Class Conflict and the National Party Split', *Journal of Southern African Studies*, 10(2), April.

Chatora, A . (2017). 'Ngugi wa Thiong'o Calls for Preservation and Inclusion of African Languages in Learning Institutions', *This Is Africa,* 3 March. Accessed on 2 October 2018 at https://thisisafrica.me/ngugi-wa-thiongo-calls-preservation-inclusion-african-languages-learning-institutions/.

Charles, Mevin. "Justice Sisi Khampepe appointed to lead inquiry into racism at Stellenbosch University". *News24*.

Published 3 June 2022. Access 12 June 2024. https://www.news24.com/news24/southafrica/news/justice-sisi-khampepe-appointed-to-lead-inquiry-into-racism-at-stellenbosch-university-20220603

Chetty, Kuben. "Female student 'humiliated' in fresh Stellenbosch University race incident". *IOL*. Published 18 May 2022. Accessed 12 June 2024. https://www.iol.co.za/capetimes/news/female-student-humiliated-in-fresh-stellenbosch-university-race-incident-dfd8c2e6-7d7c-4a82-9ed8-22a9ae4fcee2

Chigumadzi, P. (2018). 'Whatever's Happening to Interracial love?', *New York Review of Books,* 25 June. Accessed on 26 June 2018 at *https://www.nybooks.com/daily/2018/06/25/whatevers-happening-to-interracial-love/.*

Clariborne, W. (1989). 'The Birthplace of Apartheid May One Day Become Its Deathbed', *Washington Post,* 8 October. Accessed on 2 February 2018 at https://www.washingtonpost.com/archive/politics/1989/10/08/the-birthplace-of-apartheid-may-one-day-become-its-deathbed/eaba5c30-b2e2-423d-aa0c-45c5c070dfd5/?utm_term=.e55c9cc7095c .

Clifford, J. (1997). *Routes: Travel and Translation in the Late Twentieth Century.* Harvard University Press, Cambridge.

Clifford, J. (1986). "Introduction: Partial Truths," in *Writing Culture: The Poetics and Politics of Ethnography,* edited by Clifford, J. and Marcus, G. University of California Press, Berkeley: 1 - 26.

Citizen Potawatomi Nation. "Remembering The 1887 Dawes Act's Impact". Citizen Potawatomi Nation. Published February 8, 2021. Accessed 6 August 2024. https://www.potawatomi.org/blog/2021/02/08/remembering-the-1887-dawes-acts-impact/

Citizen Reporter. (2018) 'Traitors of the Volk' Trash Afriforum', *The Citizen*, 15 March. Accessed on 18 August 2018 at https://citizen.co.za/news/south-africa/1035262/self-declared-traitors-of-the-volk-trash-afriforum/ .

City Press. (2013). 'Date Set for Nelspruit Name-Change Showdown', *CityPress-News24*. 6 July. Accessed on 19 August 2018 at https://www.news24.com/Archives/City-Press/Date-set-for-Nelspruit-name-change-showdown-20150429.

Coates, Ta-Nehisi. (2015). *Between the World and Me.* The Text Publishing Company: Melbourne.

Coetzee, JM. "Idleness in South Africa" *Social Dynamics.* 8:1. 1-13.

Commission for Employment Equity. "Annual Report 2022-2023". *Department of Employment and Labour, Government of South Africa.* Pretoria: Gauteng. https://www.labour.gov.za/DocumentCenter/Reports/Annual%20Reports/Employment%20Equity/2022-2023/23rd%20Annual%20CEE%20Report.pdf

Comaroff, J & J.L. Comaroff. (2001). 'Nurturing the Nation: Aliens, Apocalypse, and the Postcolonial State', *Social Identities* (7)2. 233-265.

Connors, Steve. "Whales and dolphins are so intelligent they deserve same rights as humans, say experts" Published 21/02/12. Accessed 12/06/2017. http://www.independent.co.uk/environment/nature/whales-and-dolphins-are-so-intelligent-they-deserve-same-rights-as-humans-say-experts-7237448.html

Constitution of the Republic of South Africa, 1996.

Contraband Cape Town. *Luister.* YouTube. Published 20 August 2015. Accessed 20 January 2016. https://www.youtube.com/watch?v=sF3rTBQTQk4

Cooper, Frederick. 2005. *Colonialism in Question: Theory, Knowledge, History.* University of California Press: London.

Coulthard, Glen Sean. 2014. *Red Skins, White Masks: Rejecting the Colonial Politics of Recognition.* University of Minnesota Press: Minneapolis.

Crapanzano, V. (1985). *Waiting: The Whites of South Africa.* Random House: NY.

Crocker, Stephen. "Muskrat Falls is the Future of Contamination in Canada" *The Independent.* Published 1 August 2019. Access 7 August 2024. https://theindependent.ca/commentary/analysis/muskrat-falls-is-the-future-of-contamination-in-canada/

Crowley, Kevin. "Whites Own 73% of South Africa's Farming Land, City Press Says" *Bloomberg News.* Published 29 Oct 2017. Accessed 8 June 2021. https://www.bloomberg.com/news/articles/2017-10-

29/whites-own-73-of-south-africa-s-farming-land-city-press-says

Damon, Wilfred Barrett. "James Joyce en ek". *HERRI*. Centre For Critical And Creative Thought, Stellenbosch University. Issue 10. 2024. https://herri.org.za/10/wilfred-barett-damon/

Davenport, Rodney and Christopher Saunders.(000). South Africa: A Modern History. London: MacMillan Press.

Davis, C. (2005). 'Hauntology, Spectres and Phantoms', *French Studies*, *59*(3).

De Certeau, M. (1984). *The Practice of Everyday Life*. Trans. Steven Rendall. UC Press: Berkeley.

De Kock, Chloe. "Stellenbosch University: A Bastion of Learning Amidst Controversy". Cape Town Today. Published 16 February 2024. Accessed 12 June 2024. https://capetown.today/stellenbosch-university-a-bastion-of-learning-amidst-controversy/

De Vos, P.(2015). 'To Address Wrong of the Past Stellenbosch Language Policy Must Change', *Constitutionally Speaking Blog*, 8 September. Accessed on 25 July 2018 at https://constitutionallyspeaking.co.za/to-address-wrongs-of-the-past-stellenbosch-language-policy-must-change/.

De Vos, Pierre. "Willing buyer, willing seller works… if you have a lifetime to wait" *Daily Maverick*. Published 13 June 2013. Accessed 18 June 2017. https://www.dailymaverick.co.za/opinionista/2013-06-13-willing-buyer-willing-seller-works-if-you-have-a-lifetime-to-wait/#.WUaAYWiGM2w

De Vos, Pierre. "Maties must root out toxic and exclusionary culture exposed at Wilgenhof, but is it brave enough?" *Daily Maverick*. Published 31 January 2024. Accessed 14 June 2024. https://www.dailymaverick.co.za/article/2024-01-31-maties-must-root-out-toxic-and-exclusionary-culture-exposed-at-wilgenhof-but-is-it-brave-enough/

Demant, J & J, Ostergaard. (2007). 'Partying as Everyday Life: Investigations of Teenagers' Leisure Life', *Journal of Youth Studies*. 10:5, 517-537.

Deloria, V. (1969). *Custer Died for Your Sins*. New York: Macmillan.

DeVault, M. (1991). *Feeding the Family.* University of Chicago Press: Chicago.

Derrida, J., 1994. *Specters of Marx*, trans. Peggy Kamuf. New York: Routledge.

Dictionary-Merriam-Webster. Nd. 'Self-Defense', Dictionary-Merriam-Webster. Accessed on 10 March 2017 at https://www.merriam-webster.com/dictionary/self-defense .

Dion, Susan. 1991. "Current Federal Indian Law and Its Precedents". *Wisconsin Woodland Indian Dissemination Project.* Madison, Wisconsin: American Indian Language and Culture Education Board https://dpi.wi.gov/sites/default/files/imce/amind/pdf/current_federal_indian_law_and_its_precedents.pdf

Dirk, Nicolette. 2014. "Botman's name lives on in Stellenbosch". *IOL News.* 9 December. Accessed 14 October 2018. https://www.iol.co.za/news/south-africa/western-cape/botmans-name-lives-on-in-stellenbosch-1793028

Deumert, A. (2004). *Language Standardization and Language of Change: The Dynamics of Cape Dutch.* John Benjamins: Philadelphia.

Dlamini, N.S. (2008). *New Directions in African Education.* University of Calgary Press: Calgary.

Dominy, Michèle. 1995. "White Assertions of Native Status" *American Ethnologist.* 22(2). May. 358-374.

Doran, Justin Michael. 2017. "Review: *The Universal Church of the Kingdom of God in South Africa: a Church of Strangers*" *Nova Religion* (20) 3. 118-120. DOI: 10.1525/nr.2017.20.3.118

Dowding, K.(2013). 'Collective Action Problem', *Britannica.com.*, 07 March. Accessed on 13 May 2018 at https://www.britannica.com/topic/collective-action-problem-1917157.

Ditchburn, J. (2015). 'Because it's 2015: Trudeau Forms Canada's 1st Gender-balanced Cabinet', *Canadian Broadcasting Corporation*, 4 November. Accessed on 24 June 2018 at https://www.cbc.ca/news/politics/canada-trudeau-liberal-government-cabinet-1.3304590

Duffy, J.L. (2013). *The Politics of Ethnic Nationalism: Afrikaner Unity, the National Party and the Radical Right in Stellenbosch*, 1934-1948. Routledge: New York.

Dyer, Richard. (1988). 'White', *Screen*. 29:44-65.

Emerson, MO & Yancey. (2008). 'African Americans in Interracial Congregations: an Analysis of Demographics, Social Networks, and Social Attitudes', *Review of Religious Research*. (49)3. 301-318.

ENCA. (2017). 'WATCH: Acclaimed author Ngugi wa Thiong'o speaks at Wits', 2 March. Accessed on 2 October 2018 at https://www.enca.com/south-africa/catch-it-live-acclaimed-author-ng-g-wa-thiongo-speaks-at-wits .

Erasmus, A. 'The Sound of War: Apartheid, Audibility and Resonance' (PhD Dissertation, University of the Western Cape, 2018)

Erasmus, Aidan. "A Sinister Resonance." *Canadian Review of Comparative Literature / Revue Canadienne de Littérature Comparée* 45, no. 4 (2018): 585-596. https://dx.doi.org/10.1353/crc.2018.0061.

Erasmus, A. "Re-Cover: Afrikaans Rock, Apartheid's Children and the Work of the Cover" in *Remains Of The Social: Desiring The Postapartheid* Eds. Maurits van Bever Donker, Ross Truscott, Gary Minkley & Premesh Lalu. Johannesburg: Wits UP.

Esben, Morné. "Stellenbosch Mafia mindset plays out in racist incidents at Maties". *Mail & Guardian*. Published 28 May 2022. Accessed 12 June 2024. https://mg.co.za/news/2022-05-28-stellenbosch-mafia-mindset-plays-out-in-racist-incidents-at-maties/

Fairbanks, E. (2017). 'The Last White Africans', *Foreign Policy*, 16 January. Accessed on 18 August 2018 at https://foreignpolicy.com/2017/01/16/the-last-White-africans/.

Falkof, N. (2016). 'The Myth of White Purity and Narratives that Fed Racism in South Africa', *The Conversation*, 15 May. Accessed on 31 August 2018 at http://theconversation.com/the-myth-of-white-purity-and-narratives-that-fed-racism-in-south-africa-59330.

Fihlani, Pumza. (2017) "Trying to save South Africa's first language" *BBC Africa*. Published

First Peoples Worldwide. "Three Horrendous Anti-Indigenous Laws". Published 03/09/2013. Accessed 12/06/2017 https://www.culturalsurvival.org/news/3-horrendous-anti-indigenous-laws August 30. Accessed 10 May 2018.

Flaherty, Anne F. Boxberger . (2017). "Intergovernmental Relations among Native Nations, the Federal Government, and States" in *States, American Indian Nations, and Intergovernmental Politics*. 1st ed., pp. 17–50). Routledge. https://doi.org/10.4324/9781315619477-2

Frandsen, David. "Orania". Karoo-South Africa. (2019). Accessed 6 August 2024. https://www.karoo-southafrica.com/eastern-upper-karoo/orania/

Friesen, J. (2018). 'Gerald Stanley Acquitted in the Shooting Death of Colten Boushie', *The Globe & Mail*, 9 February. Accessed on 30 Aug 2018 at https://www.theglobeandmail.com/news/national/gerald-stanley-acquitted-in-death-of-colten-boushie/article37929427/.

Gadamer, H.G. (1969). *Truth and Method (J. Weinsheimer & DG Marshall, trans.)*. New York: Continuum.

Geertz, C., 1994. "Thick description: Toward an interpretive theory of culture" in *Readings in the philosophy of social science*, pp.213-231.

Geertz, C., 1973. *The interpretation of cultures: Selected essays* (Vol. 5019).

Geisler, Charles. 2012. "New Terra Nullius Narratives and the Gentrification of Africa's 'Empty Lands'" *American Sociological Association*. XVIII(I): 15-29. ISSN 1076-156X

Giliomee, H. (2015). 'The Battle for Afrikaans at the University of Stellenbosch', *Politicsweb*, 17 November. Accessed on 25 July 2018. http://www.politicsweb.co.za/news-and-analysis/the-battle-for-afrikaans-at-the-university-of-stel .

Giliomee, H. (2003). *The Afrikaners: Biography of a People*. University of Virginia Press: Charleston.

Gleason, G. (2018). 'Vowel against Cyber Colonialism', *McGill Daily*, 19 March. Accessed on 12 July 2018 at https://www.mcgilldaily.com/2018/03/vowel-against-cybercolonialism/

Goodwin, June, Ben Schiff. (1995). *Heart of Whiteness: Afrikaners Face Black Rule in the New South Africa.* Scribner: New York.

Graham, Lucy Valerie. 2003. "Reading the Unspeakable: Rape in JM Coetzee's Disgrace". *Journal of Southern African Studies*, 29:2, 433-444. DOI: 10.1080/03057070306207

Gressier, Cate. 2011. "Safaris into Subjectivity: White Locals, Black Tourists, and the Politics of Belonging in the Okavango Delta, Botswana." *Global Studies in Culture and Power.* 18:4. 352-376.

Griffiths, D & M.L.C. Prozsky. (2010). 'The Politics of Dwelling: Being White/Being South African', *Africa Today*, (56)4. Summer 2010. 22-41.

Grundlingh, A. (2004). 'Rocking the Boat' in South Africa? Voëlvry Music and Afrikaans Anti-Apartheid Social Protest in the 1980s', *International Journal of African Historical Studies*, 37 (3). 483-514.

Hall, Stuart, Paul du Gay. (1996) *Questions of Cultural Identity.* Sage Publishing, London.

Hall, Stuart. (1997a) "Random Thoughts Provoked by the Conference 'Identities, Democracy, Culture and Communication in Southern Africa'". *A North-South Journal of Cultural & Media Studies.* (11)1/2.

Hall, S. (1997b). Representation: Cultural Representations and Signifying Practices. SAGE Publication Ltd: London.

Hakamaki, Henry, Adnan Husain, and Breht O'Shea. "The History of Indigenous Resistance w/ Nick Estes". *Guerrilla History.* May 21, 2021. 02:01:02 https://guerrillahistory.libsyn.com/nick-estes

Hanekom, Wouter. (2013) "The Simon van der Stel Festival: Constructing heritage and the politics of pageantry" *Historia* (58)2 Durban, January. ISSN 2309-8392..

Hanson, Erin. "The Indian Act". First Nations Studies Program. *University of British Columbia.* Created in 2009. Accessed 6 August 2024.

Harrison, S. (2003). "Cultural Difference as Denied Resemblance: Reconsidering Nationalism and

Ethnicity". *Comparative Studies in Society and History*, 45(2), 343-361. Retrieved from http://www.jstor.org/stable/3879319

Hatton, J. (2015). 'Fearlessly Afrikaans and Fearless Afrikaners', *Afriforum-Afrikaans*, 3 November. Accessed on 10 September 2018 at https://www.afriforum.co.za/fearlessly-afrikaans-fearless-afrikaners/ .

Harvey, D. (1989). *The Condition of Postmodernity: An Enquiry Into the Origins of Cultural Change*. Blackwell-Wiley: Hoboken, USA.

Hosken, G. (2016). '12 Maps That Explore the Changing Racial Divide in Our Biggest Cities', *The Sunday Times*, 26 May. Accessed on 15 May 2018.

Hughes, David McDermott. 2010. *Whiteness in Zimbabwe: Race, Landscape, and the Problem of Belonging*. Palgrave MacMillan: New York.

Hugo, P. (1985). 'Waiting: the Whites of South Africa', *Social Dynamics*. 11(2), 56 -78. DOI: 10.1080/02533958508628686.

Immigration and Refugee Board of Canada. "Responses to Information Requests" Modified: 23 January 2024. Accessed 7 August 2024. https://www.irb-cisr.gc.ca/en/country-information/rir/Pages/index.aspx?doc=454595&pls=1

Johnson, Douglas H. 1982. "Evans-Pritchard, the Nuer, and the Sudan Political Service" *The Royal African Society*. 81 (323). 231-246.

Johnson, SC. (2009). 'South Africa's New White Flight', *Newsweek*. Accessed at http://www.newsweek.com/south-africas-new-White-flight-82709.

Johnson-Castle, Patricia. (2014). "The Group Areas Act of 1950". *South African History Online*. Published 19 Dec 2014. Accessed 30 June 2016. https://www.sahistory.org.za/article/group-areas-act-1950

Josefsson, Jenny. 2014. "Safe-guarding the Colonial Present: game farms on the frontier in KwaZulu-Natal's 'Battlefield Route'" *Journal of Contemporary African Studies*, 32:2, 258-274.

Keesing, R.M., 1990. "Theories of culture revisited" in *Canberra Anthropology*, 13(2), pp.46-60.

Kamwangamalu, Nkonko M. (2016). *Language Policy and Economics: The Language Question in Africa.* Palgrave: London. DOI: 10.1057/978-1-137-31623-3

Khampepe, Sisi. *Commission Of Inquiry Into Allegations Of Racism At Stellenbosch University.* Stellenbosch University. 25 October 2022.

King, Thomas. (2003). *The Truth About Stories.* House of Anasi Press: Toronto.

Koot, Stasja P. 2015. "White Namibians in tourism and the politics of belonging through Bushmen" Anthropology Southern Africa, 38:1-2, 4-15.

La Croix, Sumner. "The Decline of the Khoikhoi Population, 1652-1780: A Review and a New Estimate". *University of Hawai`i at Mānoa Department of Economics Working Paper Series.* Working Paper No. 16-22.

Lansing, P. & King, JC. (1998). 'South Africa's Truth and Reconciliation Commission: The

Conflict between Individual Justice and National Healing in the Post-Apartheid Age,' *Arizona Journal of International and Comparative Law*, (15)3. 753-790.

Larkin, A. (2015). 'Ramifications of South Africa's Dope System', *South African History Online,* 12 June. Accessed on 1 November 2017 at https://www.sahistory.org.za/article/ramifications-south-africa%E2%80%99s-dop-system-alexandra-larkin .

Leitch, RA. (2006). *Prepared for a world that no longer exists.* University of Cape Town: Thesis.

Levin, David Michael. "On Levi-Strauss and Existentialism" in *American Scholar*, 38(1). Winter, 1968-1969. Pp 69-82.

Library and Archives Canada Blog. (2016). 'Inuit Disc Numbers and Project Surname', *Library and Archives Canada Blog*, 22 June. Accessed on 03 October 2018 at https://thediscoverblog.com/2016/06/22/the-inuit-disc-numbers-and-project-surname/.

Locke, , Joseph L., and Ben Wright (eds.) 2019. *American Yawp.* Stanford California: Stanford UP

Louw, PE. (2004). 'Political Power, National Identity and Language: the case of Afrikaans', *International Journal of Social Language*, 170 (2004), 43-58.

Lukes, S. 1973. *Individualism.* Oxford: Basil Blackwell.

Mahmood, Saba. 2005. *Politics Of Piety: The Islamic Revival And The Feminist Subject.* Princeton, NJ: Princeton UP.

Maluleke, T. (2018). 'Author', *Mail & Guardian,* 11 October. Available at https://mg.co.za/author/tinyiko-maluleke-uj

Makoni, Sinfree B., Busi Dube & Pedzisai Mashiri. (2008). "Zimbabwe Colonial and Post-Colonial Language Policy and Planning Practices" *Current Issues in Language Planning.* (7) 4. Pp 377-414. https://doi.org/10.2167/cilp108.0

Mamdani, Mahmood. 1996. *Citizen and Subject: Contemporary Africa and the Legacy of Late Colonialism.* Princeton UP: Princeton

Mangcu, X. (2003). 'The State of Race Relations in Post-Apartheid South Africa', in *State of the Nation: South Africa, 2003-2004,* J. Daniel, A. Habib, & R. Southall (Eds.). HRSC Press, Cape Town. 105-117.

Mapumulo, Z & J. Eybers. (2017). 'We're running out of White', *City Press,* 8 June. Accessed on 19 August 2018 at: https://www.news24.com/SouthAfrica/News/were-running-out-of-whites-20170806-2

Mark, Peter. 2002. *"Portuguese" Style and Luso-African Identity: Precolonial Senegambia, Sixteenth-Nineteenth Centuries.* Indiana UP: Bloomington.

Mamdani, Mahmood. 1996. Citizen and Subject: Contemporary Africa and the Legacy, James Currey, Oxford.

Markell, A., Hall, M. and Schrire, C., 1995. The historical archaeology of Vergelegen, an early farmstead at the Cape of Good Hope. *Historical Archaeology, 29*(1), pp.10-34.

Massey, D. (1995). 'The Conceptualization of Place', in D. Massey & P. Jess (Eds.), *A Place in the World?: Places, Cultures, & Globalization.* Oxford UP: Oxford. 45-86.

Majavu, Mandisi. "Orania: A white homeland in post-apartheid South Africa" *Sociology Compass.* 2022;16:e13004. https://doi.org/10.1111/soc4.13004

Mawani, Renisa. 2009. *Colonial Proximities: Crossracial Encounters and Juridical Truths in British Columbia, 1871-1921.* UBC UP: Vancouver.

May, R. (2018). 'Velvet Rope Racism, Racial Paranoia, and Cultural Scripts: Alleged Dress Code Discrimination in Urban Nightlife', City & Community. 17(1): March. 44-64. Doi: 10.1111/cico.12286

Mbuli, Mbekezeli. (2014). 'High court rules in favour of Nelspruit name change', *Mpumalanga News,* 14 May. Accessed at https://mpumalanganews.co.za/174366/high-court-rules-favour-nelspruit-name-change/.

McCulloch, J. (2012). *South Africa's Gold Mines & the Politics of Silicosis.* Boydell & Brewer: Rochester, USA.

McKeague, Madelyn Lehualani. "To Raise the Health Status of Native Hawaiians to the Highest Possible Level: An Expansive Reading of the Native Hawaiian Health Care Improvement Act" *Asian-Pacific Law and Policy Journal.* 24 (1), 2022. 120-159.

Merriam-Webster. (2017). 'Stay Woke: The New Sense of 'Woke'', *Words We're Watching,* September. Accessed on 21 August 2018 at https://www.merriam-webster.com/words-at-play/woke-meaning-origin.

Milbrath, C, B Ohlson & S Eyre. (2009). 'Analysing Cultural Models in Adolescent Account of Romantic Relationships', *Journal of Research on Adolescence*, 19 (2), 313-351.

Mkentane, Odwa. "Besieged Stellenbosch University appoints inquiry into racism". *IOL.* Published 6 June 2022. Accessed 12 June 2024. https://www.iol.co.za/capetimes/news/besieged-stellenbosch-university-appoints-inquiry-into-racism-be6cf766-a57a-4543-96dc-580e125c8af1

Mkhonto, S. (2018). 'Black Tax: A Responsibility, Not a Burden', *MyNews24*, 20 April. Accessed on 21 August 2018 at https://www.news24.com/MyNews24/Black-tax-a-responsibility-not-a-burden-20180419.

Mpofu, Shepherd. (2017). 'Disruption as a communicative strategy: the case of #FeesMustFall and #RhodesMustFall students' protests in South Africa', *Journal of African Media Studies* 9(2): DOI: 10.1386/jams.9.2.351_1.

'Model C- definition and synonyms', *MacMillan Dictionary.* Accessed at https://www.macmillandictionary.com/dictionary/british/model-c.

Modjadji, Ngwako and Neo Goba. "'Apartheid was not a crime against humanity': AfriForum CEO's remark sparks outrage". *Times Live*. Published 15 May 2018. Accessed 7 August 2024. https://www.timeslive.co.za/politics/2018-05-15-uproar-over-remark-that-apartheid-was-not-a-crime-against-humanity-by-afriforum-ceo/

Moodie, D. T. (1975). *The Rise of Afrikanerdom*. UC Press: Berkeley.

Morgan, Naòmi. "Why translate Godot into Afrikaans?" *HERRI*. Centre For Critical And Creative Thought, Stellenbosch University. Issue 10. 2024. https://herri.org.za/10/naomi-morgan/

Moyo, T. (2002). 'Mother Tongues Versus an Ex-Colonial Language as the Media of Instruction and the Promotion of Multilingualism: The South African Experience', *South African Journal of African Languages*, 2002:2. 149-160.

Mlaba, Khanyi. "5 Shocking Facts That Show Why South Africa Is the 'Most Unequal Country in the World'" *Global Citizen*. Published 27 November 2020. Accessed 7 August 2024. https://www.globalcitizen.org/en/content/facts-why-south-africa-most-unequal-country-oxfam/

Mthethwa, Cebelihle. "Stellenbosch University suspends another student for urinating in fellow students' room". *News24*. Published 23 Oct 2022. Accessed 12 June 2024. https://www.news24.com/news24/southafrica/news/stellenbosch-university-suspends-another-student-for-urinating-in-fellow-students-room-20221023

Mutasa, D. (2000). 'Language Policy and Language Use in South Africa: An Uneasy Marriage', *South African Journal of African Languages*, 20:3, 217-224

Narayan, K. 1993. "How Native is the 'Native' Anthropologist?" in *American Anthropologist* 95(3). 671 - 686.

National Archives. "Dawes Act (1887)" *Milestone Documents*. National Archives. Last edited February 8, 2022. Accessed 6 August 2024.

https://www.archives.gov/milestone-documents/dawes-act

National Public Radio. (2018). *Comfort Zone*. [Podcast] TED Radio Hour. Accessed on 26 May 2018 at https://www.npr.org/programs/ted-radio-hour/606073044 .

Ndhlovu, Finex. (2010). 'Language Politics in Post - Colonial Africa Revisited: Minority Agency and Language Imposition', *Studies in the Languages of Africa*, 41:2, 175-192. DOII: 10.1080/10228195.2010.492231.

Ngũgĩ wa Thiong'o. (2017). 'Great Texts/Big Questions', *Institute for Creative Arts, University of Cape Town*, 9 March. Accessed on 7 June 2018 at https://www.youtube.com/watch?v=1bl-2F8Nj7U.

Ngũgĩ wa Thiong'o. (1981). 'The Language of African Literature', *Decolonising the Mind: The Politics of Language in African Literature*. James Currey: Melton, UK.

Ngwadla, Nkosazana. (2018). 'The Burden of Black Tax', *Fin24*, 9 May. Accessed on 21 August 2018 at https://www.fin24.com/Money/the-burden-of-Black-tax-20180309.

Nyamnjoh, F. B. (2017). *Drinking from the Cosmic Gourd*: Langaa RPCIG, Bamenda.

Nyamnjoh, F.B. (2016a). *# RhodesMustFall: Nibbling at resilient colonialism in South Africa*. Langaa RPCIG: Bamenda.

Nyamnjoh, F. B. (2016b). 'Reframing Communication in Cultural Development', in O. Hemer & T. Tufte (Eds.), *Voice+Matter: Communication Development and the Cultural Return*. Nordicom: Gottenburg.

Nyamnjoh. F. B. (2013). 'The Nimbleness of Being Fulani', *Africa Today*. 59(3), 105-134.

Nyamnjoh. F. B. (2012a). 'Blinded by Sight: Divining the Future of Anthropology in Africa', *Africa Spectrum*. 2-3: 63-92.

Nyamnjoh, F. B. (2012b). 'Potted Plants in Greenhouses': A Critical Reflection on the Resilience of Colonial Education in Africa. *Journal of Indian and African Studies*, 47(2), pp.129-154.

Nyamnjoh F.B. (2012c). Intimate Strangers: Connecting Fiction and Ethnography. In: De Bruijn M., Van Dijk R.

(Eds) *The Social Life of Connectivity in Africa*. Palgrave Macmillan, New York

Nyamnjoh, F. B. &. K. Shoro. (2011). 'Language, Mobility, African Writers and Pan-Africanism', African *Communication Research*, Vol.4 (1):35-62.

Nyamnjoh, F. B. & B. Page. (2002). 'Whiteman Kontri and the Enduring Allure of Modernity among Cameroonian Youth', *African Affairs* 101.405: 607-634.

O'Connor, J. K. (1915). *The Afrikaner Rebellion*. Unwin Brothers: London.

Ohene, Elizabeth. "Letter from Africa: Malaria, a Bedroom Battleground". BBC World Service. Published 27 July 2016. Accessed 20 January 2020. https://www.bbc.com/news/world-africa-36894631

Open Stellenbosch. (2015). 'Open Stellenbosch Alternative Language Policy', 17 November. Accessed on 07 June 2018 at https://www.facebook.com/openstellenbosch/posts/893217927394052.

Open Stellenbosch Collective. (2015). 'Op-Ed: Open Stellenbosch – Tackling Language and Exclusion at Stellenbosch University', *Daily Maverick*, 28 April. Accessed on 2 February 2017 at https://www.dailymaverick.co.za/article/2015-04-28-op-ed-open-stellenbosch-tackling-language-and-exclusion-at-stellenbosch-university/.

Ostler, Jeffrey. 2015. "Genocide and American Indian History". American History: Oxford Research Encyclopaedias. DOI: 10.1093/acrefore/9780199329175.013.3 http://americanhistory.oxfordre.com/view/10.1093/acrefore/9780199329175.001.0001/acrefore-9780199329175-e-3 Accessed 07/06/2017.

Overcoming Apartheid/Building Democracy. "Forced Removals". *Michigan State University*. ND. Accessed 7 August 2024. https://overcomingapartheid.msu.edu/multimedia.php?kid=163-582-18

Peters, Rebecca Warne & Claire Wendland. 2016. "Up the Africanist: the possibilities and problems of 'studying up' in Africa". Critical African Studies. DOI: 10.1080/21681392.2016.1244945

Phillipson, R. (1996). 'Linguistic imperialism: African perspectives', *ELT journal, 50*(2).160-167.

Pilossof, R. (2012). *The Unbearable Whiteness of Being.* African Books Collective.

Plenke, Max. "The Reason This "Racist Soap Dispenser" Doesn't Work on Black Skin" *MIC*. Published 9 September 2015. Accessed 2 October 2024. https://www.mic.com/shopping/without-a-doubt-the-cheapest-coolest-home-upgrades-on-amazon

Poyner, Jane. "Truth and reconciliation in JM Coetzee's Disgrace" in Scrutiny2, 5:2. 67-77. DOI: 10.1080/18125440008565972

Probyn, E. (1996). *Outside Belongings.* Routledge: London.

Rawls, J. (1999). *A Theory of Justice.* Harvard UP: Cambridge, Mass.

Ratshikuni, Mugabe. "Mandela, De Klerk and the apartheid apologists" *PoliticsWeb*. Published 16 Feb 2020. Accessed 8 Oct 2024. https://www.politicsweb.co.za/opinion/mandela-de-klerk-and-the-apartheid-apologists

Raibmon, Paige. (2005). *Authentic Indians: Episodes of Encounter from the Late-Nineteenth-Century Northwest Coast.* Vancouver: University of British Columbia Press.

Redkozubova, E. A. (2013). 'Slang in the Communicative Space of South-African Linguistic Culture', *Humanities and Social Sciences Journal,* 6 (2013): 218-226.

Ramutsindela, Maano Freddy. "Afrikaner Nationalism, Electioneering and the Politics of a Volkstaat" *Politics* (1998) 18(3) pp. 179±188.

Reilly, J. D. (2016). *Teaching the "Native".* HRSC Press: Cape Town.

Reality Check Team. "South Africa elections: Who controls the country's business sector?" *BBC News*. Published 4 May 2019. Accessed 7 August 2024. https://www.bbc.com/news/world-africa-48123937

Rhodes, Cecil John. "The Glen Grey Speech". The Cape House Parliament on July 30 1894. https://www.sahistory.org.za/archive/glen-grey-act-native-issue-cecil-john-rhodes-july-30-1894-cape-house-parliament

Rose, G. (1995). 'Place and Identity: A Sense of Place', in D. Massey & P, Jess (Eds.) *A Place in the World?* Eds. Oxford UP: Oxford.

Ross, F. (2017). *Raw Life, New Hope*. UCT Press.

Reuters, Tracey-Lynn. "Stellenbosch University haunted by 'chamber of horrors' and 'toxic culture' at Wilgenhof" *IOL*. Published Feb 3, 2024. Accessed 12 June 2024. https://www.iol.co.za/weekend-argus/news/stellenbosch-university-haunted-by-chamber-of-horrors-and-toxic-culture-at-wilgenhof-87a5d107-1f4d-4dfc-89f7-e910ce3d8f3c

Rushdie, S. (1981). *Midnight's Children*. Random House: Toronto.

Sahlins, MD. 1974. "The Original Affluent Society" in Stone Age Economics. Chicago: Aldine-Atherton. 1-39.

SAHO (South Africa History Online). (2011). 'Bantu Education and The Racist Compartmentalizing of Education', *SAHO*, 30 March. Accessed on 2 July 2018 at http://www.sahistory.org.za/article/bantu-education-and-racist-compartmentalizing-education.

SAHO. (2011). 'The Department of Native Refugee Camps: A Historical Overview', 31 March. Accessed on 6 June 2018 at http://www.sahistory.org.za/article/department-native-refugee-camps.

SAHO. (2011). 'The South African War 1899-1902', SAHO, 8 November. Accessed on 10 September 2018.

SAHO. (2012). 'The Prohibition of Mixed Marriages Act Commences', SAHO, 05 July. Accessed on 24 June 2018.

SAHO. (2015). 'The History of Separate Development in South Africa', SAHO, 27 March. Accessed on 15 May 2018.

SAHO. (2016). "The Natives Land Act of 1913". Initial date of publication: 06/03/2013. Last updated: 28/01/2016. Accessed 10/06/2017. http://www.sahistory.org.za/topic/natives-land-act-1913

SAHO. (2018). 'Changing Perceptions of Nelson Mandela', *SAHO*, 27 June. Accessed on 12 July 2018.

SAHO. "Glen Grey Division". Produced 16 March 2011. Last Updated 18 April 2019. Accessed 6 August 2024. https://www.sahistory.org.za/place/glen-grey-division

SAHO. "The Homelands". *SAHO* https://www.sahistory.org.za/article/homelands Accessed 12/06/2024

SAHO. "Reverend Beyers Naudé" ND. Accessed 2 October 2024. https://www.sahistory.org.za/people/reverend-beyers-naude

Said, E. (1978). *Orientalism*. Pantheon Books: New York.

Seema, J. (2016). English in Africa: A Genocide for the Development of African Languages and Literatures', *Journal of Sociology and Social Anthropology*, 7(3). 184-192.

Seixas, Peter, and Jill Colyer. "Ethical Dimensions" *The Historical Thinking Project*. 2014. Access 6 August 2024. https://historicalthinking.ca/ethical-dimensions

Seldon, Sylvia. 2014. "Orania and the Reinvention of Afrikanerdom". PhD in Social Anthropology: the University of Edinburgh.

Sguazzin, Anthony. "South Africa Wealth Gap Unchanged Since Apartheid, Says World Inequality Lab" *Time*. Published 5 August 2021. Accessed 7 August 2024. https://time.com/6087699/south-africa-wealth-gap-unchanged-since-apartheid/

Sigcau, N. E. (2004). Mother-Tongue Education: A Key to Success', *Researching the language of instruction in Tanzania and South Africa. Cape Town: African Minds*. 239-254.

Singh, O. (2017). 'Government Concern About High Emigration Rate', *Zululand Observer,* 7 August. Accessed on 18 August in 2018. https://zululandobserver.co.za/150605/government-concerned-high-emigration-rate/

Soja, E. W. (1989). *Postmodern geographies: The Reassertion of Space in Critical Social Theory*. Verso.

Soggot, Mungo. "The Rev Beyers Naudé: Courageous Afrikaner cleric who became a champion of South Africa's liberation struggle" *The Guardian*. Published 8 Sep 2004. Accessed on 2 Oct 2024. https://www.theguardian.com/news/2004/sep/08/guardianobituaries.southafrica

Smith, Candance, and Bryan Pitts. "Inside the all-white 'Apartheid town' of Orania, South Africa" Published 11 April 2019. Accessed 6 August 2024. https://abcnews.go.com/International/inside-white-apartheid-town-orania-south-africa/story?id=62337338

Smuts, F. (1979). *Stellenbosch: Tercentenary October Festival 1979*. Stellenbosch: Cabo. 'South Africa',

Stats Canada. "Aboriginal peoples in Canada: key results from the 2016 census" The Daily. Date Modified 2017-10-25. Date accessed 2019-06-29. https://www150.statcan.gc.ca/n1/daily-quotidien/171025/dq171025a-eng.htm

Stats Canada. "British Columbia Census Profile, 2021". Date modified: 2022-09-02. Date accessed 2022-09-30. https://www12.statcan.gc.ca/census-recensement/2021/dp-pd/prof/details/page.cfm?Lang=E&SearchText=British%20Columbia&DGUIDlist=2021A000259&GENDERlist=1,2,3&STATISTIClist=1&HEADERlist=0

Stellenbosch Enrolment Overview. "Official June Statistics". *Stellenbosch University*. Accessed 6 August 2024. https://app.powerbi.com/view?r=eyJrIjoiY2UzMThjNjktYzk4YS00ODg0LTk3MTMtMmM5OTI3OTE4NTI0IiwidCI6ImE2ZmEzYjAzLTBhM2MtNDI1OC04NDMzLWExMjBkZmZjZDM0OCIsImMiOjh9

Stellenbosch University. "Facts and Statistics". 2012. https://www.sun.ac.za/english/Documents/About/FactsAndStats/JH15705_Kitsfeite_Eng_PRINT.pdf

Stellenbosch Municipality. 'Home - The Greater Stellenbosch'. Accessed at https://www.stellenbosch.gov.za/.

Stellenbosch University. 'Prof H Russel Botman'. Accessed on 12 June 2018 at https://www.sun.ac.za/english/management/rector.

Stellenbosch University. 'Strategy and Internationalisation- Prof Hester Klopper'. Accessed on 23 July 2018 at https://www.sun.ac.za/english/management/Pages/Strategic-Initiatives-and-Internationalisation.aspx..

Steyn, A.S. (2016). 'Afrikaans, Inc: The Afrikaans Culture Industry After Apartheid', *Social Dynamics*. 42:3, 481-503. DOI:10.1080/02533952.2016.1259792.

Steyn, J. C. (1980). *Tuiste in eie taal: Die behoud en bestaan van Afrikaans.* Tafelberg.

Steyn, M. (2007). 'As the Postcolonial Moment Deepens: A Response to Green, Soon and Matsebula". *South African Journal of Psychology.* 37(3): 420-424.

Steyn, M. (2005). 'White Talk': White-South Africans and the Management of Diasporic Whiteness', Postcolonial *Whiteness.* SUNY Press, Albany.

Steyn, M. (2004). 'Rehabilitating a Whiteness Disgraced: Afrikaner White Talk in Post-Apartheid South Africa', *Communication Quarterly*, 52:2, 143-169, DOI: 10.1080/01463370409370187.

Swarns, R. (2000). 'For South African Whites, Money Has No Colour', *The New York Times.* Accessed 22 August 2018. https://www.nytimes.com/2000/04/20/world/for-south-african-Whites-money-has-no-color.html.

Swart, Mia. "'Apartheid was never prosecuted': S Africa's unfinished business". *Al Jazeera.* Published 27 Apr 2020. Accessed 8 Oct 2024. https://www.aljazeera.com/features/2020/4/27/apartheid-was-never-prosecuted-s-africas-unfinished-business

Swart, S. (2001). *A 'ware Afrikaner': An Examination of The Role of Eugene Marais (1871-1936) In the Making of Afrikaner Identity.* Thesis, Oxford University.

Tabata, I. B. (1980). *Education for Barbarism.* Prometheus: South Africa.

Tamarkin, M. (1996). *Cecil Rhodes and the Cape Afrikaners.* Frank Cass: London.

Teicher, J. G. (2014). 'The Human Cost of South Africa's Mining Industry', *Slate*, 9 September. Accessed on 22 April 2018 at http://www.slate.com/blogs/behold/2014/09/09/ilan_godfrey_documents_the_impact_of_south_africa_s_mining_industry_in_his.html.

The Economist (2008). 'White Flight from South Africa: Between Staying and Going', *The Economist.* 25 September. Accessed on 19 August 2018 at https://www.economist.com/node/12295535/all-comments.

Theron, L. C. 'Facilitating Adaptability and Resilience: Career Counselling in Resource-Poor Communities in South Africa', in K. Maree (Ed.) *Psychology of Career Adaptability, Employability and Resilience*. Springer: DOI 10.1007/978-3-310-66954-0.

Thompsell, A. (2017). 'Racial Classification under Apartheid', *Thoughtco: Humanities,* 7 March. Accessed on June 15 2018 at https://www.thoughtco.com/racial-classification-under-apartheid-43430.

Truscott, R. (2016). Postapartheid rhythm: Beyond apartheid beatings. Subjectivity, 9: 290.

Tsing, A.L. 2015. The mushroom at the end of the world: On the possibility of life in capitalist ruins. Princeton: Princeton University Press.

United States Census Bureau. "Welcome to Quick Facts". https://www.census.gov/quickfacts/ Accessed 07/06/2017.

Universal Church of the Kingdom of God. "The UCKG's Statement on Ilana van Wyk's book". Published 22 October 2015. Accessed 27 January 2020. https://www.bizcommunity.com/PressOffice/PressRelease.aspx?i=133323&ai=136279

USDV. 'Afriforum versus Open Stellenbosch Debate', Accessed at https://www.facebook.com/events/914477838600113/.

Van Devente, G. (2018). 'Stellenbosch Newsletter', 17 May. Accessed on 31 May 2018 at https://www.stellenbosch.gov.za/news/newsletters.

Van Rooyen, J. (2000). *The New Great Trek: The Story of South Africa's White Exodus.* UNISA Press, Pretoria.

van Wyk, Johannes Stephanus. 2014. "Buying into Kleinfontein: the Financial Implications of Afrikaner Self-Determination". Master's Thesis, University of Pretoria.

Van Zyl-Hermann, D. & J. Boersema. (2017). 'Introduction: The Politics of Whiteness In Africa', *Africa, 87*(4): 651-661. DOI:10.1017/S0001972017000298.

Van Zyl-Hermann, D. (2014). 'Baas or Klaas? Afrikaner Working-Class Responses to

Transformation in South Africa, ca. 1977-2002', *International Labour and Working-Class History.* 86, Fall: 142-158.

Vawda, A. Y. & A. H. Patrinos. (1999). 'Producing Educational Materials in Local Languages: Costs from Guatemala And Senegal', *International Journal of Educational Development* 19(4): 287-299.

Vale, P. & J. Higgins. 'State of Urgency', *Arts and Humanities in Higher Education.* https://doi.org/10.1177/1474022215618512.

Verwey, C. & M. Quayle. 'Whiteness, Racism, and Afrikaner Identity In Post-Apartheid South Africa', *African Affairs*, 111/445, 551–575. DOI: 10.1093/afraf/ads056.

Wandel, Torbjorn. 2001. "The Power of Discourse: Michel Foucault and Critical Theory". *Cultural Values*. 5(3). 368-382.

Walker, Melanie. (2005). 'Race Is Nowhere And Race Is Everywhere: Narratives From Black And White-South African University Students in Post-Apartheid South Africa', *British Journal of Sociology of Education*. 26 (1): 41-54.

Wasserman, H. (2010). 'We're not like that: Denial of racism in the Afrikaans press in South Africa', *Communicatio: South African Journal for Communication Theory and Research*, 36(1): 20-36.

Webster, Dennis. "'An indictment of South Africa': whites-only town Orania is booming" *The Guardian*. Published 24 October 2019. Accessed 7 August 2024. https://www.theguardian.com/cities/2019/oct/24/an-indictment-of-south-africa-whites-only-town-orania-is-booming

Willis, Paul and Mats Trondman. 2000. "Manifesto for 'Ethnography'" in Ethnography, 1(1). 5-16.

Wolfe, Patrick. "Settler colonialism and the elimination of the native" *Journal of Genocide Research* (2006), 8(4), December, 387–409.

Worden, Nigel. (2000). *The Making of Modern South Africa.* Blackwell Publishers: Oxford.

World Factbook. Central Intelligence Agency: USA. https://www.cia.gov/library/publications/the-world-factbook/geos/sf.html

World Population Review. "New Zealand Population 2019" ND. Accessed 2019-06-29.

http://worldpopulationreview.com/countries/new-zealand-population/

Yuval-Davis, N. (2006). 'Belonging and the politics of belonging', *Patterns of prejudice*, *40*(3).